A Father and Daughter World Cycling Journey

Michael A. Rice and Jocelyn M. Rice

A Father and Daughter World Cycling Journey
Copyright © 2017 by Michael A. Rice and Jocelyn M. Rice

All rights reserved. No part of this book may be reproduced or transmitted in any form or by any means, electronic or mechanical, including photocopying or recording, or by any information storage and retrieval system, without permission in writing from the author, except where permitted by law.

Cover design and page layout by MagicGraphix.com

Softcover: 978-0-9898845-1-8
Hardcover: 978-0-9898845-2-5

First edition published 2017

Visit our website
FatherDaughterCyclingAdventures.com

Dedication:

We would like to dedicate this book to all those in this world who are physically unable to ride a bicycle yet dream of a biking adventure.

This second book is dedicated to all those I met on the road who do not have the freedom to speak for themselves. I also want to share my sincere sympathy for the Orlando Pulse Nightclub victims, their families, and friends who were affected by tragic actions then and now. Of course, lots of gratitude for my mother and Aunti Tish for loving me unconditionally and supporting every wild move I make. *–Jocelyn*

I dedicate this book to my late Mom and Dad who let me go and gave me wings to discover this wonderful world, and also to my late sister Susan who helped instill independence within me. *–Mike*

Acknowledgements

We would like to thank the people of the world, whether road angels who came to our assistance, warmshowers' hosts who supported us with a safe place for the night, fellow riders who guided us, or drivers who respected our space. A smile is a smile no matter where in the world we met you, and your smile became a bright spot in our day. A special shout out to my father for providing the means for this epic experience of a lifetime. I am truly grateful. *–Jocelyn, August 2017*

I would like to thank my wife Andrea who let me go and live my dreams once again; my son Cary who helped take care of the house and made life easier for his mom and who maintained our website and assisted us with computer problems while on the road; my road partner Jocelyn who safely guided me around the world and for being the type of daughter that I could ride day in and day out with and still be friends. *–Mike, August 2017*

Contents

Forward 1 vii
Forward 2 xi
Introduction. 1
Preparing for a World Tour 3
Morocco 6
Spain 16
France 21
Italy 25
Slovenia. 31
Croatia 34
Bosnia-Herzegovina and Montenegro 40
Serbia 44
Bulgaria and Romania. 48
Greece 52
Turkey 54
The Republic of Georgia. 71
Azerbaijan. 75
Iran 80
Tajikistan 103
Kyrgyzstan 115
China. 118
Vietnam. 131
Laos. 137
Thailand 143
Starting our next ride 152

Mexico	166
Guatemala	188
Honduras	193
El Salvador	201
Nicaragua	204
Costa Rica	211
Panama	217
Colombia, South America	220
Ecuador	227
Peru	236
Chile	253
Canada	272
Re-entered the U.S.	298
Epilogue	331
Afterword from Andrea Rice	333
World Tour Mileage Summary	334
Final Thoughts	337
South Pole Mike	339

Maps

Morocco to Croatia	5
Croatia to the Republic of Georgia	33
The Republic of Georgia to Bangkok, Thailand	70
Washington, U.S. to Honduras, Central America and Calgary, Canada to Nova Scotia, Canada and South to Florida	151
Honduras, Central America to Chile, South America	187

Forward 1

"To move, to breathe, to fly, to float, to gain all while you give, to roam the roads of lands remote: To travel is to live."
—Hans Christian Andersen

My little brother, Mike, who stands 6'4", 210 pounds, was a bit of the quiet type. However, you knew that the "wheels were always turning" in his head. When he was 14, he sent a sketch of a future space capsule to NASA. He actually received a reply, complimenting him on his design. He later was employed with the Space Program for thirty years.

Mike once steered a sailboat from Long Beach Naval Yacht Club to Catalina Island 22 miles off the coast of California. Everything was fine, until the morning of our return, when the warning flag for high seas, deterring small craft from sailing, flapped in the wind. Mike, unabashedly, manned the helm, combating fierce winds and waves that rolled the craft into huge troughs of water. Eight hours later he crashed into the dock, caked with an inch of salt on his face. It was a testimony to his skills, strength, and endurance, that we had not lost our lives at sea. It was all so crazy and fortunate, that I said to him, "So, you want to sail around the world?" He looked thoroughly exhausted and responded with a grunt. Mike did sail and travel in the navy and with his wife, Andrea. However, the "around the world" part took the form of cycling with his daughter, Jocelyn.

Jocelyn, our niece, was always active, independent, and strong. She excelled at sports and possessed a tenacious attitude. Her beautiful blue eyes and bright smile percolated with mischief and adventure. She believed that life was to be lived to the fullest. So on this father/daughter bicycling journey, Jocelyn brought all her insatiable energy and a younger perspective. Her mapping skills made her an excellent navigator. She was a natural at cultivating a positive approach and compromise to their travels. Together, they explored the world, themselves, and discovered remarkable lessons. We all have special gifts, desires to fulfill aspirations. Acting on them is another story. So this is a quest born of creative ideas, forged in determination, sacrifice, and open-mindedness. One pedal rotation at a time, believing it was possible, living it, relishing every day.

When Mike and Jocelyn began their journey in exotic Morocco, I so wanted to join them. The land of cobras and kind Berber people, who welcomed them into their lives, pulled me into their adventures. Riding a bicycle through this remote area of camels and heat was no easy task, so I admired their tenacity from my home and relished their correspondence.

I lived vicariously through their travels, reading each blog entry, absorbing the scents, tastes, and visual sensations of each bump in the road. Their descriptions of Croatia lured me with its pristine coastline and fresh seafood with tasty sauces. Again, the uphill rides beckoned them with excitement. Their muscles strengthened and their acuity sharpened. When they visited a sacred Tibetan monastery, I heard the creaking of the huge, wooden prayer wheels, as they turned them by hand. As they climbed the stone steps beside a gigantic Buddha, carved from rock into the cliff in China, I hiked with them. Their lungs were strong with oxygen, from all the hours pedaling on the bike.

When the family decided to meet Mike and Jocelyn in Istanbul and spend time on the coast of Turkey, it was exhilarating. Bound together, exploring ancient ruins, we cherished this precious, loving family time. Hearing their cycling stories firsthand, confirmed their personal cadence. Saying goodbye was heartbreaking, but acceptance was our steadfast response.

I worried, feared for them, felt their sicknesses, pain, agony, injuries, and worried about diseases. I agonized for their safety, cried at the risks they were taking. I was glad to hear their appreciation for all the kindness people showed them. It was surprising and reassuring to hear about so many bicycle experts, parts, and shops, in the most remote of areas. There seemed to always be a gentle soul who would assist them in their time of need. I prayed for them constantly. The world has so much to teach us, if we are just willing to listen and participate. When they helped a family build a fence in Serbia, and worked with Jocelyn's cousin, Kate, in Honduras, serving remote people with medical assistance, it was vulnerable, logical, liberating, and honest. Their cycling had become more than physical motion; it was now a profound act.

Traveling changes you. It rips apart your sense of security, allows you to face raw reality and emotions, and then, heals your heart. It makes you an alternative version of yourself, a 2.0, as you acquire a super-packed adrenaline to forge forward, pushing to the next surprise. I imagine on a bicycle this feeling is even more amplified and it gives you the courage to "keep the wheels turning." It makes you trust others, yourself, and your God. Truly, their breathtaking photos of sunsets and sunrises confirmed their awe and commitment to their goal.

Mike and Jocelyn stayed with my husband Jim and I in San Diego, California after cycling from Canada to San Diego, and we treasured the time. When we took them to the border of Tijuana, I cried as we said goodbye again, and watched them cross the bridge into Mexico. As they cycled south, time and time again, stories of compassionate individuals, offering water, fruit, snacks, and retreat for the night, reassured me that they were protected on their path, as the heat rose, and their bodies were drenched in sweat and perseverance.

As their cycling continued, they experienced the Pyramids of Tikal, Guatemala. They described hiking at 4:00 A.M. through a dark jungle, and then climbing the huge blocks of steep steps, to the top where it was quiet, peaceful, and slowly watched the sliver of dawn unfold, as monkeys broke the silence with their piercing howls. Again, I was there with them, as their weary bodies celebrated their joy with gratitude. In Machu Picchu, Peru, climbing the lush green stones of ancient Inca ruins, with llamas running freely, I once again felt their resilience and appreciation.

Their bikes were a conduit for their triumphs, struggles, aches, anxieties, and fascinations. I was right there with them, screaming, exhaling, hoping, and loving. Always praying for their safe return home to their devoted family — waiting, anticipating, accepting their choices, stalwart, relieved when they completed their goal each time, until the final crossing back in Cape Canaveral, Florida.

Mike and Jocelyn's three-year cycling adventure was a remarkable achievement. It was a daunting accomplishment that took courage, focus, and unrestrained cooperation with the unknown. The world responded with challenges and delights, and Mike and Jocelyn answered the call with sensitivity and fortitude. Follow them in this book of discovery and turn the pages of adventure.

   –Patricia Haake, August 2017

Forward 2

"Traveling – it leaves you speechless, then turns you into a storyteller."

–Ibn Battuta

Every day since I can remember, my father would wake up as early as possible to head outside to do his bicycling or running routine. At first, it was just small treks of a few miles here and there, and I thought, *He's just doing it to stay in shape and avoid the heat of the day.* To me, it all would end with the same result — a hot mess of sweat, a smoothie, and a nap to recover.

The rest of the family would often still be fast asleep, maybe just barely waking up from dreaming and trying to resist the sunlight because of staying up too late the day before. These small jaunts eventually became all day adventures that gained the interest of Jocelyn. After a time, the duo found that all-day adventures were not enough!

However, these treks foreshadowed a destiny filled with full exposure to the sun, culture, and the natural beauty of the Earth that can only be found while traveling on a bicycle (not a vacation of comfort from the view of a car). They began to despise their idle time in their air-conditioned house and "real" life. And so, they planned, researched, gathered their gear, and traveled all the way across the USA to California!

As they traveled and struggled with unique challenges every day, their muscles and minds underwent a fitness that changed them into brave explorers that we read about in stories (both real and imagined).

The love for this travel formed an addiction, and their epic quest to travel the Earth on bicycles became realized — a dream that could be lived with open eyes. Fast forward to 5 years later. They have traveled 5 continents, 37 countries, and 28,034 miles!!!

How many of us would choose this journey even if we had the money, time, and health? One in a million . . . perhaps less.

However, numbers aren't everything. I implore you to search your mind and soul, and to keep the wheels turning. With hard work and your sails set high, you might find yourself in strange and wonderful places, with the wind at your back, and a permanent smile of joy affixed upon your face. There is no greater calling than a life spent exploring all our glorious Earth has to offer.

–Cary Rice, August 2017

Introduction

Mike:

"Problem... problem," dryly said the Tajik Border guard as we were trying to leave Tajikistan. We had been called into the border shack after a lengthy delay in the wind, snow, and cold. About ten miles back, while climbing toward this border crossing, we had waved down a truck to get a ride to Kyrgyzstan. Riding at over 14,000 feet in the Pamir Mountains for the last few weeks, both Jocelyn and I were suffering from altitude sickness. Along with that, Jocelyn was suffering from an intestinal illness. Since leaving the cold village of Murgab a few days ago, she had been getting worse and was now stopping on the dirt road to lay down every few miles. Camping was uncomfortable in the freezing temperatures, and it was a struggle just to have drinkable, unfrozen water. We only have a few days left before our visas expire. But at this point we were desperate as the wind was increasing and the temperature dropping. We heard an increasingly loud rumble from behind us and saw a slowly approaching truck. We were surprised because we had only seen maybe two-three cars per days on this road. I immediately waved the driver down and conveyed to him that we were sick and would like a ride to Kyrgyzstan. He and his partner readily said yes, so we loaded our bikes into his filthy truck bed and headed to the border.

When we reached the border, a guard took all of our passports and headed inside. He quickly returned with two of the passports stamped but called us inside. The guard kept his hands behind his back, slowly walked around, and kept saying, "Problem." It's funny now, but I kept thinking of a WWII movie where, "Your papers are not in order." Because of the language barrier, the minutes passed painfully slow. I was concerned about the driver leaving with our bikes and stuff, so I kept looking out the filthy window. Jocelyn figured out that the guard was looking for our Tajikistan entry forms issued to us when we arrived in Dushanbe by air.

Due to circumstances with our unexpected ride through Iran, two other visas had expired and we didn't want to pay and wait again for new visas, so we flew to Dushanbe, Tajikistan from Mashhad, Iran. Jocelyn found her form, handed it to the guard, and was rewarded with a smile and offered an apple from the basket he picked up. She picked one and the guard put the basket down without offering one to me. I started sweating as I realized I had thrown my entry form away because I didn't think it would be necessary. I didn't tell the guard that but did go out to the bikes and search through my bags even though I knew it wasn't there. This was to let the guard know I had one somewhere and for the driver to know that I was watching our bikes.

I returned inside, put my hands in the air, and said, "*Nyet, nyet,*" ("no" in Russian). Suddenly, he said I would need to return to Dushanbe to exit the country. At this, I was becoming frantic and continued to say *nyet*. In situations like this, it is important to remain calm and to smile. I did the opposite of what one should do, but I learned from this experience. The thought of biking back there was out of the question, even more so without Jocelyn. We were not going to separate. I told Jocelyn to go to our bags and pull out a $50 and a $100 bill. During our trip, we hid several hundred dollars on our bikes and ourselves. Jocelyn returned and gave me the $50 bill, which I stealthily gave to the guard. He quickly pocketed the bill but continued to say, "Problem," and pace inside the small shack. I didn't want to give him the $100 bill too, so we were in a standoff. After a few more minutes another guard entered the shack. Our guard quickly said something to the other one who immediately stamped exit on our passports as our guard left the shack. I figured that our guard was waiting for someone else to stamp us out so that it would not appear to be a bribe. We quickly jumped back into the truck and roared off. As we headed to the Kyrgyzstan border, I breathed a huge sigh of relief and wondered how we had gotten here. A father and daughter riding around the world on their bicycles stuck at a former Soviet Union country. What a fragile life a touring cyclist can live.

Preparing for a World Tour

"Hills, wind, rain, and bicycle grease are the ingredients for a grand adventure and builds character."
–Michael Rice

Our first book, *A Father and Daughter Bicycling Adventure: A Cross-Country Tour and a Six Week Tour of New Zealand's South Island* was the seed that gave us the idea of a world bicycle ride. In-between those two rides, I spent two Austral winters in Antarctica while Jocelyn continued riding her bike on another cross-country tour and several other shorter rides. While spending the winter of 2013 at Amundson-Scott South Pole Station, I avidly followed Jocelyn and her friend Rachel as they cycled from Virginia to Washington State on the Transamerica Bicycle Route to work at a Girl Scouts summer camp. A South Pole winter gives one plenty of time to think and plan the future. I emailed Jocelyn and my wife Andee asking if she were interested in continuing our ride to include an around the world journey. It was a silly question, of course, and the planning began. Any doubt that I had about leaving Andee again was erased when she happily endorsed the plan. She had been positive about my travels for the past few years and continues to be so today.

Jocelyn cycled to Missoula, Montana after summer camp to attend the Adventure Cycling Association Bicycle Tour leadership course. Her career goal was to lead bicycle tours throughout the world. This would be a great start to that goal. While at the South Pole, I ordered a new touring bike and published our first book. Jocelyn had her Surly Long Haul Trucker, an excellent touring bike. She and I kept in touch with emails discussing possible routes. We decided on flying to Marrakech, Morocco instead of the original planned start of Lisbon, Portugal. Our plan was to leave early February, which is still winter in northern Portugal and Spain. Jocelyn came up with the idea of starting in Morocco, which was brilliant to add

Africa to the trip, although I was concerned about flying into an Arab country with my daughter and two bicycles. We envisioned this travel by bicycle not so much as a cycling exercise but rather as a means to get to out of the way places, to dig deeply into a country's culture, and to meet the locals in a way normal tourists rarely do.

We both arrived home mid-November 2013 and set February 12, 2014 as our departure date. My new touring bike arrived a few weeks later at Matt's Bicycle Center in Cocoa Beach. Jocelyn took her Surly LHT to Matt's shop for a well-deserved makeover by Matt and Chris. I can't say enough about how great these guys have been on all our tours. They assembled my new bike and gave Jocelyn's a good overhaul including new rims and spokes with 26" by 2" Schwalbe tires. They also changed her chain-wheel and cogset/gear cluster gearing to match that which came with my new bike, as we wanted both bikes to have a low climbing gear and be similar parts-wise. After this and a few break-in rides, we returned the bikes to Matt for expert packing. In the meantime, we ordered and packed more new gear to encounter the year-round weather extremes and bike repairs.

We made reservations at a hostel in old town Marrakech, and they kindly arranged airport transportation to the hostel for our two bike boxes and four large duffel bags of panniers and gear. A trip like this requires many travel vaccinations. After three visits in a month to the Brevard County Health Department, our ten travel vaccinations were complete at a cost of $3,200 for both of us. All of a sudden, it was time to say goodbye again to Andee and son Cary. Ever since I 'retired' after the last space shuttle launch in August 2011, I feel like I have run away from home to bicycle the world and work in the Antarctic. Neither Andee nor I are good at saying goodbye, but I am probably worse. I know it seems cold, but I would prefer a hug and walk out the door.

Morocco to Croatia

Morocco

"On a bicycle you are inside the movie, an essential part of it. Completely reliant upon your environment, you absorb every sensation around you. You feel every change in terrain, the texture of the road, the direction of the wind, every ascent and descent, the constantly shifting weather. You smell every plant and flower, every roadkill carcass. You hear every birdcall, every insect, and animal, and the country takes you in. If you want to experience the world, get on a bicycle."

–Juliana Buhring

We arrived at Orlando International with our bike boxes and gear. When we checked in at British Airlines (BA) we were told that since we had purchased a one-way ticket to Marrakech we may not be allowed to stay in the country. We thought it strange that BA would sell a one-way ticket in the first place. Because of this, we purchased an additional fully refundable ticket from Marrakech to London to show that we planned to leave. Since we had no problems at Marrakech Passport Control, we canceled this ticket. It took Andee two months and a lot of hassle to get this refund minus a $50 service fee from BA.

We arrived at Marrakech International Airport on a connecting flight from Gatwick, London. Landing in Northern Africa was a notable moment for me, as I now have attained all seven continents! Passport Control and Customs was a breeze. Our hostel had arranged transportation and we were met by a large van. It was a crazy ride to the hostel with abundant moped and bicycle traffic. It was as if the van driver was saying, "Welcome to Morocco!" In fact, we saw a crunched bicycle lying in the street and our driver bumped into two mopeds. I quickly envisioned our future on these same roads, and it wasn't a happy thought. The moped drivers appeared senseless and didn't pay attention to any traffic or road signs. After arriving near the hostel, we and others carried everything through several narrow dark alleys too narrow for a vehicle. I kept expecting someone to run off with a bag, but the helpers were polite and efficient. On arrival at the hostel, we carried everything up three stories to an open courtyard, third-story terrace. Our room consisted of a bamboo structure with three walls, a roof, and four beds. It was cold at night and we were happy to have our minus 39°F sleeping bags. We decided to eat pretty late after we had settled in and braved the local streets for our first excursion. When we returned to our room, Russell, our Scottish roommate, exclaimed, "Well done! My hat is off to you both for surviving your first endeavor on the street, especially this late at night."

We awoke at 4:00 A.M. to the sound of Muslim morning prayers throughout numerous mosques in the city as it was blared through the mosques' loudspeakers. Right after that it was roosters and donkeys greeting the morning. The rain started, and since there were only three walls, along with a plastic tarp, we got wet. After breakfast at the hostel, we spent a few hours reassembling our bikes. We wrestled them down the narrow stairwell and rode through the streets. I must've lost a few lives during that harrowing adventure while negotiating people, traffic, mopeds, and donkeys pulling carts. Jocelyn was my wingman and kept me out of catastrophes several times. She'd finally had enough and said, "Let's get out of here, Dad!" This first foray into Morocco was enough biking for one day.

After cleaning out our bags, we covered and locked the bikes next to our little *cabana*. We felt safe in the Mama Marrakech Hostel, located in a historical *medina*. A *medina* is an old walled section of a city where people live and shop with narrow streets free from car traffic. There are more comfortable, touristy sections, but during this trip we wanted to live with the locals. Once again we ventured outside and walked to a popular market square where we enjoyed good food, a few beers, and watched many locals perform tricks and other entertaining feats. Our favorite was the classic snake charmers playing a musical instrument as a cobra rose out of a basket. It suffices to say that our world as we know it no longer exists.

Leaving Mama Marrakech Hostel for the start of our Moroccan ride.

Last year, my cousin Albert and his daughter Kathy traveled to Marrakech to participate in a charity walk across 100 miles of the Sahara Desert. We decided to hire the same tour guide they had for a one-day drive up the Atlas Mountains. Abraham picked us up for an interesting one-day tour. He also leads bicycle tours in Morocco, and we had a long talk with him about our planned route north to Casablanca and other options that he suggested. We ended up hiring him for ten days as a guide who would map our route and drive his car ahead of us. Abraham's itinerary would keep us away from the touristy areas and give us a better experience with the smaller villages and the indigenous North African Berbers. This route would take us south (instead of north as we had planned) to Quarzazate, east to Errachidia and the Sahara Desert, north to Fes, and eventually to the Strait of Gibraltar ferry. Our planned northern route to Casablanca, Rabat, and Tangiers would have put us in the land of tourists and condos.

Since we had a few days before starting this tour, we explored the *medina*. We were busy enjoying all the new sights, smells, and experiences that we had never encountered. The new food and teas were delicious and made us anticipate riding through this friendly and beautiful country on our bikes. During this time, a young guy asked me, "How many camels for your daughter?" As I looked at him, puzzled, he said, "Two Lamborghinis?" The next day at the market, an old guy came up and said, "1,000 camels for your daughter." I imagine it would take a lot of money to take care of 1,000 camels, so I said no! I figured that these guys were joking but later found out that they were probably serious.

Our first riding day was challenging as we rode over the Atlas Mountains in the rain, snow, and fierce winds. After a few knockdowns from the wind and problems with Jocelyn's loose right pedal, we limped into the village of Telouet and explored a 17th century *kasbah*, which is a type of fortress where the local leaders lived and a defense when the city was under attack. Today, many *kasbahs* are hotels. *Kasbah* Telouet was a stopping point for caravans heading to the Sahara Desert. We are both history and architecture buffs, and this ride was going to open our eyes to the immense history of Morocco. Jocelyn's pedal broke off, but Abraham was able to find a mechanic in town to reattach it. At the end of the day along a beautiful rocky valley, Abraham rode ahead and found us a room in an old Berber hotel in the town of Benhaddou.

The next day, Jocelyn's pedal broke off again in the town of Quarzazate. Once again, Abraham came through and found us a machinist who inserted new threads in the crank arm and reattached the pedal. The machinist proudly said, "This repair is guaranteed for life. If the pedal falls off again, come back." We ended up replacing the crank arm for another reason while in Istanbul, Turkey. I'm happy to say his repair held all the way there. We were able to continue to the village of Skoura where we rested comfortably in another historical *kasbah*.

The next few days found me riding along with Abraham, my bike atop his Land Cruiser, as I was sick with flu-like symptoms. I visited a pharmacy and was sold two medications. We have found that in most of the world there are pharmacies where your medical issue is diagnosed by the pharmacist who offers medication without a doctor. Jocelyn continued riding her bike by herself with us close by.

Riding through the Atlas Mountains overlooking a Berber village.

After a few days, I was well enough to get back on the saddle. The days passed with exploring many more old *kasbahs*. The locals along the streets waved and shouted greetings. We were in awe of the dated, fascinating buildings that were made out of bricks and mortar. They were decorated in fabulous artwork in the form of windows, huge ornate doors, and inside furnishings. Abraham would plan ahead for lunches and tell us to meet him down the road. He chose these picnic spots that often overlooked a small village, or sometimes we visited a local friend of his for tea. I remember one lunch where we met nomads in a cave dwelling and were served tea while watching with fascination the nomads going through their daily routine. The men tended to the animals while the women weaved carpets on old looms.

A highlight was riding through Gorges du Dades, an extremely high and magnificent river gorge. It was here we were building our climbing legs as we traversed the steep hills. We passed many villages with people yelling, "Bonjour, bonjour," to us. One of the first things we noticed in Morocco was the old French influence. It was during this ride that we purchased long scarves from roadside merchants. These turbans would serve us well in several countries, keeping the sun off our heads and giving us a cooling effect. After a few days of this, we reached a point where we would turn north or take a side trip to the Sahara Desert. It was a four-hour drive to the Sahara from here, which equates to four days of cycling, along with four days of cycling back to where we would head north. We opted to load our bikes on Abraham's Land Cruiser. Four hours later, we arrived in the town of Erg Chebbi and were in time for a sunset camel ride on the western edge of the Sahara Desert. The camel ride was a first for us, as we rode into the sunset over large sand dunes. One hour later, we were at our desert camp where we moved our gear into a huge tent like the ones you see in the movies. This two-night camp was incredible, as we spent the days exploring the dunes by hiking large ones to watch the sunsets, watching camel herds saunter by, and having our meals on a table that was carried up a small dune.

Two days later, we were back on our bikes headed north to the old historical city of Fez. It was a pleasure to be back on the bike instead of on camels! Our new energy pill is dates, of which we sampled many different kinds and purchased some to pop into our mouths as we cycled. After cycling through the cold Atlas Mountains and spending time in the cool Sahara, the desert heat south of Fez was welcomed. A few days later, we arrived in Fez and headed to the 9th century walled old-town *medina* where 350,000 people live. We toured this fascinating city before continuing north to Chechaouene in the Tassaot Mountains.

Since our tour time was short, Abraham drove us to Chechaouene, a town full of artisans that has an old-walled town *medina* just like Marrakech and Fez. The cool thing about the Chechaouene *medina* is that the entire *medina* is painted blue. He arranged for us to spend the night inside the *medina* with a family. We have been in *medinas* and have seen hundreds of interesting doors, wondering what was behind them. We were surprised how roomy it was inside the door. The living areas were on the 2nd and 3rd floors, and we had a room to ourselves. The family did not speak English but we got along just fine. We were served an excellent meal and said our goodbyes to Abraham. At night we explored inside the *medina* walls.

The following day, we biked into the mountains to Tetouan on a rainy day. The ride was stressful with all the holiday traffic, as the Moroccan schools are out and mountain travel is popular. We stopped a few times to adjust my load since I was struggling. So what does Jocelyn do? She takes my trunk bag, which contains camping gear, and adds it to the top of hers! I felt bad that she was carrying so much. We even had funny looks from the locals who noticed that I was way behind Jocelyn and carrying a smaller load. We entered Tetouan in a full gale as we were close to the Mediterranean Sea. We only made 35 miles in eight hours. By far, this was an emotional day for me as I struggled for these miles. I was beginning to have doubts of my stamina and perseverance for the upcoming miles. We rode several blocks uphill to find a hotel. We were soaked and a mess, and after cleaning up and dinner, we were fast asleep . . . until the hurricane-force winds pounded against the hotel window.

I was up most of the night listening to the howling wind and watching debris fly down the street. We considered sitting it out for the day, but Jocelyn's weather search on her phone showed the forecast winds dropping down to gale strength as a cross or tail wind. We left for Ceuta, a small, northern town in Morocco, which is Spanish territory. The rain finally stopped, but the winds were ferocious as we negotiated our way north. We were forced off the bikes several times because of the wind. Eventually we made it to the border, were stamped out of Morocco, and entered Spain. Once in Ceuta, we searched the port to find a ferry to Gibraltar. That did not exist, so we hopped a ferry to Algeciras and were told a ferry from there would get us to Gibraltar. Initially, we boarded the wrong ferry and were told, "Two ferries down." So we cycled like madmen to make it just in time. Onboard this high-speed jet ferry, we bought two beers, sat down, and wondered where Algeciras was! I figured it was in Algeria, and Jocelyn thought we may be back in Morocco near Tangiers. What was funny was that neither of us cared. So I retrieved our map and discovered that we were headed across the Strait of Gibraltar to Algeciras, Spain. All of a sudden, we saw what had to have been the Rock of Gibraltar. Some say adventure results from poor planning. If that is true, we will take the adventure any day.

Jocelyn:

I never even thought about how surreal flying into and starting our bike tour in Morocco would be until we strapped our boxes on a van and drove fluidly into the old *medina*. No lines were painted on the road, meaning no lanes to follow. Everyone drove with erotic precision. I considered coming into this country with a bit of naïve behavior, which helped me tremendously.

Somehow, I felt at home sleeping on the terrace of a hostel. Russel, our roomie, and I had hash smoking sessions while my dad and I would watch the tortoises with their painted shells walk across our stuff. We'd drink wine, listen into the dark secretive air, and wonder where we would find ourselves again. Wandering the *medina* at all hours of the day was a thrill. After the first few days, we started recognizing locals and they'd wave back. We were sort of blending in! We partied some too, ate Burger King once, and visited the main shopping square for many meals.

After meeting Abraham, I knew our lives would change. He informed us that our original route out of Marrakech would be boring and touristy. We didn't want that. He convinced us, and we eventually did see the real parts of Morocco and its people.

We stayed at a *Kasbah* across the riverbed from Ait-Benhaddou, a village famous in many movies such as *Gladiator*. We met traditional nomads near Ait Youl where I bonded with the elderly woman over our dry hands. I bought a six-meter-long turban from a blind village man near the village of Gorges du Dades.

Dad and I rode camels into the Sahara Desert as the sunset danced upon the ginormous sandy gods of these lands. We were treated to meals atop several dunes, and I enjoyed doing yoga on a new dune every day. It was only two days, but I felt like time stopped and my dad and I were here to stay. The solitude, the fresh air, and the heat soaked our bodies into a realization that this tour would be very special. Here we are, together, exploring new land physically, emotionally, and mentally. Our guide led us to the Gnaoua people, a very musical tribe filled with love and appreciation for the desert.

Breakfast at our campsite in the Sahara Dessert.

The city of Fes was so visually challenging because of all the alleys and streets. We literally walked the entire length of Fes from right to left, traversing through the old town and *medina*. Over 350,000 people live here, and there are 9,000 passageways. Almost every door has a *khasma* symbol positioned overhead to protect from the evil eye. The tile work can be simplistic and yet so precise and mind controlling.

Considering that Morocco was our first foreign country, it was a euphoric experience.

Exploring the narrow alleys in blue-washed old town medina of Chefchaouen, Morocco.

Spain

"To my mind, the greatest reward and luxury of travel is to be able to experience everyday things as if for the first time, to be in a position in which almost nothing is so familiar it is taken for granted."

–Bill Bryson

Mike:

We disembarked from the ferry after it moored in Algeciras and cycled through the port area. We stopped and asked a policeman for directions to the Gibraltar ferry and were told that it didn't exist. We continued cycling into town and found a hotel with a beautiful view of Gibraltar and the beaches. After cleaning up, we decided to spend two nights and plan our Spanish ride up the Mediterranean. My first order at a local cafe was comical. I pointed to the Spanish beer on tap and said "Two beers please." We ended up with two pieces of toast with butter. I returned to the girl and said, "*Dos cervezas, por favor.*" She smiled and gave me two beers. What was I thinking!

Our initial ride out of Algeciras was on a four-lane motorway, as we misinterpreted the on-ramp signs. We later found out that the sign with a red circle around a bicycle meant "No Bicycles Allowed". After several miles on this busy road, Jocelyn noticed a parallel frontage road that turned out to be a pleasant ride along the Spanish countryside, which eventually guided us to a pretty two-day coastal ride until we met a warmshowers.org host in the town of Fuengirola. Warmshowers.org is a website where cyclists around the world host touring cyclists. The host offers the cyclists a place to stay, which could be a spare bedroom, a couch, or space to lay out your sleeping bag. Others will offer a backyard for camping. The host also prepares dinner and/or breakfast. Through this, the touring cyclist has a safe place for the night along with informative conversation about local cycling knowledge. Usually dinner conversations turn to the entertaining 'Tales from the road' where you each share world cycling experiences. Our hosts, Fernando and Veronika, helped us carry our bikes and gear up to their apartment and served us a delicious dinner as we talked about bicycle touring. The next morning, they guided us to the start of a Spanish mountain ride to a national forest. We soon parted ways with our gracious hosts and began an all-day climb north into the mountains. It was a beautiful day, and the riding was slow but strong. We encountered groups of friendly 'roadies' who passed us saying, "*Hola*" and "*Bueno*." A roadie is a cyclist who rides a fast, lightweight road bike or is fanatical about road bike racing. After several hours and thirty miles, we found a hostel for the night.

We continued north into increasingly steep climbs where I started walking. I hadn't walked my bike since New Zealand where bicycles are called "push bikes". I still remember stopping at a pub on the South Island and talking with the bartender. We told him that we were bicycling around the South Island. He looked surprised and said, "It's all uphill from here, mate!" Several years later, I can honestly say that the world is all uphill! Because of this we only rode seventeen miles, but that took us all day. We found a mountainside hostel in the small town of La Joya. Everyone we saw with bikes walked them as the streets were just too steep. When we stopped at a bar for a quick beer, customers asked us where we had come from. When we said, "*Algeciras*," they said "Aiii!", put their hands up, and shook their heads.

After restful sleep in the tiny mountain village of La Joya, we began riding east through many peaks and valleys. I was climbing better today, while Jocelyn owned the hills. It was such a beautiful, clear day with a small headwind that we decided, after passing village after village, to keep going and see how far we could get. Around 6:00 P.M., after 36 miles, we came upon our first Spanish lake — Presa de la Vinuela — along with a campground. At the reception area, I noticed there were mobile homes available for just a few euros more. Since the tent camping areas were only covered concrete pavilions, we decided to stay in a mobile home for two nights.

Two nights later, we returned to the Mediterranean and continued east for several days along the hilly and windy coast. We occasionally had to ride on the busy A7 Highway where I was twice thrown against the guardrail by cars and trucks passing too close. There were also many frightening tunnels we had to negotiate, as most tunnels in the world do not have a shoulder, and some do not have working lights. At times, it was a battle between the steep coastal hills and strong headwinds, but we persevered. We had heard that Spain is the second-most mountainous country in Europe behind Switzerland. We were conquering one climb after another as we worked the headlands, dropped down into canyons and up another headland. Our last hosts had told Jocelyn about the web's maps.me phone application. Now she was able to download country maps and use them without Wi-Fi. These maps were excellent and showed the smaller roads that Jocelyn, our tour leader, used to navigate us around the world.

In the small city of Aguilas, we met another warmshowers host. Benno from the Netherlands had a fabulous 6th floor apartment right on the waterfront. It was here that we had our first real Spanish late-night dinner experience. Up to now we have been eating *tapas* (snack food) at bars, because the Spanish don't eat dinner until 8:30, which is way too late for us. We arrived after 8:00 and it was soon filled with families. Once you are seated, the table is yours until closing.

The next day, we climbed out of the valley with a super-fun ride as I have finally found my climbing legs. After a *cerveza* break, we met a cycle-touring couple from Germany who were biking west. They were living in Australia and had moved back to Germany but could not find jobs, so they did the next best thing — get on their bikes and tour! They told us about the route they had just ridden, and it sounded interesting, so we took their advice and rode off-road to the beach, went swimming in the Mediterranean, off-roaded around the coast, back to civilization. It was a fun way to celebrate my 61st birthday! The scenery was beautiful with old ruins and eroded beach-rock formations. We soon found ourselves in the town of Puerto de Mazarron and a campsite with rental bungalows right on the beach. At this point, we agreed on a break after seven days of riding. We visited the local super *mercado* (market) and moved in a bungalow for two nights. We had dinner at an excellent American restaurant run by a fun Scottish couple with an excellent Spanish cook. After five weeks on the road, Jocelyn and I were craving American food and we found it.

After a relaxing day on the beach, we rode to the city of Cartagena. During the last several days, we have been told that the 170 miles from Cartagena to Valencia is busy and the train was recommended. We found the train station and decided to take the advice of others. We purchased our tickets and found a hotel close by the station. We spent the rest of the day exploring the historical city of Cartagena.

Our first experience on a Spanish train was good, and there were slots in the passenger carriage where bicycles (*bicicletas* in Spanish) are hung. Four hours later, we arrived in downtown Valencia during a weeklong carnival. We negotiated through the streets full of Mardi-Gras-type revelers and thought about spending the day to enjoy the festivities but could not find a place to stay. As we navigated out of Valencia, we encountered fireworks and explosions throughout the city, which seemed like it was under attack.

As we continued toward Barcelona, the headlands and valleys were not as steep as the previous weeks. We also encountered many smaller farming roads, bike paths, and bike tunnels that eventually led to a busy Mediterranean Sea cliff-side ride around a peninsula. It was Sunday and there were many people out for an afternoon ride, and since there was no shoulder, it was a bit intimidating. On a hillside outside of Barcelona, we met another warmshowers host. Alba and Gerard were at work, so a neighbor let us into their home. We spent the afternoon cleaning our bikes, reading, and napping until they returned. The next day we drove with them to their downtown Barcelona office. A few weeks ago, we had mailed our large, heavy four-season tent home, and Andee mailed our smaller one to us. We took a bus to the airport DHL office and found a package for us which included our tent. We returned to Alba and Gerard's law office, dropped off the package, and then spent the rest of the day exploring compelling Barcelona rich with Roman history. Navigating out of Barcelona was busy and interesting, as Jocelyn expertly led our way inland through the surrounding hills because the airport blocks the coastal route.

Jocelyn:

Most of the coast of Spain was a fast and boring ride. The cliff side kept my mind in a dream state, and the left-breaking waves of many surf spots pulled me in. I wanted to play but found no surf shops around to rent a board. We ventured in and out of the hills on the coast and inner farmlands. It was fun but too much at times. My dad had to walk more, slowing our pace and breaking us down.

After taking a train trip into Valencia, our lives were turned upside down. I mean the college students that were sitting next to us were talking about the first drink they wanted and how many drinks they were trying to have, and I just looked at them with awe and sadness. I wanted to be their friend. I didn't even know we were stepping off the train into a land of festivals and parties. It was, in fact, the last day of *Fallas*, the biggest party in Spain. It was complete madness, and many streets were closed. People were dressed in all sorts of festive attire. I felt like we just walked into a fairy tale, and then we started to bike. We circled the old city and saw the Torres, two towers that represent the old city gates. We eventually found the road N340 and started heading north, but it wasn't till we got out of the city that I started to hear very intense sounding bombs! The Spanish have the most intense fireworks; one even knocked me off my bike!

After many hair-turning cliff-side climbs, we made it to Castelldefels, a beach town just outside of Barcelona. We arrived a day ahead of schedule for our warmshowers host, so we took our time finding the cheapest hotel in town. It was a bit difficult because it's a nice touristy town. When we did find one, my dad couldn't stand up inside! But for one night it worked. What we didn't know was that a *futbol* (soccer) game was going to be playing on every TV because it was two popular teams: Barcelona vs. Madrid. We happened to be right above the bar of this hotel, so we watched as Barcelona won and the town went nuts. I didn't sleep much that night and woke up with a massive hangover. I told my dad I had to sleep past 11:00 A.M., and of course he got upset with that, but sometimes sleep helps me.

March 12, 2014

There are times when the path might turn a little rocky, and I don't know where it might lead, but it is always worth a shot and a great view. We managed to make it to the top and skip six miles of road today. We didn't have to jump a fence either!

France

"It is by riding a bicycle that you learn the contours of a country best, since you have to sweat up the hills and coast down them. Thus you remember them as they actually are, while in a motor car, only a high hill impresses you, and you have no such accurate remembrance of country you have driven through as you gain by riding a bicycle."

–Ernest Hemingway

Mike:

We followed our hosts' advice to enter France from inland and not the busy coast. After two days, we had an easy climb up the southern end of the Pyrenees Mountains and entered the open border of France. Twenty miles later, we were in the town of Perpignan where we found a small motel for the night. We were up early for our first full day in France. We didn't get far when Jocelyn said, "Dad, there's a bakery!" After hearing so many appealing things about French pastries, we just had to stop. Inside the shop, we had a difficult time choosing our treats, since it all looked so good. Once outside, we tore into each of our bags. With all our cycling and burning of calories, it doesn't matter, at least on me anyway, as Jocelyn kept complaining about gaining weight. The delicious pastries fueled us for several miles. We stopped at a winery for lunch and bought an extra bottle for camping. On this day, we spent eleven hours on the road cycling to the historic city of Beziers.

In the morning, we enjoyed a walking tour of the old part of Beziers. The city dates back to 575 B.C. At the top of the hill is the Cathedral of Saint-Nazaire, which is a fascinating cathedral/fortress built in the 1200s. After a few hours we were ready to roll out of Beziers, and Jocelyn found our way to the coast and the first of many bike paths.

France is known for good bike paths and also for signing where bikes cannot go. There were a few times when bikes are allowed on major roads for a mile or two just to connect with another path. We spent the next two days traveling along the coast through small villages and fishing ports. Eventually we made it to Port de Plaisance and another warmshowers host named Brian (and two friends) who recently cycled around the world over three years and 33,000 miles. We stayed with his family and were visited by Morgan who rode with Brian. Brian's parents cooked a delicious meal, and the wine and conversation flowed while talking about world travel. As we said in our first book, a trip like this is all about the people you meet along the road.

The next morning we cycled inland and stopped to explore the 12th century walled town of Aigues-Mortes before cycling through the mostly-flat wine country. Aigues-Mortes is a striking, walled medieval town sitting on the flat marshes of the Camargue and is considered the purest example of 13th-century military architecture. It looks today pretty much like it did in the Middle Ages. The town of neatly straight-lined streets is surrounded by a fortified wall with four corner towers and a dozen fortified gates. We spent a long day riding before entering a wooded area and setting up camp. Jocelyn was happy to be camping, but I was a bit concerned with our first stealth camp as I would rather be in a campground. We had a few heated discussions on this subject while in Spain, as Jocelyn would rather be camping most of the time, whereas, at times, I enjoy a shower and bed at the end of the day. It came to a point where we each wanted a different type of trip — Jocelyn more rustic and me more comfortable.

At one point in Spain we actually thought about splitting up. This would happen on and off around the world. With two people in tight and sometimes stressful situations, the emotions can run high and the anger results in saying things that we shouldn't. Fortunately we were able to regain a levelheaded position and stay together mostly because of my wife's, Jocelyn's mom's, intervention. Sometimes the emails and Skype home would fly during these difficult times. Andee had the cooler head every time and kept our emotions in check.

The following day we headed back into the mountains for two days before dropping down to the coastal city of Frejus where we arrived in a full gale. Our search for campgrounds found two that were closed for the season, so we ended up in a hotel well after dark. The morning brought rain as we cycled into the French Riviera and had breakfast in Cannes. The red carpet was nowhere to be found for us, so we continued riding this lovely coastal area with many small towns. The wind was down and the hill work fun. We soon arrived close to Nice and searched for our next warmshowers host. As we were riding, a car stopped and our host Sandrine jumped out and gave us directions. What a coincidence that she just happened to be driving by. Our hosts Ludovic and Sandrine prepared an excellent meal with some fine French food.

The next day Ludovic took us on a tour of the walled Village of Saint Paul, one of the oldest medieval towns on the French Riviera. It was quite a treat to be driven in a car. We said farewell to another excellent warmshowers host and quickly found the bike path to Nice and beyond. It was a beautiful sunny day, and since it was Saturday the crowds were heavy as we cycled around Nice's main square including Notre Dame Cathedral. We cycled through many historic areas before heading to the town of Beausoleil, next to Monaco.

The steep hill climbing was robust as we searched for the apartment of our next host Ludovic and his wife Marisol. Ludovic spent five years hitchhiking around the world, including hitching a ride on an icebreaker to Antarctica. After settling into their apartment, they drove us the mile to Monaco and left us to explore this tiny country or principality. Monaco is the smallest country in the world, the most densely populated country, and also the richest. We were in awe as we wandered the expensive streets, explored the humongous yacht harbors, and unsuccessfully tried to enter Monte Carlo Casino made famous by James Bond.

Jocelyn:

For some reason I wasn't overly excited to cycle into France. I had heard that the French are rather rude if you don't at least try to speak their language. I tried to learn some beforehand, but I ultimately resorted back to reading off the cheat sheet I'd made and had strapped to my bicycle handlebar.

The second day was eventful. We chowed down with two pastries each for breakfast. I then proceeded to get us lost on several roads, literally zigzagged till we found ourselves on a highway that didn't allow bikes but we didn't get kicked off. Thankfully we found a winery to stop and enjoy lunch. Maynadier wine in Languedoc was a pleasant stop. We explored and tasted many wines and then walked next door to their restaurant with our seven-Euro bottle and had delicious spaghetti with raw egg yolk on top.

France has shown us some amazingly-built bike paths. I was astonished to find them, too. Our first stealth camp experience together was in France. We finally camped! Yay! Found an epic wild camp spot with this rusted fallen apart truck. It only took us over a month and a half to camp, and a huge fight about different spots where we could camp at, but I hope we continue to camp now, even if my legs are all scraped and bloody from the bush and I have many splinters in my hands. This is the type of adventure I'm looking for! I love to camp, but my dad, on the other hand, likes a warm shower, a bed, and perhaps a beer after a long day of riding. I have found that I have adopted some of his desires. I just want the beer or wine at the end of the day!

We stayed with two influential people in France, Brian from Solidream.net and Ludovic the founder of Travel with a Mission (travelwithamission.org). (both websites are in French) If it wasn't for my friend Terry Leo, we wouldn't have had such amazing connections and fun times swapping travel tales and experiences!

Italy

"My father showed me that the benefits of bicycling run much deeper than physical fitness. We've stumbled across a basic world rhythm initiated by those pedals spinning around. There's a youth force living in the suspended energy of that age-old diamond frame."
–Joe Kita "The Key to Happiness" –*Wisdom of Our Fathers*, 1999.

Mike:

We took an additional day off, rode the train back to Nice, and spent the day playing tourist. We wandered through old town Nice and enjoyed the sights, sounds, and smells of an old French city. After one more night with our hosts, we were back on the road to Italy. The border was again open, and we quickly noticed that the Italian coast was a lot like Spain with the steep headlands and valleys. At the end of the day, we found a campground that wasn't open yet but the owner let us pitch our tent. It was a pretty site that overlooked the Mediterranean Sea. It was raining the next day as we climbed through headlands and arrived in the major port city of Genova. Genova is Italy's leading port, with a long history of maritime power that began when it defeated rival Pisa in the 10th century. The riches that flowed into the city in the 16th and 17th centuries still show in the marble palaces. Since it was rush hour, the traffic slowed us down, but with Jocelyn's navigation, we were able to find a hotel in the busy downtown area bordering the historical waterfront. We don't like riding after dark, but this was one of those days that required it. The first order of business was to find a fine Italian beer and what else — pizza! For some reason we wanted to watch the movie, *The Godfather*.

Genova is full of forts and interesting monuments, but since it was still raining we decided to continue east. It took over three hours to cycle across the sprawling city. Once we were out of the city, we turned south along the scenic Italian Coast. The coastal road gave way to the mountains, which we started climbing while keeping an eye out for a place to camp. We were both out of water as we rode into the village of Mattarana where we stopped at a restaurant to refill our water bottles. Jocelyn noticed that there were rooms above the restaurant, so I immediately inquired and it was also a hotel! On the premises was an award winning restaurant where we enjoyed an excellent dinner.

Riding toward the mountains in picturesque old Northern Italy

Our goal for the next day was another warmshowers host in the small village of Bargecchia, west of Pisa. We passed many small towns until we reached the Mediterranean Coast once again. Throughout Italy and the smaller towns, we enjoyed the sound of church bells and I always looked to see if the bells were really clanging (not electronic), and they were. The coast of Massa consists of miles and miles of beach clubs preparing for the upcoming tourist season (May to September). Our host, Perla, said that she used to work there and families are charged up to $6,000 for the summer at their beach resort consisting of chairs, umbrella, showers, changing rooms, etc. This does not include lodging and food. Occasionally there is a 'free beach' that is clearly marked. There are even sprinklers on the beach to give it the groomed look.

We found our way to Perla's house high upon a hill. She was an enjoyable host and cooked us a delicious Italian meal that we savored along with two bottles of wine from a vineyard where she used to work. She had two dogs that we thoroughly enjoyed as we are missing ours. Perla has traveled around the world, working and cycling, and is planning a five-year world bicycle tour.

After a delicious Perla breakfast, we left early for Pisa on a back route mapped out by her. In Pisa, we visited a famous leaning tower with hundreds of others and then made tracks to Florence. At first, the riding was fairly flat but soon turned hilly and we continued charging. We arrived in Florence on a busy Friday evening at 6:30 P.M. and soon found a hotel. We had thought about taking a train to Rome, but it sounded way too touristy for us, and besides, the Rome trains were on strike.

Throughout our trip along the Mediterranean, we have always been one step ahead of the tourist season. It was now April and one month from the start of the busy season. We have been fortunate with this and sometimes have cycled through seemingly deserted towns that were just waiting for tourists. The result was less traffic, fewer people, and cheaper prices.

Florence is a city that easily excites the senses and your intellectual admiration. Florence is beyond beauty. We spent two days walking the streets where there is always something inspiring to view along with delicious food and wine to savor. We would have liked to have spent more time in this city, but we are meeting family in Istanbul, Turkey at the end of May, in about six weeks, and we must continue moving.

From Florence, we headed north toward Venice and spent an afternoon in another historical city of Bologna. We researched access to Venice and discovered that it is difficult, safety wise, to arrive by bicycle, and in Venice bicycles are not allowed on the streets. Later we would find out how true this was. With that information, we rode to the Bologna train station and hopped onboard the Trenitalia to Venice. A few hours later, we exited the train and immediately realized we had to find a place for our bikes as the streets were narrow and packed with people, and the pedestrian bridges that connect the many islands are difficult to negotiate on a bike. We quickly found a hotel, stored our bikes, and spent the rest of the day and night having fun as tourists. Venice is a spectacular city on the water. We wanted to ride one of the famous gondolas, but the price of a boat ride was ridiculous and insulting. The next morning, we wrestled our bikes over 25 arched bridges to the ferry side of the island. Only once did a gentleman offer to help Jocelyn. After that, most people stared at us, as it was difficult to wrestle our bikes up and over steps. Between this, we guided our bikes through narrow alleys. Jocelyn used the maps.me app on her phone and expertly led our way to the ferry. The ferry dropped us off on the mainland, and after pushing hard over steep hills with the snow-filled Italian Alps in the background, we were within fourteen miles of the Slovenian border.

Jocelyn:

Now we have finally traveled into some massive hills. We cycled all day and maybe saw just ten cars during that time. One lengthy climb took us over three hours. We made it to the top with a limited amount of water. Dad and I discussed our options to camp or to continue down the hill. It was just about an hour after dusk, so a heavy, dark, black, foam shadow moved over all objects in its path, including us. I could tell that my dad was feeling anxious, and I wished we could just stay up on top of the mountain for the night. Cycling in complete darkness was out of the question, but we had a goal.

Before going up the massive hill to our host, Perla's, house, we decided to stop at this corner bar right off the street. We sat on the street next to an old man who was bundled up, and I was dressed in shorts and a tank top. The old man talked to us for a very long time as we stuffed our faces with popcorn. I don't know anything he said, but it was important. We finally made it to our goal, Perla's home!

Perla was our warmshowers hostess that went above and beyond in inviting us into her lovely home on top of a hill where you could indeed see the Leaning Tower of Pisa. We were welcomed with wine and good, wholesome food that would fuel us for the adventures ahead.

Jocelyn posing with the Leaning Tower of Pisa.

April 15, 2014

This morning in Venice, after 18 bridges with steps ranging from 8 to 25, we made it to the ferry. Carrying a Surly bike is tough, and I give props to all the guys that bring in supplies to Venice. I bruised my right hip from placing the frame on it, and I bruised my knee from my bike rack. Oh, and my pedal decided to attack my calf several times! Only one man offered to help me while walking through Venice. SAD.

Prepared for a cold and wet ride.

Slovenia

"If you reject the food, ignore the customs, fear the religion and avoid the people, you might better stay at home."
—James Michener

Mike:

We crossed into Slovenia and started climbing immediately in this eye-appealing country and soon found a lunch spot. We ordered the local favorites, which was a combination of enjoyable fish dishes. Our server gave us a sample of his homemade 'schnapps' made from grape skins after the juice is removed. As evening approached, we were at a closed campground in Ajdovscina. While we discussed our options, a mother and her two young children walked by and said the camp was closed but that we could pitch our tent nearby in her backyard garden. At that warm offer, we followed her home and set up our tent while playing with her children. Her husband soon arrived, and we were immediately welcomed into their home for an evening of food and wine. It was a pleasure to stay with Marko, Melita, and their two girls Zoya and Rina. We discussed our upcoming route north to Austria and were told there may be one border crossing open as it was still early in the season. Marko and Melita had bicycled that route through Austria and Hungary, and they had also bicycled south through the Balkan Peninsula on their honeymoon and highly recommended that route because it was prettier and a lot cheaper. I had read about the Balkans in my research on routes, and it did sound interesting.

After breakfast and continued route discussions we decided to travel south through the Balkan Peninsula. Every host we have stayed with has suggested this route instead of Austria, Hungary, Romania, Bulgaria, Greece, and Turkey.

Jocelyn:

I don't think we actually knew we were cycling into Slovenia until we crossed the border with the sign saying so. Vineyard after vineyard with the Alps in the background was most of the scenery along with buildings taken over by vines and moss.

I somehow saw that there was a campground and went there after only like thirty miles in the country. The campground was closed, of course. But we met Melita, Zoya, and Rina, a young family, and were welcomed into their backyard. It's been awhile since someone actually opened up to us like Melita, and I was shocked. She was lovely, and we followed her to her soft, green area in her backyard next to their large garden.

While Marko, her teacher-husband, and Melita cooked us dinner, I read *Zoja*, a book with depictions of the world, and she thought I was an Australian aboriginal like a picture in the book. We laughed for a bit, and I realized I was much tanner than any individual she has probably ever met! We owe many thanks to this family for pointing us to the opposite direction we were indelibly going to ride.

Croatia to the Republic of Georgia

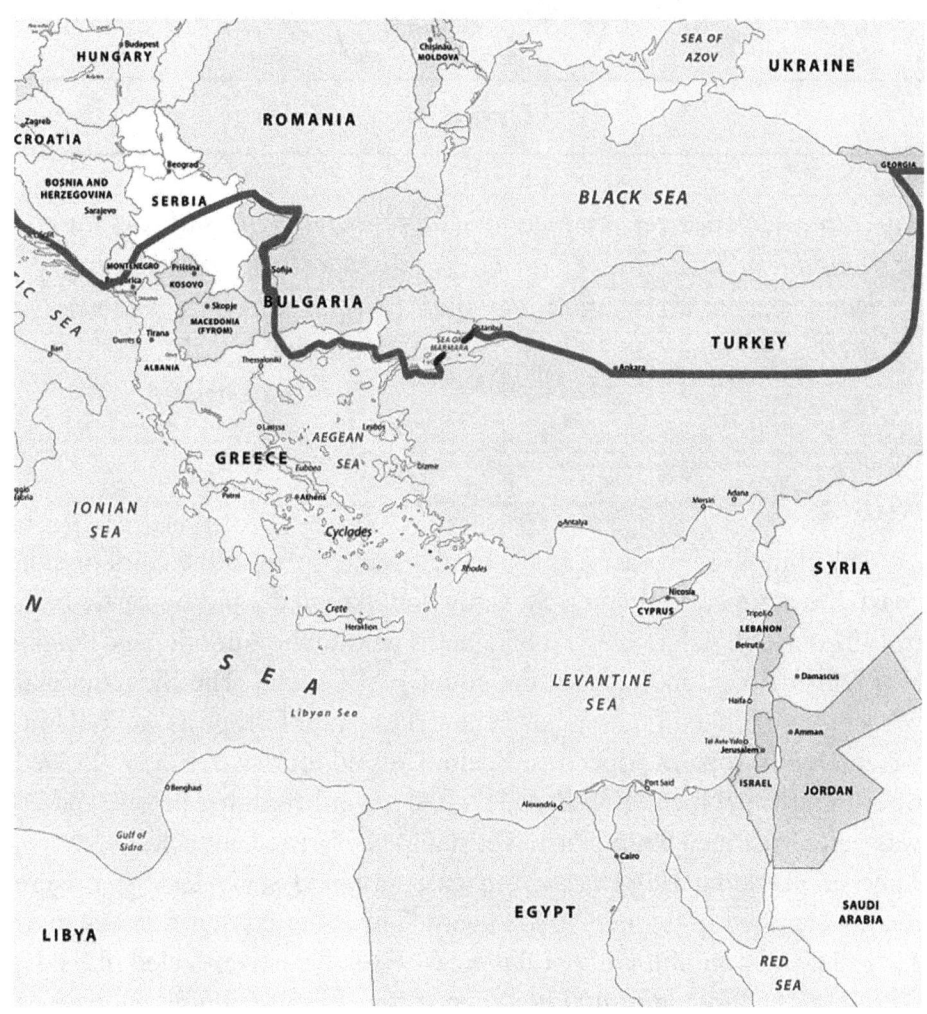

Croatia

"A bicycle does get you there and more...And there is always the thin edge of danger to keep you alert and comfortably apprehensive. Dogs become dogs again and snap at your raincoat; potholes become personal. And getting there is all the fun."

–Bill Emerson

Mike:

The climbing increased as we turned south down to the Adriatic Sea coast. We stopped in Stanjel, Slovenia and explored a hilltop castle built in 1402. After lunch, we found bike paths next to the Adriatic Sea, thanks to a fellow biker, and entered the country of Croatia. The Slovenia exit border guard looked for a Spanish entry stamp into Europe as we told him we entered Europe in Algeciras, Spain. He said tourists are only allowed three months upon entering Europe. I had never heard that before, and he was quite frustrated that Spain never stamped us in and neither did France, Italy, or Slovenia. He returned our passports and said, "Go." We were readily stamped in by the Croatia guard. The roller coaster ride began as the terrain was rolling without flat areas. We have never cycled like this, so it was challenging at first but soon it was fun. It certainly slowed us down, and toward sunset we found a campground.

Easter Sunday found us in a cycling rhythm as we crossed over the showery Croatian Mountains to the other side of the peninsula where we found the sun and a rocky coast. The towns we passed had interesting war memorials where we stopped many times for pictures. On the coast, we turned north, rode up to the city of Rikeja, and then followed the road south. We spent several days negotiating with the traffic in the rain. The drivers passed us within inches and didn't seem to care about their speed or if cyclists were on the road. After a few days with the rain increasing, we decided that it was too dangerous to ride, so we stopped at a hotel. The next day was clearing as we climbed all day through a sparse part of the country that included only one small town. Toward sunset we rode into the town of Karlobag. Since the nearest campground was fifteen miles away, we rented a room from a private home at a small price in this cool little town. We spent a few more days riding and camping down the coast at empty campgrounds before arriving in the large port city of Split. We were interested in island hopping, and after two hours of navigating the city streets we found the ferry dock. We bought a ticket to Vela Luka on the island of Korcula, and at 3:00 P.M. we were aboard for a three-hour, 62-mile ferry ride. We arrived in Vela Luka, found a hotel, and enjoyed the evening exploring and eating.

Around every bend on the Croatian Coast was a beautiful fishing village and harbor.

After more than three months, our bikes required attention. My rear wheel was wobbling and the rear brake pads were worn. Usually a wobble in the wheel is caused by loose spokes with a need for wheel truing. Jocelyn knows how to true a wheel, but this didn't solve the problem so I replaced the brake pads and turned my attention to Jocelyn's bike with a vibration on the rear wheel. After removing the rear wheel, the chain twisted into a knot that we could not straighten. This is called a 'Gordian knot', and no matter what we did, we could not remove this knot so we decided to remove the chain. I could not find our chain removal tool, but a mechanic friend of the hotel clerk came to help us. It was way past checkout time, but the clerk said, "No problem." Jocelyn tightened her spokes and trued her rear wheel. The mechanic was able to remove the chain and install a spare. I also cleaned the grease and crud from both bikes. Finally, at 4:00 P.M., we were repacked and ready to go. When a heavy downpour started we decided to spend another night. We walked to the corner market for food and then settled down for the night.

The next day was sunny as we cycled thirty miles to the other end of Korcula and boarded a twenty-minute ferry ride to Orebic on the Peljesac Peninsula of Croatia. Neither bike was working properly as we nursed our way across the island. Jocelyn's chain was skipping on the rear gear while climbing, almost causing her to fall several times. In our accommodations for the night, we used Wi-Fi to research bicycle repair in the next major city of Dubrovnik. Jocelyn found that there is only one bicycle mechanic in the city, and since the road to Dubrovnik is over another mountain range, we decided to ride the morning bus.

We arrived at the bus stop for Dubrovnik at 6:45 A.M. and waited in the heavy rain. The bus appeared and was full of school students, but the driver kindly found a place for us and our bikes. After a three-hour trip over the mountains, we were in the ancient city of Dubrovnik. We reassembled our bikes, and then I walked the streets and asked about bicycle repairs. Finally, after inquiring at a dozen shops, I heard about the one bicycle mechanic from a scooter shop. The scooter rental guy called him and gave me directions to his garage. Thanks to this, we found his garage, and thanks to another gentleman who translated for us. Tony, the only bicycle mechanic in a city of 300,000 people, worked on our bikes, and Kreso offered us a reasonable apartment if needed. We took Kreso up on his offer, and after Tony completed repairs on our bikes, we were led to an apartment for the night. This gave us our day to explore the old town of Dubrovnik.

There is one thing you learn quickly on a trip like this. I am not a real social person and can be quiet. I guess I could be called somewhat of an introvert. But in a foreign country you throw all that out, because when you need help, you have to just 'Go for it' and walk up to strangers on the street, shop keepers, or police to ask for help. There can be no holding back when your trip depends on finding what you need. Both Jocelyn and I have always sought out help, and we are happy to say that most people in the world are friendly and want to help. In our experience, we have found that you must ask multiple people because they will answer even if they don't know. If you get two answers relatively the same — that's the way . . . maybe!

We walked to the walled town of Dubrovnik and enjoyed a few hours exploring the town that dates back to the 7th century, although there are records of a wooden city in place in the 3rd century before Christ. Dubrovnik is a mighty fortress surrounded on three sides by water. It also has a history of being ruled by many countries. It was a fun day to blend in with other tourists, knowing that our bikes were safely locked in an apartment. Dubrovnik is a bit too pretty though, with excessive restoration. There is a fine line between the two, and we like old stuff to look — old.

We woke to more hard rain and waited in our rental until 11:00 A.M., but it never let up. Croatian drivers and riding bicycles in the rain just don't match, as we had many close calls in the past few weeks, and since there is a large, busy hill to climb out of Dubrovnik on the way to Bosnia, we decided to take a weather day. We spent the day cleaning out our panniers, watching two movies, and visiting a Mexican restaurant down the street. We basically did nothing, which most bicycling tourists do when bad weather sets in.

The next day brought the sun and we left early for our ride to Bosnia. We are going to miss the coast but have decided to cycle inland to discover Romania and Bulgaria. Changing our route is one thing we do well. Nothing is set in stone with us, and we like it that way. This quote says it well:

"I see my path, but I don't know where it leads. Not knowing where I'm going is what inspires me to travel it."

–Rosalia de Castro

Jocelyn:

Tuesday April 29, 2014

Sincere Notice to: Cars, Trucks, Semi-trucks, buses, RVs, horse/pony drawn carriages, motorcycles, tractors, mopeds, and camels, etc.

My name is Jocelyn, and I am your friendly touring cyclist. I am traveling through your homelands on a bicycle with just two wheels, four bags, and myself. I wear a helmet, my bags are bright red, and my clothes are usually brightly colored. You can find me "hugging" or riding close to the white line. Sometimes there is a shoulder, a bike lane, or even a bike path, but for most of the time there is a single white line and you. I understand that you are larger than me; your vehicle is more powerful and can run me over. But why must you scare me like you do? I am, after all, a human being, with loved ones just like you, with a heart maybe bigger than yours, and an actual brain. I know it's hard to believe that I choose to cycle day after day, sunrise to sunset.

Sometimes you make me feel like I'm going into battle. I wave at your obnoxious horn honks; I share the peace sign in response to your angry screams. I stay close to the white line and hold on to my handlebars with white knuckles. Maybe you don't know what resides on the other side of the white line? Well, let me tell you: there could be a curve, a guardrail, sharp rocks, nails, snails, a cliff, a ditch, a pedestrian, or, often times, water.

Many things can be obstacles preventing me from being on the "right" side of the white line. Sometimes when you honk, or you speed by pushing me closer to the cliff, or race past sucking me into your vacuum vortex, I become more fearful because you don't give me any room. I'm trying to enjoy your countryside, and see the world from my slower-moving bicycle. You must know that I am allowed on the road, just like you. All I ask is for all drivers to be more than cautious and join the 5% that always move over at least two feet to pass around me. Hey, that's less than a meter, and I know the distance takes a moment for you to register a change in your steering. Please take a breath and slow down for just a few seconds while you pass me. Somehow,

I know how close you are when my left calf muscle tightens and my heart starts to beat faster. It won't take but a few minutes of your time to notice when the passing lane is clear and then just go slower around me! Is that too much to ask? Can you live with your conscience knowing you might cause harm to an innocent world traveler?

I am a human life riding on this painted white line, and I try to stay among the living. I'm not just a foreign object, a deadbeat cruiser without any ambitions, or another species of animal. Oh, one more very important reason for being a thoughtful person. Would you also look out for my dad, as he is a little slower and usually behind me, somewhere. He is the reason I am sharing this journey of a lifetime, and I don't want to see his "bucket list" cut short.

Heartfelt greetings and simple requests from the world touring cyclist,
Jocelyn

Bosnia-Herzegovina and Montenegro

"After your first day of cycling, one dream is inevitable. A memory of motion lingers in the muscles of your legs and round and round they seem to go..."

–H.G. Wells

Mike:

We entered Bosnia after a short ten-mile climb. The views of Bosnia from the mountains were fantastic. After lunch in a small town, the rain started again but fortunately backed off during our climb to Montenegro. The climb was a fairly easy 4,500 feet that continued for many miles, and the summit border crossing took almost 2½ hours. After a quick descent, we stopped at a café for dinner. A few miles later, Jocelyn found a quiet spot to wild camp.

After a wet and cold wild camping night we were on the road at 6:00 A.M. A few hours later, we stopped in a distant restaurant to warm ourselves from last night's cold. We were quite miserable and were only able to eat a little but did warm up after several cups of hot tea. After another few miles on a wet, muddy road, we decided to stop for the day in Niksic, Montenegro. We found a hotel, spread out the tent to dry, and had our laundry done. Usually we wash our clothes in a sink, a shower, or a river. After six weeks, it was a real treat to have our clothes laundered as they smelled awfully bad. We had breakfast in Croatia, lunch in Bosnia, and dinner in Montenegro!

We left Niksic expecting more rain and slowly climbed to the local ski area. The views were majestic as we rode along the sparsely snowy roads. We were enjoying classic European hairpin turns and climbing until a spoke popped through and slashed the rear tube of my bike. My bike was still jumping badly when using the rear brakes, and I suspected a bad rim, and Jocelyn's chain was jumping around on her gear cluster — still. While changing the tube, I noticed cracks emanating from most of the rim's spoke holes. At this point, I walked my bike because my rim was cracked, while Jocelyn rode ahead to find an accommodation suggested by people in the last town of Savnik. She found a cabin available in a campground where there was also a restaurant.

Montenegro achieved after a long, wet mountain ride.

We woke early to work on my bike. The rear rim was badly cracked and needed to be replaced. The restaurant owner kindly attempted to call his friends who spoke a little English but to no avail until a customer came in who did speak some English. Through her, we found a bike shop in the capital city of Podgorica and a gentleman with a trailer who could drive us. After negotiating a price with our driver, we were driven back seventy miles to one of only two bike shops in Montenegro.

The Podgorica bike shop immediately saw the problem and said that they could replace the rim. We followed their suggestion for an inexpensive hotel down the street, as my bike won't be ready until the next day. This journey shows how a stranger in a strange land feels. When times seem difficult, there is always a local to come through and help even through the language barrier.

Once the repairs were complete we were off again toward Serbia with a new rear rim and chain. We climbed for two days in the increasing rain and were soon riding in the snow. It was cold, and after a scary tunnel ride of 3,400 feet, the cold descent began. The long tunnel did not have any working lights or shoulder. Jocelyn was riding point, and the cars were easily passing us. I yelled out to Jocelyn, "I sure hope a truck or bus doesn't come our way." Right when I said that, a series of buses and trucks were headed toward us. I was panicking and recorded the entire tunnel ride on video. If there was ever a time when I thought *This is it for us,* it was now. I think I closed my eyes for several moments. At the bottom of the descent, we stopped at a restaurant where we each had two bowls of hot soup. About fifteen miles from the Serbian border, we found a warm motel room.

Jocelyn:

May 1, 2014

Even though the entire afternoon consisted of rain, Bosnia has absolutely stunning views. The pictures don't do it justice.

We climbed for two hours in the pouring rain, ran out of water besides my emergency water, and I opted to get even more soaked filling my bottles at a waterfall off the rocks. The water was delicious, so let's see if I get sick! For the remainder of the day, I was soaked head to toe. Got strange looks from both border patrol stations, but we eventually made it to the Black Mountain we'd been staring at all day! We pulled into a small café around 6:00 P.M. and stayed an hour to warm up and eat. No rooms to rent inside, so I found an excellent stealth camp area and quickly set up camp and we were in our sleeping bags by 8:00 P.M.! I stayed soaked the entire night. This morning, we broke down camp before 5:30 A.M. and have already ridden 20 miles until I found this cafe we're at now. I need loads of coffee for sure.

May 3, 2014

My face is constantly like this now. With every beautiful view I see, my jaw drops, my eyes twitch every which way, and it's only after inhaling several bugs that I realize what a dork I must look like. Happy face!

Today from Berane we continuously climbed into the mountains! "All I do is climb, climb, and climb all the way up. Got downhills on my mind, I can't ever seem to find — HAYYYYYYYY!" Snow falls and sticks, and its making our breathing seem rather heavy. I'm a bit cold, as my base layer under my windbreaker is just my tank top and a fishing shirt because I wasn't prepared for this snow pass and yet I chugged along in second gear!

Personal Journal Note:

I prefer living outdoors. I like vegetables, but I eat meat regularly. I like to work out all day long. If I'm not cycling, I'm eating or sleeping. I like cuddles only sometimes. I also don't care for meaningless conversations, and if I feel like you aren't even listening, I'll just shut up. I prefer silence. I am fearless. Except for Alzheimer's disease, nothing scares me. I like climbing mountains and hate straight roads, but I'll beat you any day on a solid straight road. I'm secretly competitive and love to have fun. I'm crazy in the mind, and I'm working on that. Since coming down with some bug, I've only ridden 32 miles and it was all uphill, and I climbed into the snow of 5,000-foot mountains. My dad ran into major bike problems and had to walk for some time, so I rode ahead. Some locals waved me on to find a small A-frame cabin that I paid only 30 euros and we slept in fire warmth. The next day in a matter of 30 minutes, we found a man capable of driving us to the capital to a bike shop. We're waiting on our bikes now, and I'm watching MTV San Francisco Real World. Smh (shake my head), and everyone here is laughing. Still smh. I went from mountains to city. One day I shall stay in the mountains for good.

High in the mountains crossing from Montenegro to Serbia.

Serbia

"I seek to learn about the world around me. I seek to learn about what I actually am. I seek to learn how to be a proper human being."

–Ringu Tulku Rinpoche

Mike:

For the first time in three weeks the day was bright and sunny. We stopped in the border town of Rozaje to convert our leftover marks (Bosnia) and kunas (Croatia) to euros and to purchase fruit. We climbed out of Montenegro and into our 10th country, Serbia. It was quite apparent that we were more than welcome from all the friendly honks and waves. The riding was easy and the countryside beautiful as we followed a swiftly flowing river down in a deep gorge. We passed through many short tunnels, and as Jocelyn was playing "The Sound of Music" on her portable speaker, it truly seemed that "The hills are alive with the sound of music…" At the first town, we stopped in a restaurant and asked if they took euros. They did and we had a delicious lunch and our first Serbian beer.

After lunch we had a long climb and then a drop into a huge, beautiful valley and our first city of Novi Pazar. During this climb, I had another rear tire puncture but could not find the source. So we installed a new tube and arrived in town to search for a few more spare tubes and a currency exchange. We did stop at two bike shops, but they didn't have 26-inch tubes. Fortunately, Jocelyn spotted a third shop that looked fully equipped and I purchased two spares. This was an excellent stop, as once again we witnessed as how this journey is about the people we meet. The shop's owner, Sead, didn't speak much English, but his daughter, Seida, spoke it well and they were immediately interested in our ride. They came outside to meet Jocelyn, and we were invited into their next-door home for Turkish coffee and sweets. We had a pleasant time visiting with them while learning about their life and them ours. Sead gave us a gift of spare brake pads. His wife Fetija bought us sweets for the road. Seida led us to a currency exchange. They recommended a nearby hotel, and Seida showed us the way and talked to the hotel staff about our need to lock up the bikes in a storage area. We talked with them on the street that evening as we strolled through town and were invited to breakfast.

At 4:00 A.M. we woke to the sound of morning prayers from the Mosques' loudspeakers. We haven't heard this since Morocco. But this time it was joined by all the local dogs howling out of tune. The dogs were hilarious! It was a quick walk to Sead's home for a delicious Turkish breakfast. The family loaded us down with fresh bread, apples, and other goodies. Seida gave Jocelyn a beautiful embroidered bag and Sead gave us additional spare bike parts. We left Novi Pazar around noon and started weaving our way through the high mountains and valleys along a swollen rushing river. We sadly saw this river full of trash. Seida had told us that Serbians dump their trash anywhere outside of towns because there is no proper dump or pickup. The rain of the last three weeks was apparent, as the river was swollen and flowing over the banks. Our ride continued for many hours and turned out to be one of the best rides of our trip, as the riding was fun and the scenery stunning. At sunset we arrived in the town of Zica and immediately found a homestay where we rented a room for the night. We locked our bikes in an office and were served a delicious meal.

The last few weeks I have heard and tolerated loud squeaks once every revolution from my bike's crank arm. I finally had time to research the issue, which pointed to a loose crank arm or bottom bracket failure. While riding out of Zica, we spotted a bicycle shop and decided to let them look at it as we didn't have the tools to disassemble the crank arm and the constant squeak was irritating. During the disassembly, nothing was noted as being loose so the mechanic installed a new bottom bracket. I am happy to say that this solved the problem and once again I had peace and quiet while cycling.

Two days later we stayed with another warmshowers host near the Bulgarian border. Viktor, his wife and daughter built a modern and ecological ranch house. They warmly welcomed us to their farm and invited us to stay in the home's loft. We were up late after a fine meal and talked about our upcoming route through 'the old country' of Eastern Europe.

We stayed with this friendly family in Novi Pazar, Serbia. When we left, they loaded us down with fresh food and gifts.

Viktor's farm is only two miles from the Bulgarian border. He knew the owner of the local bike shop and suggested that Jocelyn's wheel be checked because from now on there would be few bike shops. He had also planned to spend the day working on a friend's ranch. We drove the Surly to the Zajecar bike shop and then joined Viktor and his friends for the day. It was a real hoot to join in this endeavor along with several others, as we enjoy spending time with the locals. We sat around a large table for breakfast, which consisted of beer, wine, brandy, and bread. About two hours later, the owner said, "Time to work." We worked all day shaving timbers for fence posts and setting them. After a long day, a huge barbeque was set aflame and a grand meal was enjoyed with more wine, beer, and brandy. We returned to the bike shop to discover that Jocelyn's rear rim was also cracked. This was a second failure of our rims and the inside cracks were apparent. I outfitted both bikes with the same rims. The mechanic said that the failure was due to weight. I had researched touring rims extensively, but obviously these are not good rims for touring with heavy loads. The good news was that the rim was replaced, but the bad news was that it was replaced with the same model as it was the 'best' rim the shop had in stock. What's funny is that we have been in Serbia for four days and have visited four bike shops! We had a pleasant time in Serbia and consider this country one of our highlights and will miss the people.

Jocelyn:

First views of Serbia consisted of epic downhills, sunshine, and cloudless riding through several Serbian towns with more modern housing. But what I don't understand is why they dump their trash in the rivers and not in a dump! Trash litters the riverbed. Oh, and Dad got another flat tire! I was too busy jamming out until the hitchhiking man I passed whistled so loud for me to hear. I joked going by him and pointed to my back and said, "Hop on!" He laughed, and so I thought he was trying to get me to come back to pick him up until my dad yelled out about his flat. I took out the flat tube and began inspecting it but couldn't find the puncture till the man said, "*Voda,*" (water)! And I just turned and said, "You're so smart!" There was an open well filled to the top just ten feet away. I then I found the puncture, thanks to the water, and enjoyed the old man's company as Dad changed his flat.

May 7, 2014

The rest of the ride went like this: We peddled on and on and stopped for two beers. We called it a *pivo* (beer in Russian) crawl, and we ate a picnic lunch from the Seida family of apples and bread. We got many honks, waves, and thumbs up! And even two calls of, "Good luck!" The truckers all moved over as we rode on forever. It wasn't like any other ride before. We raced the swollen river along many winding roads, and yes, even the buses moved over and a few honked and waved too! We're tired after this fun ride, and eating a splendid dinner. We've both decided, today was our favorite ride of this tour, by far the best, by far the farthest and the most enjoyable.

We rode many miles with just over 100 km. I pushed my dad hard and we averaged 12.6 miles an hour. We started at noon, arrived at a hotel at 7:00 P.M., and paid $30 U.S., and that's 3,000 *dinars*! Our dinner last night was 1,000 *dinars*. I freaked out about the cost and then did the calculation and realized it was like $12 U.S. Thanks!

Bulgaria and Romania

Mike:

We left Victor's farm early and were soon in Bulgaria. We immediately noticed the changes Victor had talked about. There were high razor-wire fences and tall guard towers. The border guards were abrupt, making it a bit intimating to enter Bulgaria, while checking out of Serbia was friendly and easy. We were surprised that no visa was required and that it is still a free world so far on our trip. The towns we passed were ill-kept and dirty, but the countryside was still scenic. We rode to the city of Viden and had lunch along the Danube River but were uncomfortable with people staring at us and seeing all the trash strewn about. Cycling through town took us over broken-up roads and past eroding buildings. We crossed the Danube River Bridge into Romania and were surprised at the immediate difference in friendly people and cleanliness. In our first Romanian town, we checked into a hotel and noticed a local festival that was in full swing, and we anticipated sampling the regional food. After visiting three ATMs attached to banks, we were unsuccessful in acquiring the local currency. We would later find out that one of them took several hundred dollars from our account that later would be attributed to bank fraud. This was the second time our account was compromised. The first was the ferry ticket office in Ceuta, Spain while purchasing a ticket to cross the Strait of Gibraltar where $1,200 was stolen from our credit card to buy art in Asia.

The next day was stormy and the forecast wasn't any better, so we rode east for our only Romanian day ride. We had planned to visit Transylvania and the castles to the north, and we inquired about storing our bikes at the hostel and then boarding a train or bus, but it just didn't work out. Family is meeting us in Istanbul toward the end of May, so we will head south. The ride was wet and fun as we rode through the countryside with many villages. The locals were friendly as they smiled and waved. In the village of Bechet, we stayed at a hostel close to Port Bechet. The proprietor told us that a touring cyclist who recently left had attempted to board a bus to Transylvania but was denied boarding with her bike. The next morning we checked out of Romania, and I asked when the ferry to Bulgaria left and was told around noon. There were three cars lined up and two hours to kill, so I decided to move some weight from the rear panniers to the front to relieve pressure on the rear wheel, while Jocelyn stretched out the tarp to take a nap. After I removed everything from my bike, the cars boarded the ferry. We quickly threw everything together and were the last to board. The ride to Bulgaria wasn't even a mile across the Danube River. We re-entered Bulgaria and I finished the weight redistribution outside the border crossing.

After a long day of wet roller coaster mountain riding, we made it to the large mountainside city of Vratsa. Shortly after arriving, a major storm system covered Vratsa so we quickly found a hotel. We received a cold shoulder at a nearby restaurant and were actually laughed at, but the hotel owner was friendly. This was a bit disturbing to us since this treatment also happened in Viden. The next day, the thunderstorms continued and our goal of Sophia through a mountain pass was also weathering the same storm. The forecast was the same for the following day. At this we decided to take a weather day off.

Bulgaria is quite depressing. The old Communist world is apparent everywhere. The farmed countryside looks like anywhere else in the world, but there is starkness, almost ugly, in the towns and cities. We walked this morning between storms and couldn't get over the 'ruins' on the roads, buildings, or sidewalks. All trees, bushes, and weeds were fully overgrown. It makes us appreciate what we have at home.

Our weather-break day activities consist of eating junk food, drinking a few beers, watching television, and catching up with Wi-Fi. It is interesting that the further east we travel the more English television there is. In general we get bored and look forward to the next day's ride. We continue to have occasional arguments. Some think that we are on a vacation, and in some ways that is true. We argue, we cry, we each have our quiet times, but we also laugh, we smile, and we gaze in wonder as we discover and live in this world with our bicycles, which is incredible in itself as our whole world is contained on these two vehicles. Jocelyn is an excellent navigator and keeps us on track. She is my wingman and is always looking out for me. We are good and still going strong together. I see us as Felix and Oscar on the television show *The Odd Couple* with me as Felix and Jocelyn as Oscar.

The next day the thunderstorms continued. During our walk around town yesterday, we had noticed a train station so today we decided to try and reach Sofia by train. 'Try' is the key word here, as in so many places in the world, it can sometimes become a huge challenge. If unsuccessful, we would just ride. Through a comedy of translations and running around the depot, we had tickets in our hand for the 8:39 A.M. train to Sofia. When the ancient-looking train arrived, Jocelyn immediately called it the 'scary train' as evidenced by the train's abundant odd graffiti. It quickly arrived, and without the kind help of others we could not have loaded our bikes on time as the train left so suddenly. The conductor barked orders in an intimidating manner. We struggled heaving our bikes onto different cars and stood by each for the 67-mile trip. We would have liked to sit and watch the countryside pass by, but we were busy moving each bike as passengers used the stinking WCs (water closet). The only spot for our bikes were at the end of each carriage right next to the WC door. The ride was so rough that we fought to hold the bike with one hand and the carriage wall with the other during the entire trip.

We arrived in Sofia and welcomed the elevator to the main crossover but soon found that we were stuck with no working elevators to go up to the main street. We manhandled each bike with panniers (about 100 pounds each) up two flights of stairs. Add to that the rude people trying to squeeze by us and you get the picture. We were soon on our way out of Sofia when two Bulgarians stopped us on the street and asked us about our trip. They were cyclists and warned us of gypsies. This is the first time in Bulgaria that we have made friends, so we were happy to talk with them and they asked if we needed anything. During the rest of the day there were several friendly Bulgarians that talked with us.

We climbed out of Sofia in the pouring rain. After twenty miles on a new freeway, we stopped at a modern Shell gas station with a McDonald's to take a break from the wet and cold. It seemed as though we were in a different world. I sat and watched the people as they returned to their dry cars and sped away. *How pleasant for them*, I thought. There were many times we became a bit emotional while watching normal life happen as we sometimes struggled each day. But at the end of the day, we were reminded of this special trip we are experiencing. I smiled as we sped away on our bikes and powered through another twenty miles of the rolling wet hills and were rewarded with scenic, magnificent, snow-topped mountains toward the end of the day.

We rode into Dupnitsa after 7:00 P.M. and decided to call it a day, and we found a hotel. We quickly washed our clothes in the sink, set them out to dry, and enjoyed a filling Chinese dinner.

The next day it was — surprise — raining again. We slowly prepared for our ride, hoping the rain would stop. It did for the start but then continued throughout the day. There is only one busy road heading south, and we gained a hard 57 miles in the traffic, rain, and wind. We spent the night in Sandanski, the last town before Greece.

Jocelyn:

I'm amazed at how dirty the villages are here. Somehow we cycled into a parade and no one stopped us! We cycled and waved and kept cycling till my dad decided to stop at about the end so we could watch in the back. It was some kind of like government cult parade. How funny for us. I mean me being me and then us just cycling with no care in the world. It was ironic I suppose. Once we found out about the destruction they wished upon our country, we quickly cycled out of the town without fueling up with water or food.

Bulgarians pushed us out so quickly and then the Romanian bank stole our money. Not funny, but we found more love and appreciation over the Danube River in another real way. The people were friendlier, less dark natured, and we found people who would give us water. Romanian people waved, let me sit on their benches, and enjoyed our giggles.

It took us a few hours to go across the Danube from the Romanian side, so I suntanned. I laid out a tarp and settled down on the ground in my sports bra and tights. My dad took his time organizing his things, which I knew exactly where all his things were in all his panniers, but he didn't!

Back in Bulgaria we found it to be a dark and sad place. We rode on a train that I literally thought we were going to die on. At this hotel, I worked out in the gym where men were smoking cigs and doing dead lifts at the same time. There were statues representing strength and perfection, which I found contradicting considering their choices. Every person I actually tried to talk with would calmly say they hated me.

May 11, 2014

I'm always missing my friends. I love you all, and, oh gosh, I'm so thankful for the technology these days. I look at it as a great advantage in my life to connect to my friends around the world to show you the "Real World." Others think differently and think down upon such things. But for me, cycling on the road every day, all day, it's nice to see familiar faces and be able to talk with old friends.

Greece

Mike:

Due to road construction the main road to the border was closed. We made a detour through another valley thanks to the recommendation of a stranger who stopped when we were looking for directions. After several extra detour miles we were back on our original route, passed the border town of Kulata, and entered Greece our thirteenth country in ninety days. We immediately noticed the difference in road quality, shoulders, and driver attitude. Several hours later we arrived in Serre, where we found the last room available in an old city hotel. While we were discussing with the clerk where to put our bikes, an older gentleman walked up and asked in perfect English, "Is there a problem?" The clerk replied to the man in Greek who then said to us, "Take your bikes to your room." We later found out he was the owner. Due to European elections and a car race, the city was full and rooms sold out. We visited a local sports pub and watched Barcelona vs. Madrid soccer with many fanatic fans. The pub was full to capacity but the manager warmly welcomed us and sat us up front among other patrons.

Sunday morning in Greece . . . sun shining bright, rolling farming roads on a blissful day, a lunch spot, and a Skype session with Andee, climbing hills to the coast, seeing the sun glisten off the Aegean Sea from a mountain pass, rolling into a quiet beach town, a room overlooking the sea, excellent spaghetti, salad, and tasty white wine, sharing dinner with a fellow Dutch cyclist that rolled in after us, and a beautiful Grecian sunset . . . enough said, except that we decided to stay another day to swim and relax. It is days like this that a touring cyclist is thankful for.

We had a rest day yesterday, if you call preparing for the Asian portion of our trip rest. After Turkey, it is no longer a free world as Europe has been. Most of the Asian countries require tourist visas, which is a cumbersome process with some countries requiring a costly "Letter of Invitation". We started the process that will pretty much dictate where our route will take us. This requires visiting many embassies in Istanbul. The trickiest part is estimating entry and exit dates for each country. I visited a computer store with a color scanner and had many documents scanned thanks to a generous business owner. After that, we performed bike maintenance and then visited a market for fresh fruit. We were able to catch up with email and swim in the Aegean Sea while having a few beers on the beach.

Our two-day stay at the family-run Hotel Syrtaki (named after the dance in the movie *Zorba the Greek*) in Orfinio Beach was enjoyable. We were the only guests and treated like family. But that comfort can only last so long and we quickly returned to the road. Ever since Spain, we have been ahead of the tourist season and enjoying the quiet coastal towns. A rare tail wind pushed us past the large city of Kavala and toward Turkey. The coast is absolutely stunning and our picnic lunch was so picturesque that we just wanted to stay and swim. But we continued to the city of Xanthi after a long and exhausting day of seventy miles. Another early start found us in farmland where we met three more touring cyclists — two Aussies and a Kiwi, headed the opposite way. We continued toward the major city of Alexandrupolis. After fifteen miles we both bonked due to the rolling hills, headwinds, and little food. We split our last apple and tried to hitchhike, but there were no takers on this quiet road. Bonking is a complete loss of energy due to physical stress and poor nutrition. We helped each other to continue and rode harder. We didn't want to ride another four hours until dark to wild camp, so we continued climbing — or Jocelyn did. I was so proud of the fact that I hadn't walked up a hill since Spain, but I ended up walking a few steep ones in Greece. We continued pushing until reaching the pass and had a magnificent fast ride to town where we found a hotel.

Jocelyn:
May 21, 2014

Toughest day thus far. It was the hottest day, too. We cycled 76 miles in 7 hours. We had picnic breakfast and lunch with one stop to enjoy a Fanta Orange in a butcher shop. My dad started bonking with over twenty miles to ride. I stuck myself right behind him as we climbed a cliffside, and we actually didn't think we'd make it. But we did and rode the most epic downhill back to the coast and will enter Turkey tomorrow!

Turkey

Mike:

The ride through busy Alexandrupolis was uneventful, and we were soon riding in the countryside on the way to the Turkey border. After thirty miles in four hours, we made it through rolling hills and headwinds reaching the Greece border checkout after a brief but cooling thunderstorm. The ride into Turkey was interesting as we passed several military units on bridges through four check-in stops. Several times we were stopped while taking pictures and told, "No pictures." At the "Welcome to Turkey" sign, we quickly jumped off the bikes and got our "Turkey Achieved!" picture. We passed through the final armed gate and started our journey to Istanbul. In a week our family would start arriving, which brought us anticipation and easier miles.

Turkey achieved!

Two days later we cycled into our first major city of Kesan. We found an ATM, acquired Turk *Liras*, and ate a quick breakfast. We tried to stop at other places but were told that Jocelyn was not welcome. We noticed that in Morocco and now in Turkey that there are 'Men's' places including shops and restaurants where females are not welcome. We caught on to that and found a small cafe run by women where we were both warmly welcomed. Back on the road, we were stopped as tanks and other military vehicles rolled down the street. We had heard that there were government protests in a neighboring city and this military unit was sent to quell the protests. We climbed into the mountains for a valley ride to the city of Gelibolu. Along the way, we stopped at a small market, bought sandwiches, and asked if there was beer. The man looked outside and all around before digging into the refrigerator and pulling out two beers hidden behind a line of Coke. Alcohol is not illegal in Turkey, but few people have it and the shopkeepers don't want to be seen selling it. From Gelibolu, we caught a four-mile ferry across the canal between the Sea of Marmara and the Aegean Sea.

We exited the ferry and rode to the small town of Lapseki. The town was filled with chaos as people were massed on the street, some physically hurt and many crying. With sirens wailing, ambulances and fire trucks were rushing around town. As we rode through town, we had no idea what was happening and heard an explosion. We stopped at a hotel but the clerk would not tell us anything and he just wanted to sell us a room. Both of us had bad vibes about this as outside the hotel there was a group of about forty crying girls. We thought we were witnessing a riot and continued to another hotel where the clerk picked up a Turkish flag and abruptly moved it around. I said, "Earthquake?" and he nodded his head. I remembered while riding from the ferry the rear of my bike wobbled as if I had a rear puncture. I was looking at the road which was smooth, but my rear continued to wobble but there was no flat. A few seconds later the wobble disappeared and I didn't think anything more about it. That must have been the time of the earthquake. After lunch, we found a hotel and expected aftershocks but never felt a thing and slept well. Most of the hotel was filled with traveling Muslim women. Before bed, we visited an ice cream shop next door and enjoyed our cone in the hotel lobby. Soon, several small groups of women giggled down the stairs as they rushed to the ice cream shop and rushed back to their rooms with a treat. It was almost as if it was illegal for them to eat ice cream.

Exploring old town Istanbul, Turkey with my son Cary and wife Andrea.

The next day the steep rollers started early as we climbed inland. Toward the middle of the day, the terrain flattened out somewhat as we rode to Bandirma. Eleven hours later we rolled into the city after sunset and found a room. Once again we will take a road less traveled with a ferry from the port city of Bandirma to the old town of Istanbul (Constantinople). We had heard from many touring cyclists that this is a much better route than taking the busy highway that runs directly into Istanbul from Greece. Our plan was to purchase Istanbul ferry tickets and then spend two nights camping on the Marmara Sea at a bicycle-friendly campground. All went well and we had a quiet and clean campground on the beach for two nights. Two days later, we boarded the 'fast' ferry that turned out to be like flying on a plane as passengers were not allowed outside and the seats were similar to an airliner. On arrival, it was an instant shock in this fifth largest city in the world of fifteen million people. The old city is built on a series of steep hills. We had made reservations, rare for us to do that, at an apartment in the city, and with Jocelyn's accurate navigation we soon found our accommodation for the next four nights. We navigated our unloaded bikes to Bisiklet Gezgina, a touring bicycle shop on the Asian side of Istanbul, for necessary maintenance and outfitting for our upcoming Asian journey. We cycled and walked our bicycles to the Bosphorus River Ferry that crosses from Europe to Asia and then rode several more miles to the small shop.

Family members visited us in Turkey. Mike, wife Andrea, my cousin Albert's wife Lou, cousin Albert, sister Tish, son Cary and Jocelyn.

Our family, including Andee, son Cary, sister Tish, my cousin Albert and his wife Lou, arrived during the next several days and we all stayed at the same hotel. We explored all the famous sites of Istanbul for the next few days. A few days later, we boarded a flight to a resort on Bosbuk Bay and the Aegean Sea in Southwest Turkey. During the seven days, I worked on paperwork for obtaining visas for Azerbaijan, Turkmenistan, Uzbekistan, Tajikistan, plus the Gorno-Badakhshan Autonomous Oblast (GBAO) permit (a military pass) necessary for traveling the Pamir Highway in Tajikistan. Georgia and Kyrgyzstan are still free countries. The week was wonderful spending time with family, visiting the ancient ruins in Didmya, Temple of Apollo, and the old cities of Priene and Ephesus. We were enthralled exploring and studying the 3,000-year-old civilization.

Swimming every day in the Aegean Sea was an added bonus. All too soon the week was over and we returned to Istanbul and different hotels but were together for a few more days in this magical city. Everyone except Andee left a few days later, and we started visiting embassies and applying for visas. Our future Silk Road journey was waiting, and we were excited to think about our future ride.

We spent a few weeks with family in Istanbul and left our bicycles for an overhaul at Bisiklet Gezgini touring bike shop with owners Basak and Rahman on the right. To my left is a Japanese cyclist also touring the world. To Jocelyn's right is my cousin Al's wife Lou and my sister Tish.

Andee, Jocelyn, and I moved to a hotel on the Asian side of Istanbul to be closer to Bisiklet Gezgini bike shop. During the three weeks at the shop, all four wheels were refit with Rigida 36-hole rims with Shimano XT hubs and DT Swiss double-butted spokes as even the new rear rims from Montenegro and Serbia were showing signs of stress. The Rigida rims were advertised as 'bomb-proof', and I am happy to say we completed our world ride without another rim or spoke problem. Jocelyn's kickstand was removed, and where it was attached to the frame were severe indentations along with cracks on the chain stays. The Surly frame obviously wasn't safe to ride anymore. We learned that Surly had published a safety notice not to use this kickstand. The shop had a Dutch Santos Travelmaster 2.6 frame in stock that fit Jocelyn. All of the other components were moved to the new frame. We mailed her Surly LHT home where she eventually turned it into a fixie — a bike with no freewheel, therefore no coasting, or brakes. The addition of front dynamo hubs that powered new front and rear lights completed our refit. Thanks to Bisiklet Gezgini bicycle shop and Cecil, Alexios, Basak, and Rahman for their impressive service. They are at the crossroads between Europe and Asia and have the touring experience and technical expertise to refit touring bicycles.

It has been 22 days since we last rode and are feeling out of shape. These three weeks have been fun with the family but too long a break. It was time to say goodbye to my wife of nearly 35 years. For a few seconds I thought we had gone far enough riding through Europe and maybe it was time to go home. But the riding bug took over as Jocelyn and I have many thousands of unridden miles to ride and the Silk Road awaits us. We said our goodbyes, shed a few tears, and rode out of town. Cecil suggested we take a ferry to bypass a huge industrial and traffic area east of Istanbul. It was a good choice, as we ferried this fifteen miles from Pendik to Yalova. Our next goal is the capitol city of Ankara where we will continue our visa work. We left Bisiklet Gezgini at noon, and after thirty miles and the one-hour ferry ride, we were tired so called it a day at a hotel in the city of Omangazi. We were glad but somewhat melancholy to be back on the saddle.

Jocelyn working on her bicycle chain in Northern Turkey.

We left Omangazi on a Saturday morning and toured the ancient Roman walled city of Isnik in Northwestern Turkey. This was one of our favorite forts as the walls and gates were crumbling and looked authentic. In fact, as we rode through Isnik I could 'sense' the ancient civilizations come alive. This entire area looked like it was frozen in time. For the next several days we rode east through the mountains to Ankara, the capital city of Turkey. Camping was easy as we passed many lakes and mountain villages with friendly locals. The climbs were sometimes exhausting but the scenery striking. Fruit stands were plentiful and we stopped often to replenish with fruit during the heat. While climbing over a mountain pass, we noticed our speed had decreased because our tires were sinking into the melting asphalt. We were soon trying to overcome the smelly, oozy mess that was sticking onto our tires. Whenever we put our feet down, our shoe and sandal soles became covered. We tried weaving on several areas of the road but our tires became even more covered with loose gravel. In the early afternoon we arrived at the village of Goynuk after only seventeen miles and decided to stay and get an early start when it was cooler. It was market day and we enjoyed sampling the local food, vegetables, and fruit.

The rest of our trip to Ankara was through many mountain peaks with fun climbing and lots of good honks from the villagers. We stopped to rest in one shaded area, and an older couple on a horse-drawn cart stopped and gave us their lunch for the day. We tried to say no but they insisted as they emptied their food basket to us. The kindness of the Turks sometimes overwhelmed us.

The closer we were to Ankara the packs of roaming dogs increased. While riding, these packs would suddenly appear at our heels and the chase was on. We made lots of noise and had rocks ready to throw at them. Fortunately we had not been bit yet — and I mean yet. The mountain climbing of the last week turned into a *High Plains Drifter* ride at 3,000 feet. We eventually dropped down in elevation and into the desert. The traffic increased as we entered the city of Sincan, a suburb of the vast capital city of Ankara. We had difficulty finding a room as we rode through the city center until a kind stranger stopped his car and offered help. We told him we were looking for a room, and he motioned to follow him. He slowly drove through the hectic traffic so that we could keep up, while the other drivers were patient, and finally pointed out a hostel and waved goodbye.

The capital of Turkey is situated in an area of awfully steep hills, and riding a fully loaded bicycle around Ankara is arduous at best. We headed toward the Uzbekistan Embassy twelve miles away. After two hours we only made about half that and considered other options. When we stopped, several people stopped and asked, "Problem?" It's interesting that in the last few weeks whenever we stopped our bikes people would pull over and ask if we needed help. The driver of a panel truck offered us a ride and we loaded the bikes, but since I was boxed in by the bikes I stayed inside the enclosed truck back and Jocelyn rode in the cab. It was a wild ride and I started feeling sick, probably from carbon monoxide poisoning as I was weary and wanted to fall asleep. I soon recognized this and banged on the wall. The truck stopped and I made it out okay. The generous man left and we sat on the curbside thinking about our options. We did have a warmshowers host lined up but didn't think we could make it another 12 miles and we wanted to try and get a visa in our pocket. Suddenly, we realized we were sitting in front of a hotel, obtained a room, and a taxi ride to the Uzbekistan Embassy. At the embassy, we were told that it was not "Visa day," as they were open but not working visas. After that, we walked to the Kazakhstan Embassy and started their visa process. Turkmenistan is now off our route due to their highly inflated $750 each five-day transit fee. We had heard that cycling through Turkmenistan in only five days is difficult and requires riding at night. In fact, two Aussie girls we later met arrived a few hours late in their transit. They were detained 24 hours and fined before they were able to exit.

We spent a week in Ankara, Turkey with Deniz (in the yellow, back row on the right) and Banu (blue in front of Deniz). They are both professors at Middle East Technical University, Ankara. We joined them and the school's Orienteering Club for a day of adventure learning how to navigate in the woods.

The next morning we returned to the Kazakhstan consulate before our appointment with the Uzbekistan consulate. We presented our applications and were told to deposit $160 USD each at the local bank. We rushed to the bank only to find that it didn't open until 10:00 A.M. We found an English-speaking person in line and asked to use his Turkish ID number to perform this transaction. In Istanbul, we successfully performed a bank transaction when a man volunteered his ID. All bank deposit transactions in Turkey require an ID number and foreigners must use a Turk's ID. Armed with this $320 receipt, we rushed back to the Kazakhstan consulate who said, "Come back in a week." Curses — another delay!

We hired another taxi for the ride to the Uzbekistan consulate on the other side of town. At our appointment time, another citizen took us to another bank where we were able to use her ID to deposit another $320. We returned to the consulate and our visa was approved. Another taxi ride took us back to our hotel where we had lunch, loaded up the bikes, and rode through the steep hills to a warmshowers host. We ended up not using either of these visas because by the time we completed our unexpected Iran ride the Kazakhstan and Uzbekistan visas were expired.

We met our next hosts Deniz and Banu. At their apartment, we also met Mark from the UK who was also working the visa process and headed our way. Deniz and Banu were generous in allowing us to stay a week.

The visa delay is frustrating because we need to arrive in Azerbaijan on the fixed entry date of July 23rd. The distance from Ankara through east Turkey, up through the Republic of Georgia to the Azerbaijan border is approximately 1,100 miles. After much discussion with Deniz, he recommended a partial train trip to cover some of this distance. Without the train, we would be required to ride 78 miles a day without a day off. That is not going to happen in this mountainous country. Mark's entry date to Azerbaijan is two weeks later than ours. As you can see, visa applications are a real thorn in the side for touring cyclists.

Thanks to Mark for helping plan our route through the Stan countries. I miscalculated our Tajikistan visas entry date by three weeks. We went to the Tajikistan consulate but found out that only the Istanbul office where we received the visas can change the dates. After talking with the Istanbul consulate madam by phone, we mailed our passports to her. Mailing passports while in a foreign country is not to be taken lightly, and all you can do is hope that they don't get lost. In the meantime, we returned to the Kazakhstan consulate a few days early and our visas

Turkey

were ready. We had to wait until our passports were returned to have the Kazakhstan consulate place and stamp the visas in our passports. Two days after mailing our passports to the Tajikistan consulate in Istanbul, I received an email from the consulate saying that our corrected visas and passports had been mailed back to us. Riding our bicycles is so much easier than the paperwork.

We rode to the train station and purchased tickets to the eastern Turkey city of Erzurum. Fortunately, Kyrgyzstan north of Turkmenistan is still a free country and we can enter anytime. From there we will apply for our China visas and have our fingers crossed. I have to admit that the visa process has been frustrating to me, but I have learned to accept these roadblocks and have made peace with the visa process.

In the meantime we visited the fascinating Ankara Castle. The earliest records show it was conquered around the year 1027 but that it was built much earlier by the Romans. The city views are stunning. Deniz and Banu are professors at Middle East Technical University and invited us to visit the school twice to participate in the university orienteering club. We have been enjoying our hosts and their friends along with our roommate Mark from England. One day we made tacos for "Taco Tuesday". They were a big hit thanks to Jocelyn who learned how to cook fresh taco shells from Andee. It took a bit of looking, but we found fresh flour tortillas and avocados. We even smashed pinto beans and made refried beans.

On the 4th of July we left our superb hosts Deniz and Banu. The stay was longer than we intended but our mission was accomplished as we had now obtained all the required visas through the Stan countries. Since it was early, we stopped by a favorite restaurant Cafe del Mundo on the way to the train station. After a delicious lunch, we were told by the manager that our meal was free because we are traveling the world by bicycle. At the train station we had to jump through hoops to get our bikes aboard, as it was, "Yes, no, yes, no," while talking with various people. I finally found the conductor right before the train arrived and he said in English, "No problem." He and others assisted us with loading the bikes and panniers into the luggage car. We have learned to put on a big smile and never, ever lose your patience with transportation officials. The overnight train took longer than expected as we took an out of the way route through Southern Turkey. This was Jocelyn's first overnighter on a train and she loved it. Sleep came easy with the slow rocking movement.

In Erzurum we reloaded our bikes and quickly started climbing as we headed northeast. The rain soon began as we reached another mountain summit. The descent was epic and allowed us to put on the miles, so we reached the mountain village of Yusufeli. We wanted to camp, but since it was raining so hard and cold we opted for a hotel. The next several days we climbed north toward the Black Sea. It turned out to be a long, hot, and dirty ride through a major road construction project that included 41 tunnels and a new dam. We cycled through all the tunnels and were thankful that we'd had a dynamo hub and new lights installed in Istanbul. Most of the travel was over washboard roads being worked by massive earth-moving and tunneling machines. The dirt flew as cars and trucks passed us. After a few days, we dropped down to the Black Sea and the town of Hopa where we found a seaside hotel. We ate dinner at a beachside restaurant that was full of Muslims sitting and staring at tables full of food. We were served our meal and immediately started eating while the Muslims waited for sunset before they could eat. Some of them stared at us while we ate. It was a bit uncomfortable, but soon the mosques' loudspeakers announced sunset and everyone ate.

High in the mountains on our way to the Republic of Georgia.

Jocelyn:

May 26, 2014

A Turkish man is in front of us and a German man with an RV and mountain bike is across the way. He is going to the market to pick up more beer for us and the camp owner, haha. Our tent is a few feet from the Sea of Marmara. Wish I could stay here all summer since it's so nice. And cheap! Minus the bugs!

Just went to the market and got six Tuborgs, which is a much better beer than Efes. I've tried a lot of beer so far on this trip, and I still can't figure out my top five. I'll get back to you on that one. I wish I could have kept a bottle of each beer I've had. I'd make a shadowbox of beer caps from around the world. Might I add that I'm sitting on a sandbag wall in the sea typing this, and my dad just fell down in the water. It's pretty funny! LOL

Wowzers to this sunset and view. Had to take the shades off for this beautiful sunset! We were walking in the water to the nearby restaurant and I was amazed. Like who walks in the water to a restaurant? I don't know of any place near *my* hometown!

May 29, 2014

Yesterday we arrived in Istanbul. We met another touring couple from Bellingham, WA on the ferry and that was neat. The ferry sucked because we were all cooped up inside for over two hours. Somehow, following our disembarking, I found our apartment that we are staying in Fatih, old town Istanbul. It's a studio that is so cute and nicely furnished. Right away we stocked the fridge with fruits and veggies.

Today we quickly learned how terrible it is to try cycling in Istanbul. It's challenging and way more hilly than San Francisco! Plus, the roads are cobblestone, and after bouncing around, we luckily boarded the correct ferry toward our destination in Kadikoy. I navigated us to find the most amazing and beneficial bike shop ever. They are a bike shop specifically for touring, Bisiklet Gezgini, so we dropped off our bikes for an overhaul. I'm so excited to see my bike again in three weeks, maybe more excited than seeing my family in a week! He he!

June 4, 2014

Well, folks, this was the bad news that I found out yesterday over email and have now seen my Surly with my own eyes. Each of the frame arms (chain stays) where my kickstand was attached were deeply compressed with small cracks. Those compressions were about to be a major accident. It's sad :(but it's from the weight on my bike. Apparently, a Surly notice says to not use a kickstand anywhere because the frame isn't as strong as you'd think. I am upset that I can't take my Surly around the world, though I'll turn her into a fixed-gear fun ride when I get back home!

My new Santos frame is thicker, so I will be using a kickstand, but not the same type. With continuing discussion, decided to snatch the 21-inch Santos aluminum tour frame at Bisiklet Gezgini bicycle shop. I'll be retiring my lovely Surly. I was being picky about the new frame color, but black is going to have to do because I don't have six weeks to have a frame built and shipped. I'm very bummed, as I love my Surly, but I'm excited to see about all the Santos Travelmaster hype of a world-class heavy touring bicycle! Note to readers: Definitely take your kickstand off and check it out. I'd toss it, too.

June 5, 2014

My mom, brother Cary, Aunti Tish, my dad's cousin Al and his wife Lou, are all here in Istanbul. We're back together and I am happy to have my Mommy here with me. Today we visited Bisiklet Gezgini again! Haha, can't stay away because it's an amazing good happy energy on the Asian side of Istanbul in Kadikoy. We met Yoshi from Japan who is also cycling around the world!

June 15, 2014

Happy Father's Day (again!) We've celebrated three times now in different countries! Without my Papa, my dreams wouldn't have been made possible. Because of his hard work and dedication with the space shuttle program and working at the South Pole, Antarctica, I am able to guide him toward achieving his ultimate bucket list during retirement. I am furthering my resume for my dream job! I'm so grateful for him and my mother. They truly have always supported me through all my wildest times!

I'm so grateful for the relationship I have with my brother Cary. He is my best friend, and for him to come celebrate and join in my adventures shows how genuine and supportive he is. My artist brother is an amazing photographer, and I can't wait to see where we go in our lives! I hope he'll join me in an adventure of our own, maybe to the West Coast of the U.S.A.! I love you Care Bear.

June 20, 2014

It's time to start part two of our adventure! My new Santos Travelmaster bicycle is looking colorful even with its black frame. Thank you, Bisiklet Gezgini, for all of your help.

June 22, 2014

Today's climb was absolutely stunning and a bit challenging. Riding up to the mountain, I said to myself, *Challenge accepted*, though after achieving that mountain I didn't realize there was a larger guy right behind it. During the remainder of the afternoon, we moved along the side of the mountains climbing with some little declines of joy. The shot with my handlebar is the first actual downhill, and I topped off at 45 mph! Such a thrill, until I ran right into a pothole. I'm thankful it wasn't deep, and all I could think was, *Who would put a pot hole there?* Lol. We both achieved the 2,200 ft. climb!

The mountains here are never-ending. It's so fun, and I just get giggles all over. But let's talk about the cherries, another best fruit here in Turkey. At this one section of the peak, a little man with his tractor and tiny fruit stand resided right next to a beautiful waterhole fountain. We stopped and ate an entire bag of cherries, washed our faces, and filled up our bottles. I should have washed my body; I've got dirt all over! And I definitely got a stomachache after this; probably too many cherries!

June 24, 2014

I've ridden on many terrains with a loaded bike, but I have never ridden on what I faced today. The grueling pain from melted asphalt is unlike anything I've experienced. There really isn't anything like it. The way it melts and pulls you back with all its force really is agonizing. And to think it was only 87 degrees today. After a hill pass and 17 miles, my body and mind were shot. I didn't want to continue because it wasn't fun.

Okay, it was fun at first when I imagined the asphalt bubbling and my enormously heavy tires popping every single one, but once I stopped and put my feet down and got stuck it started to become a pain.

I have a Beanie Baby called Spumoni on my handlebars. She was given to me the last time I saw my Gramma Polly. I've had her with me during the entire trip, and until the beginning of part two, I never had her out. But I realized she needs to see the world with me, so now she's got a front-row seat, even if it gets a little bumpy! We had three descents like this today: 3,900 feet to approximately 1,700 feet and up climbing again. Yesterday was one of the most beautiful morning rides we have ever ridden. *"Life itself is a privilege, but to live life to the fullest - well, that is a choice."* –The Traveler's Gift.

June 26, 2014

No matter how grueling and hot and testing it was, it will always play an important role in my memories of this trip and of Turkey. Even though I became very depressed and couldn't control negative thoughts clouding my mind, I kept true to my love for bike touring. The heat and the hills are testing our limits, but that's just it; we have no limits! Bring it on; give it to me dirty! I like it that way!

July 4, 2014

Ankara, Turkey. We're back on the road, baby!!!! We have less weight, more stickers, and I doodled on my pannier. We're now just hanging out at the Traveler's cafe, Cafe Del Mundo. We have a few hours to kill before we load up on a night train ride to Erzurum. A bit long of a ride, which is unfortunate, but sometimes you have to give up the distance because of time constraints. We are not giving up the miles, as we will make that up somewhere on this world tour! :)

July 5, 2014

I now have a new name for my bike, Master Yukito! I put a bunch of country flags on it that aren't going to last long since they aren't car decals. Oh well. Trying to cover the huge Santos logo as fast as possible. It's too fancy and expensive looking! We had a lot of the usual, "No, you can't take your bike on board," and then, "Well, if you can take it apart, then maybe," and finally, "Okay, it's fine, but you just have to pay extra."

It's nothing new for us, though it's very stressful. The key is to control that stress and be as nice, polite, and happy as possible. I'm still trying to teach my dad this way. He'll sometimes freak out, which isn't going to get us anywhere. We finally talked to the train conductor and he agreed that we could put them in the cargo car. So we strapped them in and ran to our car, which was seven cars away, the last one! Just barely made it on to our "express" train that will take us 22 hours from Ankara to Erzurum. The train was the slowest-moving train I've ever been on.

I feel completely myself when I am on my bicycle. The unknown of where I am, where I'll go, or what I will face is always thrilling. It's strange to think that I enjoy sleeping in a new place every night. I'm an original soul and I'll always challenge my body, mind, and spirit to learn more, become more, and be true to myself.

July 7, 2014

Today was a day I saw a completely different side of Turkey with the varying shades of green that were mesmerizing and in fact made me run off the road a few times! Crazy how we were in dirtballs yesterday. We stopped at a small park along the Coruh River, and I got a chance to swing away until I started feeling sick. Many kids ran alongside us as we cycled by the small villages, and the climb was a lot of fun! I jammed out to some good-ole bluegrass and folk, which is always fun to groove along to. We reached the Black Sea after an epic downhill where a semi-truck and I raced down together. When I finally was able to slow down and let him pass, he cheerfully honked and waved. The people here are some of the nicest and honest people I've met thus far on this world tour. We're heading into Georgia tomorrow. I'll miss Turkey; we've enjoyed every day, over a month and a half!

The Republic of Georgia to Bangkok, Thailand

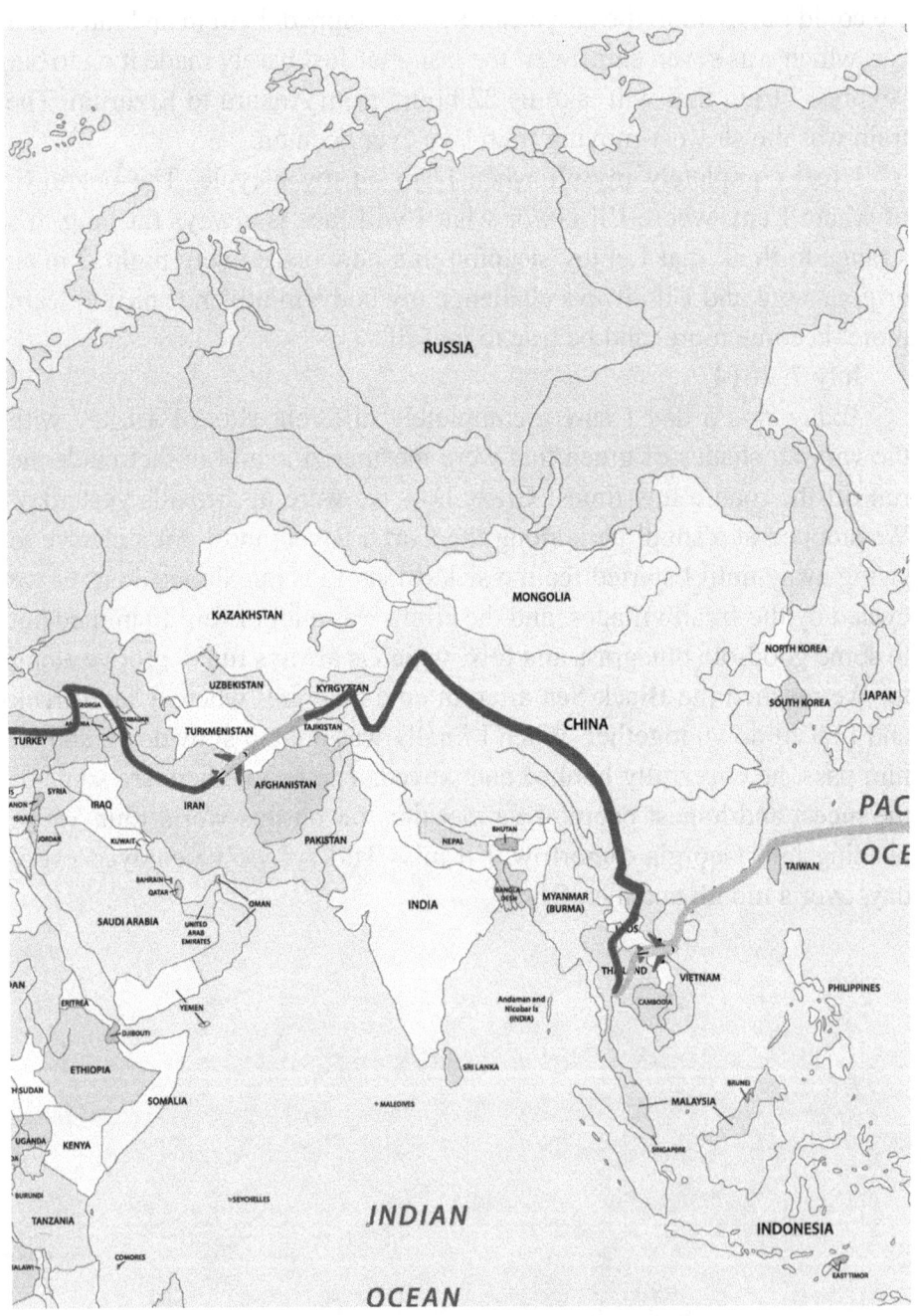

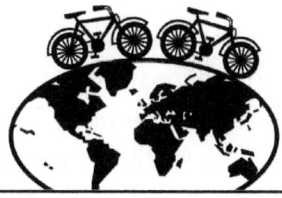

The Republic of Georgia

"Stop worrying about the potholes in the road and enjoy the journey."

–Babs Hoffman

Mike:

The border to Georgia was only seven miles away where we exited Turkey and were directed by Georgia passport control to remove all our panniers and pass them through x-ray. For all other countries, we have simply ridden the car lane through borders. We rode twenty miles to the port city of Batumi and found an inexpensive apartment to rest in before our mountain ride through Georgia.

Midafternoon: The large seaside city of Batumi is a combination of New Orleans, Las Vegas, and Disney World. Batumi is a strange city with huge monument-type buildings, many abandoned and right next to blighted high-rise apartments. In the evening, we walked to the Batumi Pier rising over the Black Sea. During this walk, we encountered a 'Disney World Main Street' kind of atmosphere complete with lighted dancing waters, abundant families, street vendors, hidden speakers playing nature music, and of course alcohol in the street New Orleans style. Russian is the common language here, as all of the Stan countries and Georgia were part of the old Soviet Union.

We rode out of Batumi and into the local mountains for our trek across Georgia. Cows roam freely so they were everywhere once we started climbing. Sometimes they move but most times just stand there and stare. We passed a winery and Jocelyn shouted out, "What do you think, Dad?" Of course I said yes and we enjoyed tasting fine Georgian wine along with lunch. We spent the next several days in the mountains negotiating the mostly dirt road which paralleled a large river. The over 115°F heat parched our thirst, and we replenished our water from many roadside hoses that drew water from this river. We stopped at villages for fruit and cold drinks and enjoyed sitting with the locals and seeing who talked the most English. Once their limit is reached, they abruptly say, "Goodbye," and walk away. We did enjoy talking or attempting to talk Russian, but there are several dialects and it can be a bit confusing.

The climbing was a bit more intense as we headed to a ski resort in the village of Shuakhevi. We took a break with a room and then continued several more days to the large town of Akhaltsikhe. Cycling through the mountains was difficult and hot on the rocky dirt road. We made a serious mistake by not filtering the roadside water from the occasional hoses because we were so parched. This mountain ride lasted many days and we were passed by taxi vans loaded with people who drank from these hoses. Occasionally there was a village store, but they did not carry bottled water. The day after arriving in Akhaltsikhe, we were both sick and spent three nights in a hotel recuperating with lots of rest, bottled water, and ramen noodle soup. We also visited a pharmacy and purchased several electrolyte drinks. The locals are obviously immune to this water where the cows are plentiful and outhouses dump. On our last day we were feeling better and toured the 9th century medieval Rabati Castle. This castle was our least favorite of the trip as it was as clean as the Disneyland Castle.

After four sick days we were back on the road and remained strong until after lunch when we were sick yet again. We both desired a hotel instead of camping tonight, and after 66 miles we found a place to rest. It was a rough day, but we were proud of our miles.

We then discovered that our Azerbaijan e-visa was not yet ready. The ride to Tbilisi was long and rough as we alternated on the road and gravel shoulder. The traffic was frightful with often four lanes of traffic on the two-lane road. Georgia doesn't appear to have or enforce any traffic regulations, and drivers have a 'free for all' attitude. We witnessed three lines of cars (on a two lane, one each way, road) heading for us with the two closest to us both trying to pass slower vehicles in the other lane. Several hours later we arrived at a small market with a public water fountain. Since it was close to dark, we asked the proprietor if we could pitch our tent on the property and she readily agreed. This was not our best decision to be camped roadside along the busy, noisy highway.

We arrived in Tbilisi, Georgia and continued to the town of Rustavi where we found a hotel to wait for our e-visa. There were many bicyclists staying in the same downtown hostel waiting in Tbilisi for their e-visas, and it was here that we met Mark again who we had stayed with in Ankara, Turkey. From Rustavi we returned to Tbilisi by taxi and enjoyed meeting many touring cyclists and sharing lunch with several.

We also found out that our Iran visa has been approved and is ready. We had no idea that it was still in work as we had applied several months ago. Because of this route change, we will miss ferrying across the Caspian Sea to Kazakhstan. I have read many biking blogs and Iran is a favorite country for touring cyclists.

Jocelyn:

Our day ride from Batumi was so full — full of adventure and appreciative shouts from locals. Cows roamed the road with little traffic as we slowly climbed up the gorge. I decided I wanted a swim and walked up the roadway to ride the river current back down to my bike. I was in a dream state feeling so happy to have swam, so happy to have eaten delicious food and enjoyed good wine at the winery, that I felt like this was quite a plush lifestyle we were living.

After only forty miles, we noticed that the sun was setting rather quickly. I rode by this shack right next to the river's edge and saw a man outside waving at us. I figured we could possibly camp on his property. He was obviously selling cold drinks out of his outside fridge, so I was sure he had something cold to drink. He, in fact, had cold drinks and invited us in for dinner. Dinner was horrendously fried sardines with homemade *chacha* (vodka). We drank too much *chacha*. Our host that owned the one-room shack that was falling down the cliff side slyly encouraged us to drink an entire bottle with him. My father and I felt ill after a disgusting meal with the man that probably drugged us with this liquor. Neither of us can fully remember the evening, except for moments of a horrible assault. I wish I could erase that experience that tarnished a good day of cycling. I am a stronger woman today and want to remember the many kind people who assisted us on our journey. Perhaps some time in the future, I will discuss my personal memories of this roadside nightmare.

We were quickly back on the road at sunrise. The farther away we rode, the harsher the road became, and I found myself just glued to the rocks and feeling nothing. Here is when we started to climb to a mountaintop, but we didn't make it and the road became even worse to the point that my dad decided to walk. I wanted to get farther and farther away from where we came, so I kept peddling until I realized I was too far ahead and should walk with my dad. Surprisingly, this nice little man pulled over with his van of people and told us to get in. Several of the men jumped out, threw our bikes and gear on top, tied it down, and we took a ride for ten minutes until a suspension bracket broke. Luckily, a man in the nearby village had a semi-new bracket and welded the thing on. One hour later, we all were back in the hot van, all 15 of us. People were sitting on other people's laps. We were immersed into this way of travel, and I was so thankful when we arrived at the top of the mountain.

For the past few days my life has been on hold in a hotel dealing with that traumatizing event, illness from mountain water, *chacha*, and visa troubles. The event is still ever replaying in my mind. I'm currently able to eat crackers without the normal vomiting, diarrhea, and headache. And we have successfully obtained an Iran visa, and with all fingers crossed, we will pick it up in Baku, Azerbaijan eleven days from now.

Today's been like this: no clouds, eating flies, and sweating. I'm now taking the conscious effort to stay covered. Being a white woman, tattooed, blue-eyed, and strong looking has been a battle from the start of this trip. The Republic of ☐Georgia has taught me a valuable lesson, to keep my body visible to myself. I don't want to "ask" for any more trouble. This is my personal vehicle, and I should treat it with the utmost importance. Along with my bicycle, my body deserves the respect and nurturing needed as it is taking me on this journey of a lifetime!

Azerbaijan

"One's destination is never a place, but a new way of seeing things."

–Henry Miller

Mike:

In Georgia, I let Jocelyn down by not being there when she needed me most. I, too, succumbed to excessive drinking. As a dad, you have nightmares about your daughter being harmed. I failed my daughter. I did not know what had happened until later that day when I asked Jocelyn what was wrong. We had just cycled into a town and were drinking a Coke outside a market when she told me. My heart ached for her and I hugged her tightly. My heart still aches to this day. A lesson to world travelers' — be aware of your surroundings and do not excessively indulge in alcohol.

We spent several days exploring Rustavi, watching movies, reading, and resting since we were still recuperating from our intestinal illness. After four days our e-visas were approved, and after a twelve-mile ride, we crossed the border into Azerbaijan on our visa entry date. When we crossed the border, Jocelyn was still not feeling well. We continued to the first town and at the top of a hill we spotted what appeared to be a restaurant where we could maybe get some cool water. The restaurant had a dubious motel attached, but there was air-conditioning and we needed a good rest. There have been other times on this journey where we were stressed at the end of our day, but all of a sudden everything worked out. After dinner we retired early. Jocelyn had read on warmshowers.org that within three days of entering Azerbaijan one must register with immigration or pay a fine when exiting. The next day the restaurant/motel proprietor drove us to a government building where we spent the entire morning trying to register. It was a confusing process requiring us to get copies of passports, visas, travel plans, etc. It was easy checking into Azerbaijan through passport control, but this immigration part was tedious. Supposedly we were required to register for immigration or face a fine of $300 USD per person when we exited the country. After three hours of paperwork and about $5.10 USD, all was put in an envelope for mailing. Out of this, we had an official-looking signed receipt showing that we had registered — for something anyway.

We didn't get on the road until 1:00 P.M. We were both exhausted, and after fifteen miles we entered the town of Agstafa and immediately stopped at a hotel. Rashad, the manager, was friendly, and since he is an avid mountain biker and spoke a little English, we had something in common. There was quite a crowd outside the hotel when the word got out that there were American cyclists in town. Rashad helped carry all our gear and bikes up three flights of stairs to a comfortable air-conditioned room. We walked to a local market where once again the words "Welcome to Azerbaijan" rang out from various people. We decided to rest an additional day. Rashad and I spent the day watching biking videos, and I helped him with his English. He then reciprocated with my Russian.

We spent several more days riding to Baku through the heat and biting flies. When we couldn't find a room, we camped. The desert doesn't cool until early in the morning, so camping was uncomfortable. The wind was variable, always strong and the traffic burdensome. I believe that this was the first time we had ever been bored while riding. We passed many towns and frequently stopped at stores hoping to find something cool to drink. Most stores had drinks in coolers, but either the cooler didn't work or it was unplugged. The food didn't appeal to us because most of it contained questionable meat. Since leaving Turkey, meat isn't refrigerated and we didn't want to deal with that and our weak stomachs. Our go-to food was fried eggs or whenever we could find a noodle soup without meat. We arrived in the hectic, oil-rich city of Baku during rush hour. Our research indicated that Baku is one of the most expensive cities we have cycled in. With hostels at $46 USD per person, we were hoping that our stay would be short. The downtown area was crowded with expensive, large chain hotels. We stopped at a few hostels that were full until finding a hotel. At $120 per night, it offered a safe place for our bikes plus a full breakfast. The location was also central, with many shops and restaurants nearby, and the Caspian Sea was only a ten-minute walk.

The next day we took a taxi to the Iranian consulate only to find out that our visas were in Erzurum, Turkey. That is where we left the train from Ankara. The Iran consulate said that we should return to Erzurum to retrieve these visas. When we explained that we were on bicycles, he said they would be expired by the time we returned there. We asked if there was a way to transfer the visas to Baku. He didn't know but said, "Come back tomorrow." The hotel bill is starting to increase. The next day we were told, "Yes, it can be transferred but not until next week." When questioned why and we were told, "Ramadan just ended and Turkey is on a one week holiday." There goes the hotel bill again. We didn't ask why this consulate isn't on holiday. "Come back tomorrow," he said. Once again we took another taxi ride to the consulate only to be told by the guard that the consulate was on holiday. For the next few days we asked the hotel manager to call on our behalf. When the consulate was working again, we taxied there and were told that the Erzurum consulate does not have our visas. At this point I believe the consulate manager was feeling sorry for us. He gave us new forms to complete and to return tomorrow with $50 USD each. When we returned the next day he invited us into his office and asked us about our ride as he gave a worker our passports and the $100 USD. He was friendly and when the worker returned, the manager inserted visas in our passports, stamped and signed. It was that quick! He talked to us about the problems our governments have and hoped that someday there would be peace and free travel between our countries. As we were leaving, he wished us the best. We were thankful to the Baku Islamic Republic of Iran Consulate manager who befriended us and became interested in our journey and took it upon himself to make this happen. We walked out of there with huge smiles on our faces! We are going to Iran!

We enjoyed six nights in a comfortable hotel near old town Baku. In-between our consulate visits, we explored this ancient and historical city. Baku is famed for its medieval walled old city, which contains the Palace of the Shirvanshahs, a vast royal complex listed as a World Heritage Site as one of the 'pearls' of Azerbaijan's architecture. After seven days we were back on our bikes joining the morning rush hour traffic. We quickly worked our way out of Baku, and I mean quickly because we had to keep up with the flow or get bogged down. Once again Jocelyn kept the pace through many one-way streets and roundabouts while I just followed. Once outside of Baku, we shifted into our cruising mode with the flatness and tailwind. Our speed was up as the hours drifted by. Several hours later, it was getting late and while looking for a camp spot we were flagged down by a guy standing near a small mosque. We stopped, and as I looked around I thought this would be a good place to pitch our tent. With our point-it-book, we showed him our tent. After a, "*Da, da,*" we followed him to a small cabin and he invited us to sleep inside on the two cots. The large property consisted of a house, mosque, animals, and fruit trees. Once the temperature dropped at around 3:00 A.M. we slept well. In the morning, Sevda, the caretaker, collected eggs from the hens, bought fresh bread, and prepared a breakfast spread. I collected grapes, plums, and apples as Jocelyn cooked the eggs. After a delicious breakfast, Sevda sent us off with a sack full of fresh fruit. We tested our rims with our ten-liter bag of water at 22 pounds and an almost equal weight of fruit!

By 10:00 A.M. it was already over 110°F, and we stopped at a market for two cold beers. After discussing that in a few days we wouldn't be able to stop for beer, we bought two more just because we could. We continued for a few more hours until Bilasuvar where we found a hotel about nine miles from the Azerbaijan-Iran border. We walked through town and enjoyed the small town atmosphere as Jocelyn looked for a headscarf for our upcoming trip.

It was time for a run to the Iranian border. About a mile away, we were chased by three dogs that surprised us as they charged from a ranch. The larger one grabbed my right ankle and chomped down. In all our miles and after being chased by hundreds of dogs, it finally happened. I was able to yell and momentarily scared the dog so it let go. We stopped about ¼ mile down the road to check for damage. There were four punctures but not much bleeding. It was scary looking back to see all three dogs standing on the road staring as in daring us to come back. We continued to the border with my ankle swelling and the pain increasing.

Jocelyn:

July 18, 2014

Riding on a major highway isn't fun at all. The constant zooming of cars, trucks, and mopeds gives me a headache, and it's a bit mindless, really. Without the heavy headwinds, I'd probably forget I was even cycling because I can get so lost in some wild daydream. While I was chugging along, I came across this horse that was standing right off the highway, not tied up, starving, and very sad looking. At first he was very scared of me, which he has all the right to be. But I pulled out a couple of apples a man gave to us earlier and started to feed him. He really enjoyed them. The juice frothed upon his dry lips and he started to get very friendly with me. He smelled my hair and let me pet him :) What do you think? Should I trade him in? Santos for the Second Chance horse? I was sad to leave him, and just before I left, a truck with 20 stacks tall of hay slowly drove by giving me a death stare and frightening Second Chance. I'm always learning from my animal soul mates. He taught me how to appreciate a gift while allowing the fear to still be present.

July 29, 2014

Bike hitching to get to Baku. We said, "Fudge these popsicle sticks," to the heavy headwind and lame-ass big road. Sometimes hitchhiking is a must. I hit a wall in my mind and just stopped, almost like when Forest Gump just one day stopped running. I got off my bike, walked a mile, rode a little more, and then hung out on the side of the road as many people stopped to see if we wanted a lift. So that's when I started sticking the old thumb out. Shortly after, we got a ride into Baku in a very nice passenger van!

I travel to live out my personal legend.
I bicycle because it is my passion.
I seek the unknown of the days.
I share smiles with the world.
I believe in the ride I live.
I discover to share.
I love to inspire,
You.

Iran

Mike:

When we exited Azerbaijan, the guards didn't ask for a $300 exit fee so whatever paperwork we'd filled out earlier in Azerbaijan must have worked. We entered the border city of Bileh Savar, Iran and were warmly greeted by the border police, and the police chief escorted us to passport control where we were warmly greeted and welcomed by several members of *Faridad Pars Arya* (FPA) Tours, which translates to "God's gift to the Land of Persia." Americans are required to hire an Iranian tour agency and a government licensed guide to enter the country. Our original contact, Ali, the president of FPA, and our email contact, Hamid, from Tehran were there along with our licensed tour leader, Ehsan, and driver, Afshin. Along with them were various other dignitaries who wanted to greet us. We have never been so warmly welcomed anywhere in the world.

Iran achieved!

A very friendly and warm welcoming in Iran.

Our thirty-day travel tour was designed to visit as many historical and archeological areas as we could while cycling. Since we were originally going to enter Iran from Turkey instead of Azerbaijan, we loaded our bikes and gear for a 400-mile car ride directly west across the top of Iran toward east Turkey and the town of Chaldoran where the over 2,000 year old Gharah Klisa (Black Church) is located.

My ankle was hurting more, so I told Ehsan, our guide, about the dog bite. He was immediately concerned, and at the next town we stopped at a pharmacy where I purchased antibiotic pills and a topical ointment. I'm glad that we'd had rabies vaccinations in Florida. We stopped for a late dinner and then set up camp at the restaurant.

The next day was another two-hour drive to the Black Church. The Saint Thaddeus Monastery is an ancient Armenian monastery located in the mountainous area of Western Iran. The monastery is visible from a distance because of the massiveness of the church, strongly characterized by the polygonal drums and conical roofs of its two domes. One of the Twelve Apostles, St. Thaddeus, also known as Saint Jude (not Judas

Iscariot from the last supper), was martyred here while spreading the Gospel. We had attracted quite a crowd and took the time to pose with everyone who wanted pictures with us. Our first ride in Iran felt satisfying as we rode the rolling hills through the mountains. That evening we stopped at a park where once again we camped near the town of Ivughli. It is interesting how late Iranians stay up at night. We were camping at a park and there were families arriving after midnight cooking with their kids running around playing.

We continued riding through the high desert with Afshin and Ehsan following us. Our first major city was Tabriz where we checked into a hotel and were greeted by Hamid, a tour guide. We also exchanged $360 USD to over 13,000,000 Rials. At this I exclaimed, "We're millionaires!" We toured the oldest indoor bazaar in the world. This over 800-year-old bazaar is mentioned by Marco Polo in his travels. Tabriz is at the crossroads of the ancient Silk Road a popular trading route through Asia for hundreds of years. Tabriz is full of fascinating history but is a real puzzle to navigate as the traffic lines don't mean anything and people dart everywhere as the signals are ignored. We ended the day in a massive park swarming with families after 11:00 P.M.

We were off to a good start on our cross-country journey of Iran. The goal of this ride was to cross the entire country to Mashhad and explore points of interest. To make this work in the allotted thirty days, we want to cycle at least fifty to seventy miles per day. We agreed to load the bikes atop Afshin's car to visit points of interest off our cycling route. As we have said before, this trip is not a bicycle exercise but an exploration of the world. After our stay in Tabriz, we elected to explore more in and around the city, so we took the day off to play tourist. The most interesting part of the day was exploring the prehistoric cave village of Kandovan. There are about one hundred people that still live in caves dug out of the volcanic rocks. That night, we had one of our best camps yet in a beautiful quiet river gorge.

The next three riding days were challenging but enjoyable. The temperature had been in the triple digits since we arrived, and the hills are steep like Spain. The headwinds add to the challenge, and we always seem to be going the 'wrong' way. Iran's countryside is similar to Morocco but the people are more friendly and generous. We were always invited for *chai* (tea), and if we stopped at every offer we would still be in Iran!

When we do accept the offer, it usually involves *chai*, food, and fruit with families gathered for roadside or home picnics.

Sitting with new Iranian friends for a picnic lunch.

In one town I left the hotel to find a market for cold drinks. The hotel was situated out of the main town in an area for car repair shops, and after walking up and down the block I could not find a market. A gentleman appeared from a shop and spoke the greeting, "*Salam.*" I replied with, "*Salam,*" and then said, "Market?" He pointed the way, so I walked in that direction. After another long walk, I couldn't find anything so resigned myself back to the hotel. As I turned around, the kind gentleman was on the street with his truck and motioned for me to get in. I did and he drove to the market, helped me select the items, made sure I paid correctly, and gave me a ride back to the hotel. It was all done with a big smile and his hand touching his chest (heart). Not a word of English transpired except for the international word, "Market." We would find this heartfelt gesture throughout Iran.

During the next several days we camped and stayed in people's homes. In the village of Istisou, which means 'hot water', we visited a bathhouse with a hot mineral pool that was separated with a wall for males and females. We both made several new friends in this community pool, and most attempted to meet us and say, "Hi!" Jocelyn told me she was quite the celebrity as the Iranian women swam to her and admired her many tattoos. Tattooing is illegal in Iran, but there are renegades who sport them. Nearby, we were invited to stay with a family in a one-room house. After dinner, they left and we had the house to ourselves. We felt bad that they had vacated, but Ehsan said they were honored to have us stay in their home.

A very happy Jocelyn riding the Iranian Mountains.

We cycled past dozens of small villages and occasionally found an open market. There were many times that we stopped in markets for food or drink where the proprietor would say, "Free." One afternoon, we camped near a river where nearby a large family was enjoying a picnic lunch. Two of them walked over and invited us to join them for a meal.

We did, and it turned into quite a party with many friendly people. We posed for many pictures and were truly touched by this awesome family. The older lady of the group looked like my late mother-in-law Polly. I knew Jocelyn was thinking the same as I saw tears in her eyes and knew she was thinking about her Gramma Polly. She'd passed before our New Zealand ride in 2012. There were many times on our trip when we could not communicate, but the smiles and laughing was all that was needed. When they were leaving, we all hugged and then settled into our camp. There are countless people we met that we will never meet again, but our memories of them will last our lifetime.

Camping is popular in Iran, and unlike the States, it can be done in any park, city, or roadside. After several days of cycling we opted to load the bikes and drive to Katalehkhour Cave about 100 miles to the south. This world famous cave is known as one of the most beautiful and spacious caves in the world with its four levels and eighteen miles that have been surveyed. It was formed during the Jurassic Period and was just discovered in 1951. Presently, 1.5 miles of the cave are open to the public. We walked in awe through the entire open area, exploring all the unique and stunning formations. It was slow going as some areas were a tight squeeze. Since we didn't exit the cave until after 9:00 P.M., we decided to camp outside the cave. A few hours later the police arrived, woke Ehsan, and asked if, "The Americans," were okay. They must be keeping track of us.

The next morning we drove back to Zanjan, unloaded our bikes, and continued cycling east. The wind wasn't as strong as yesterday, so we had a good ride and traveled through many small towns until deciding to camp at another roadside park. It was Friday, the Iranian day off, so it was crowded with families picnicking. The Iranian workweek consists of one day off, Fridays, with all other six days at work and school. The shops and business are open late too. While we were sleeping in our tent, families were still arriving after midnight to picnic and play like it was noon.

We continued toward Tehran and met Hamid of Faridad Pars Arya Tours while eating lunch alongside the road. He cycled with us to the city of Karaj where we stayed with the owner of FPA Tours, Ali, and his family, including our driver, his son Afshin. In the evening, we were served a delicious Iranian dinner prepared by Ali's wife and daughter.

Before dinner we visited a dentist as Jocelyn has been complaining about a sore tooth while brushing and flossing. The dentist's office was packed on a Saturday evening. We were finally seen after 8:00 P.M., and she had excellent care as an examination was performed and X-rays taken. It appears that there is a beginning of a small cavity on one of the molars, and we agreed that nothing needed to be done at this time. Once again, the generosity of the Iranian people was apparent when the doctor tapped his chest and said, "No charge."

After dinner, we discussed our upcoming trip options with Ali and his team. Since we decided to cycle through Iran, most of our other 'Stan' country visa dates did not line up anymore. Our Tajikistan visa dates line up well, thanks to the change we made in Ankara. We opted to spend a few more days in Iran. We also decided to fly from the eastern city of Mashhad, Iran to Dushanbe, Tajikistan and bypass Turkmenistan and Uzbekistan to save dollars and visa waiting time.

We spent an extra day at Ali's home and rode a train to the city of Tehran and then a subway into the city of seven million people. Afshin and Ehsan accompanied us, so navigating the city was simple. We explored the older and historical areas of Tehran, including the 250-year-old Golestan Palace also known as the Flower Palace. The entire palace is a massive work of beautiful art with stunning statues, colorful mosaics that convey stories, and bedazzling gold-lined walls and ceilings. There is also a huge gallery full of historic black and white pictures showing the history of the palace and those that lived here. Since that time, all the kings and Shahs of Iran have resided here. This palace was overrun during the 1980 Iranian Revolution. We had originally wanted to cycle into Tehran but were recommended not to because of the traffic and smog. We enjoyed lunch on a crazy busy intersection of downtown Tehran. I can't imagine a more interesting place to people-watch than from this sidewalk table. As the buses rolled by, we were disturbed and disheartened at the sight of women sitting/standing at the back of the buses. We talked with our guide Ehsan who said that it is the law. There are also 'Women Only' subway cars mainly for security and women can ride in any of the cars, but if they wish to be with women only, they ride in this car. After visiting Tehran, we were glad we did not cycle through the city as the vehicle and pedestrian traffic was confusing and hectic at best and we were overcome with headaches by the dense smog.

Back in Karaj, we met many members of the Ofogh Bicycle Club and rode with them to a park. The ride was a little hectic with all the traffic, but we safely made it to a park. It was so much fun being welcomed by the many members who all greeted us with shouts of, "Welcome to Iran!" In fact, that was a common greeting throughout our entire Iranian ride. The club presented us with club T-shirts, and they all signed a beautiful Iranian flag which is now a treasured souvenir. We presented them with a small signed American flag.

After a delightful stay with Ali and his family, it was once again time to resume our riding. Afshin drove us away from the hazy Tehran area, unloaded our bikes, and we began a series of mountain climbs. On our first day in Iran, while riding in the car, there was the distinct odor of leaded gasoline at our first gas station stop. I haven't smelled that odor in years, and Jocelyn has never smelled it. Leaded gas in the U.S. was phased out in the early 1990s. Afshin and Ehsan questioned why we cycled with our panniers when we could have simply left them in the car. We tried to explain to them that we were touring cyclists and we always carry our own load, but they never did understand. They did carry large plastic bottles of cold water for us, and we stopped often to refill our bike bottles. After a lunch of two eggs, we started our climbing. The roadside restaurants, if you can call them that, do not offer many options. Instead of some greasy meat, we prefer simple scrambled eggs. The heat was soon on us but the climbing was fun, traffic light, and the mountain colorful. A few hours later we stopped in a small town park and set up camp. The fire department personnel from next door came over and offered us their refrigerator, stove, and beds. Since we had already pitched our tents, we opted to stay in the park.

The next morning there was a reporter from the local newspaper waiting to interview us. During this time, many other people came to 'see the American bike riders' and ask for pictures. Sometimes we feel like celebrities. We were soon climbing again heading east. This day we peaked at 7,600 feet and treated ourselves to lunch at a restaurant at the summit. After lunch, the wind started blowing hard and the dirt flew over our bikes. Our descent in this wind included a few ten-percent grades that we actually had to peddle down to keep moving. After a few hours of attacking this wind, we arrived at another inviting park and decided to camp for the night. The next day we climbed even higher as we headed to the Semnan Desert. Once again the views were magnificent, as we reflected on how lucky we are to be bicycle touring in Iran. The descent down to the desert was 'scary fast', and we soon found ourselves in the town of Semnan and a hotel. After three days of climbing, this was a relief.

Desert riding in Iran.

The next several days were spent riding through the Semnan Desert. The temperature was in the lower triple digits so it wasn't as hot as expected but the dry headwind parched us. The miles were slow until the wind switched to a strong tailwind and we reached speeds in the low twenties. About fifteen minutes later the wind switched once again to head us. Our destination for the night, Mehmandoust, which means a guest hospitable village was soon in sight. At this point, little did we know what that truly meant.

We rode up to an ancient 11th century tower that is still proudly standing, although there is nothing recorded about its previous use. We planned to camp next to this tower and adjoining ancient cemetery but were soon joined by an Iranian couple who were visiting family in the village and they invited us to the family home for *chai*. We cycled to this home where we were soon joined by about twenty family members for delicious *chai*, fruit, nuts, bread, and homemade jam. The family was so pleasant and generous, and we all enjoyed the time together. They invited us to spend the night, but since they were so many staying in a tiny house, we decided to camp at the tower. When we returned to the tower, we met another man who invited us to stay inside the mosque community center. We cycled to that and it was an ideal location for sleeping and cooking since it had a kitchen and also a bathroom. As we settled in this center, the man's family brought us dinner. As the evening progressed, several others visited and gave us fruit, nuts, and bread. The generosity was amazing and sometimes a bit emotional.

A very old tower in Mehmandoust, an Iranian town that translates to "A guest hospitable village."

Our ride through the desert continued through the cities of Shahrood and Bastam. The wind in the desert spins 360s during the day, so sometimes we get headed, tailed, and then headed again. We have never ridden in such fluky winds before. We decided to leave the desert and ride back into the mountains. The climbing was easy in the much cooler weather. The summit was about 8,000 feet, and as we looked at the epic downhill on the other side we heard thunder. We haven't been rained on since Erzurum, Turkey! Thunder means lightning, so we started our downhill run only for it to be spoiled by an awfully eroded road, the worst we have ridden in Iran. Many of the hairpin turns were down to one lane due to landslides. So our epic run turned out to be an epic bust as we were jarred and shaken all the way down. Since I use my brakes too much on a clean downhill road, I was favoring them too much here. Needless to say, I was happy to be back at sea level where we found what we thought would be a great camping site.

That night we entered our tents at 8:00 P.M. for what we thought would be a long-needed rest. The locals had other plans though as they started appearing at 10:00 P.M. for their late-night park playing and dinner. Even though the park lights were not working, it was packed with kids playing and adults cooking. I still don't understand this late-night ritual, and it seems as though no one works in the mornings. Maybe they are just bored since there is little for them to do in the smaller towns. The families near us started leaving around 1:00 A.M. and then several intoxicated men appeared and took over the small pavilions as the families left. After this, the motorcycles appeared and raced around the park. They all finally left around 4:00 A.M.. Ehsan said that there is an old Farsi saying: "Some people are born cows and die donkeys."

The next two days we continued heading north and a little east as we rode toward Mashhad. We did find a much quieter campsite the next day. Except for a family of wild boars, we were the only ones present. We left the mountains and climbed once more into the high desert at around 4,000 feet. This desolate area was still pretty in its own way. But the heat was back as it was almost 120°F. Jocelyn and I drink about ten liters of water between us each day and we are glad that Afshin carried water in a cooler. The miles became difficult in the heat with continued headwinds. Throughout Iran, drivers would slow alongside us and pass us water and fruit as we were riding. And it was always, "Welcome to Iran."

Jocelyn is a real trooper, as she is required to be completely covered except for her face, feet, and hands. There were a few times she unbuttoned a bit to try and get more airflow, but Ehsan would see this, stop, and tell her to button up. There were a few times I saw tears in her eyes as she struggled with this and the way women in Iran are treated. There are few women that ride bicycles in this country, so Jocelyn is quite the celebrity as seeing a woman on a bicycle is not only rare but is almost revolutionary. It is not against Islamic law but just not done.

One of the highlights of this trip was exploring all the ancient structures along the Silk Road. As traders traveled this road hundreds of years ago, the caravans wanted a safe place to spend the night. In the deserts of Iran are caravansaries, also known as the first 'motels'. These were tall, walled forts made out of mud, clay, and straw. A caravan would enter and negotiate a price for staying there for however long they wanted. There were armed guards along the walls for security. There was also food and water available at various structures inside the walls. Whenever we rode by one of these, we would stop and explore as they are totally open and free. We were always the only ones exploring these. Along with this, many of the towns we stopped in had beautiful mosques and palaces to explore. Another favorite stop was the apple and peach orchards where we stocked up on fruit. Most times the workers tried to give us the fruit, but we insisted on paying as Ehsan told us most orchard workers are poor. We also rode by several archeological research sites that we investigated. One of them was a 3rd century city that was destroyed in a 1308 earthquake and discovered 100 years ago.

As we continued toward Mashhad we stopped in the village of Sayid Abad. Ali had arranged for a family friend to host us. We were warmly welcomed with *chai*, cold melons, and grapes. A few hours later, we feasted on a traditional Iranian meal of chicken and rice. The living room of most Iranian homes is interesting as there is no furniture except for an abundant supply of comfortable pillows.

The next morning we decided to stay and explore the local villages and were invited to our host's brother's home next door. We hopped on our bikes and explored the communities. It was a fun ride and we explored a unique 7th century astrological tower called Radkin Tower. The sunlight entered a hole in the top and the time of year was calculated. We returned in the midafternoon for a delicious lunch of spaghetti and salad prepared and served by our host's wife and several neighbors. We also had our laundry done — a real treat! After that, our host took us to a local ice cream maker's shop for a unique tour of how the shopkeeper has spent the last 40 years making ice cream in this village. That evening, we again feasted with the large family on a traditional Iranian barley soup. Dinner was served at 10:30 P.M., the normal time, with a cold melon dessert at midnight. These late nights can be tough, but the family camaraderie is fun to participate in. We were soon fast asleep on our sleeping pads in the main room.

After a two-night stay in Sayid Abad, we were ready for our final Iran ride toward Mashhad. Once again we changed our route to enjoy one more mountain ride and enter Mashhad from the south. After backtracking about twenty miles, we once again started climbing. It was a fun climb in a desolate area. The road was broken up and patchy, so we let air out of our tires for a smoother ride. We continued until we found an isolated place to camp. The following day was the same until we dropped out of our final mountain into a busier valley. We explored a few tourist sites before finding another camping spot. Our goal for cycling in Iran was 1,000 miles. We reached that riding into Mashhad, and Iran was our first one thousand mile country since New Zealand.

In Mashhad we stayed in Ehsan's family apartment with his mother Zohreh, father Hosein, and sister Nooshin, while waiting for our Tajikistan entry date flight. The hospitality of Ehsan's family was wonderful, and I gained a few needed pounds with Zohreh's delicious traditional Iranian cooking and abundant fruit. I started the ride at 215 pounds and am now down to 185, below my high school graduation weight back in 1971. Jocelyn and I enjoyed the after lunch nap times too.

Mashhad has one of the world's five Islamic Holy Shrines. This one is dedicated to the eighth (of twelve) *Imam* (leader), Riza, and a decendent of the Prophet Mohammad. This artistic and breathtaking mosque is the largest in the world. Muslims from all over make this destination a pilgrimage. Ehsan and Zohreh treated us to an unforgettable tour of this shrine as it prepared for Riza's birthday celebration.

Our last few days in Iran were wonderful with Ehsan's family, along with meeting and sharing lunches and dinners with many of their friends and relatives. Our Iranian journey ended with the way it started — great hospitality and the friendliest people we have ever met. It was sad and emotional to leave as we had many new friends who we will probably never see again. I was happy to see how Jocelyn was taken in by Nooshin (Ehsan's sister) and her friends. It was as if they had known each other all their lives. We were so welcomed and relaxed in many homes that most of the women went uncovered. In Iran, women do not do this unless in the presence of their fathers, husbands, or brothers as long as there are no non-relative males in the room. At the end of our Iran ride I asked Ehsan if he knew how many Americans are currently in the country. His answer of, "Including you two, there are ten Americans in the country now," shocked us. What an honor and a privilege it was to enjoy this beautiful country.

We arrived at the airport three hours ahead of our 7:00 A.M. departure time. We were glad for the extra time as it took 2 ½ hours to reach the gate. It was a scramble to find the right cash for the extra baggage and also to pay a fine of $30 each to extend our visa as we were three days over the expiration. A few days earlier we had tried to extend our visas at a government office, but the paperwork required was overwhelming and we were told, "Pay extra on departure." Passport control for exiting was a real mess with the supervisor under a constant barrage of arguments with other passengers, locals trying to leave Iran. The bikes had been packed as freight two days earlier, and we had ten bike bags with us. Each bike cost about $100 to pack and fly, and our extra baggage fee was $66. Total cost of the flight to Dushanbe was under $700 total, which is way under the cost of $1,150 estimated for Turkmenistan and Uzbekistan visas. All of a sudden we were at a gate. There were only two gates, and we asked several airport personnel for the correct gate number. They were all wrong. We knew we were on the correct plane when we spotted our bike boxes being loaded. Departing Iran was bittersweet as we were excited about upcoming Tajikistan but sad to leave Iran with 33 days of good memories that will last a lifetime.

Imam Reza Shrine is very beautiful.

Jocelyn:
August 9, 2014

We were surprised to see a very large gathering of people as we walked across the border into Iran! Over twenty people were taking pictures of us. Even the border patrol personnel took pictures with us where there was a clearly posted sign that said, "No pictures!" Faridad Pars Arya tours made us this huge banner that we were able to keep as a memory.

So many people were around, and once word got out that Americans were there, people would come up and take pictures of us while I was eating and enjoying mass amounts of goodies and *chai*. Mr. Pam, a well-to-do man, brought us breakfast and all this chocolate. I don't know what he was thinking, as it all melted in ten minutes. For a while this morning, I forgot that I was in Iran to cycle across, and it was just so nice lounging under a tree and being forced to eat everything. I kept pinching myself to make sure I wasn't dreaming. No joke — absolutely the most beautiful terrain, and this was just our first day riding!

Leaving Tabriz, we decided to take a break day and visit the Kandovan Village, a 13th century cave village. The caves are made out of a natural volcanic rock that has compressed to form a cone shaped home. Modern day cave dwellers! It was very neat to see. We left and drove some 50km to just outside of Maragheh. Our camp spot for the night was under apple trees facing the most beautiful gorge with mountains displaying an assortment of colors.

For once the night was very chilly, and I didn't sweat while laying on my sleeping bag! I realized that the full moon perhaps was altering my mood, and I took a step back from myself to reevaluate the Now. We rode on a very busy road, with many trucks. My nose was burning terribly from the black clouds I rode into. Many times on the road we saw young boys riding motorbikes, so at lunch, after meeting this fella just nearly 10 years old, I asked Ehsan what the driving age was. It's 18 years old. After just fifty miles, we decided to stop and get a lift into Istisou Village, a remote village next to the Charaoimagh hot spring, the village where not more than twenty families reside under an assortment of large trees with an ever-flowing mud and water ground. We stayed in the hot spring owner's home, our "warmshowers" host for the night! The house is one giant room made out of brick and mud.

August 13, 2014

While checking out an epic camp spot next to a river, we sat under an old fallen down bridge. Along came a large family of twenty who were having a picnic just on the other side of our stealth spot. A man came up to my dad and said, "Welcome to Iran! Will you join us for some *chai*?!" So we did just that. We dropped our gear and headed into the family circle. They all took pictures of us, one by one. Dad with all the men, myself with all the women, me with the little kids, and then the oldest of them, their grandmother, waved over to me to sit next to her and eat the entire watermelon they gifted us.

In Iran we were hosted by a family in a tiny village. Jocelyn made some new friends.

Now... I don't know how else to say this but to burst out in a scream and tears! I FOUND MY GRAMMA POLLY! This woman, I believe, is my resting Gramma in the way in which she whispered and jibber-jabbered with me, the way she touched my arm, and how she smiled with the spirit in her eyes. Sitting next to her, I felt her spirit alive and well. After two cups of *chai*, an entire watermelon, and a bowl of spaghetti, oh, and two more melons as gifts, this lady and I kissed cheeks, kissed on the lips, and I kissed her hands. The last thing I'll remember is seeing this woman climbing up the rocky hill as she looked around for me desperately to say one last goodbye. We exchanged a wave and a touch to our hearts.

August 23, 2014

Riding yesterday wasn't fun; it felt more like a grueling chore and I didn't like that feeling. The 20mph+ winds head on, with the dry desert heat, and long boring uphills weren't the slightest eventful. That is until we reached our camping spot near an ancient tower and cemetery in Menmanduost Village. This small village literally means "Friendly to guests" or something along those lines. The use of this tower isn't well known, and it's said they used it for ritual ceremonies inside. In minutes, a family drove up and welcomed us. They didn't live in the village but were visiting family and they welcomed us to stay with all 24 of them. We graciously declined but said yes to *chai*, of course! That's like a hidden rule: Always accept a *chai* invite. :)

August 28, 2014

We rode out of Ramen with tired eyes and sore legs, and Dad confessed that he didn't even want to ride! This is new for him, but some days I don't want to ride either. It's a lot of factors controlling that sad idea. But instead of calling a break day, we rode strong. During lunch, we were surrounded by many people and for about 15 minutes women from all over ran to get a picture with the crazy American woman — me. At four hours in, I didn't even feel like I had just ridden 40 miles. The only indication was underneath all these dang clothes, an ever-flowing waterfall of sweat. It reached 120°F! What does one crazy American do when temperatures reach that degree? I made sweet tea :) in Iran!

For dinner we had potatoes on charcoal and beans and tuna. With an early start on the road at 8:00 A.M., we got in a solid thirty miles until the wind decided to go buck wild, and that's when Dad's right knee started to really bother him. It's been bothering him for a while now, and that's not a good thing. Hoping this hotel will help him rest and his knee feels better tomorrow. For now, I will enjoy the Wi-Fi and catch up on classwork! Being a student while traveling around the world is definitely a challenge.

Sept. 4, 2014

Zohreh, our guide, and Ehsan's wonderful mother and I walked down the streets of Mashhad in our *chadors* as we rehearsed the Muslim saying (a requirement to enter the mosque) before we entered the Imam Reza Shrine, the largest mosque in the world: *"Ash hadu an la ilaha ill Allah wa ash hadu anna Muhammadar Rasul Allah,"* which translates to, "I declare, there is no god but Allah, and I declare that Muhammad is the Messenger of Allah." Once inside, we were immersed in religion. It was indeed packed, as Imam Reza's birthday is Sunday! He was an Islamic leader and direct descendent of Muhammad. Many people were praying and bringing their sick loved ones to be healed. There were processions of funerals with men carrying coffins through the crowds. While taking photos, I had to hide my thumb tattoos and cover my face with my *chador* the entire time. I never got all the way inside to see Imam Reza's tomb and circle, because the people were about to stampede and they had to shut the doors.

Posing in front of Imam Reza Shrine, the largest mosque in the world, in Mashhad, Iran with Ehsan's mother Zohreh.

Jocelyn wrote the following on women's rights in Iran:

Our 1,000 mile bike ride across Iran is over. It's common to feel a bit changed or refreshed after riding across a country, but this country brought about so much more. The emotions I felt, without a doubt, tremendously altered my state of mind and being. I knew that having to remain covered the entire time was going to be a bit difficult; it was in fact more difficult than expected. Women go about daily covered from head to toe in 100°+ temperatures — smiling and happy, or so it seems. For some it's okay to take off the *hijab* while in the comforts of their own home, but they can only do so if the men in the house are close family members; husband, son, or brother. If another man is there, she must remain covered. Her body is a beautiful gift and hers to own. It quite possibly can be the purist and most controlled right they have for themselves.

Many times I watched, questioned, and mostly always was taken aback by the traditions of Iranian culture. While riding, at one point I broke out in tears, crying for women, crying for the way things are. It's the 21st century, but these people live in the 12th century. I cried for remembering every time I was told I had to button up my shirt, fix my *hijab*, cover my hair more, and keep my legs covered. It's disgusting to me, but yet normal here. In this way, I acknowledge Iran for enriching and showing me how to embrace the beauty I have and am. For if it wasn't for the constant smiles and love from the women I met, I'd quite possibly never come back to this country. I've further learned that I won't stop fighting and I'll tell the truth behind the scenes of women's rights around the world, which are surprisingly, still, just barely nothing.

We were hosted by many families while traversing Iran and were served delicious dinners. On the left is our guide Ehsan, and then the couple who hosted us. To the right of Ehsan in the T-shirt is his driver Afshin

Everywhere we stopped in Iran we were treated like celebrities, especially Jocelyn as it is very rare for a woman to ride a bike. Our guide Ehsan, (Americans must hire a guide to tour Iran.), is in the white T-shirt.

What a friendly family waving goodbye to us.

While exploring the town of Mehmandoust, we were approached by a couple who invited us to their home so we took a fresh fruit and pistachio nut break. Pistachio farms are abundant in Iran.

Outside of Tehran, we joined the Ofogh Bicycle Club on one of their weekly rides. We had a fun time with them and exchanged signed flags and received club T-shirts.

Ehsan knew a bike shop owner in Zanjan where the owner (blue shirt, fourth from right) gave each of our bikes a free tune-up.

Tajikistan

Mike:

The flight was pleasant and interesting, because as soon as we were in the air, most women, including Jocelyn, removed their *hijabs*. About ninety minutes later we landed in Dushanbe, Tajikistan. Checking in was easy and we found our bikes in the cargo office. The next two hours were spent reassembling our bikes. Then we left the airport to find our warmshowers host for the next several days. But before that, we stopped at a restaurant and had a beer with lunch in this Muslim country. We remarked that it is refreshing to be in a country where there is choice, since alcohol is available and women have a choice to cover or not.

Our host Veronica had a large house with a courtyard and is open to hosting cyclists heading east and west. She is generous to open her home like this with everyone pitching their tents on the lawn. The entire yard and house is gated, so it is safe and comfortable. We talked with several cyclists about our next route. We will head to Kyrgyzstan through the Pamir Mountains, which is a popular cycling route along the Silk Road.

Due to family obligations, our world journey plans have changed such that it will no longer be nonstop. Our new goal is to fly home from Bangkok, Thailand by Christmas with Jocelyn returning to school for the spring semester. The following May, we will continue from North America to South America. This will give me time at home with Andee who I have neglected along with my house.

During our stay in Dushanbe we were able to obtain our Pamir Highway permit. There are several areas of this highway that are patrolled by the military, as the highway sometimes approaches within sixty feet of Afghanistan. At these checkpoints, 'your papers' are checked and the permit is required. "Built in the 1930s to supply the furthest outposts of the Soviet Empire, the 800 mile Pamir Highway is a high-altitude adventure in one of the most remote and mountainous corners of Central Asia. With several climbs to over 12,000 feet, on disintegrating roads and washboard tracks, it is a strenuous but hugely enjoyable undertaking. The spectacular mountain scenery is more than matched by the amazing hospitality of the Tajik people." –Tim Barnes

Finding the local police office and the bank to pay the 20 *somonis* each (about $4) was an adventure in itself because all the building names are in Cyrillic. We also found the post office and mailed a few things home. Paperwork in Tajikistan is similar to that in the States during the 1960s. Forms are duplicated with carbon paper, no computers, scissors to cut forms, etc. Most of the world since Turkey has been like this.

While in Dushanbe there was a huge multi-country business conference being held that included all the Stan countries, Iran, Turkey, China, and Russia. Ten presidents, including Russia's Putin, were meeting next door to our host's home in a large military compound. Needless to say, the biking has been difficult from many road closures depending on the time of day. The Tajik police are everywhere and none friendly due to all the restrictions. The last two days in some areas you cannot even stand on some of the sidewalks as they shout, "Keep moving!"

We believe the next few months will be a cycling challenge with the language barrier and different foods and cultures. The visa work is much more demanding too. Unfortunately we are both sick again. I flew from Iran with a cold that has now turned into an upset stomach including diarrhea. Veronica, our gracious host, invited me to stay in the first floor bedroom close to the bathroom. What a relief, as camping and diarrhea do not mix, especially when it involves a walk to a squat toilet. Jocelyn had the tent to herself, which she thoroughly enjoyed, but this morning she was curled up sick on the living room couch. When we arrived, most of the others cyclists were sick with the same symptoms. After some discussion, we attributed this to the stress of getting here. We stayed in Dushanbe longer than planned. Sometimes this is the way of a cyclist as they progress east. We feel fortunate to be in this friendly French family home, eating, and sharing group meals, taking walks and rides, sipping a few beers, and generally great napping. Comparing notes and bicycles of the international cycle touring community is fun and informative. One of our Dushanbe highlights was visiting the many bazaars and market days to find interesting trinkets and food.

An excerpt from Jocelyn's journal

Today I am thankful for being alive.

Yesterday, Dad and I and the Canadian couple, Nick and Virginia, embarked on a twenty-hour jeep ride through two mountain passes on a messed-up, sometimes paved, sometimes rocks, and mostly potholed road. It is common for cyclists to be driven this portion to the start of the Pamir Highway due to visa constraints. Just five hours in we came to a sudden stop, thinking it was just a flat tire. We all jumped out and quickly found out that the entire left front wheel and brake drum had broken off. My dad was sure that it would take a few days to repair, but I assured him that one of the skills in these parts is being innovative and always having lots of hands to help out. We all hoped for the best and hung around with the locals for three hours. Eventually, it seemed to be all fixed so we headed off again. The mountains started to get larger and larger, and we finally reached the Pamir River with the Afghanistan border.

Once the sun set our driver quickly became sleepy. This worried us all for our safety. The road had no barrier to block us from slipping over the cliffside into the river. It became frightening as he insisted he was good. I personally took on the job of watching his eyes blink rapidly and then close for sometimes too many seconds. I decided that if I noticed him fall asleep I would be in reachable distance of the emergency brake. We eventually got him to sleep for fifteen minutes as we walked around outside in the rather chilly temperatures. But I am afraid that's when things got worse. He kept driving less than a few inches from the cliffside, freaking us all out to the point of yelling and a revolt against moving on. Once more he took our advice to take another nap, this time longer, and everyone but myself napped in the car. I stared up at the stars in awe of the amount I could see so clearly and saw one shooting star! I rested my back on a tree and closed my eyes, but I continuously shook from the colder weather.

At midnight our driver was once again falling asleep and erratically driving all over the one-lane road. That was enough for me! We yelled once more, and I pulled the emergency break, Nick took the keys out of the ignition, and we all got out of the car. The driver then pulled a knife out and that changed the entire situation as he now had all of our lives, even more so, in his hands. The four of us discussed our options, which eventually led to saying our prayers and hoping we'd survive the night.

We arrived in Khorag at 4:00 A.M., 22 hours after leaving Dushanbe. Exhausted, we quickly hauled all our gear into a local homestay and fell asleep. Grateful.

Mike:

Tajikistan, Afghanistan, and Pakistan share the Pamir Mountains, the highest mountains in Central Asia. There are two routes to take from Khorag through the Pamir's to Kyrgyzstan: the Pamir Highway designated M41, or by an alternate route through the Wakhan Valley which eventually meets up with M41. Both routes are challenging, but the Wakhan Valley route is even more so because of the lack of a paved road after thirty miles. This route also takes you along the Pamir River and the border of Afghanistan.

"A journey through the Wakhan is the very essence of adventure travel. Around every turn in the road are tantalizing mountains, unknown wilderness, and fascinating villages and nomad camps. With every step deeper into the mountains, you discover a whole new world of adventure. Walk along the road, wander through villages, explore the inviting mountain passes. Travel with the gracious and hospitable people who live here. Experiencing these mountains firsthand is incomparable and unforgettable." –a tourist brochure.

At times we were just a stone's throw from Afghanistan and only a few miles from Pakistan. The Wakhan Valley road is hilly and mostly cracked and shattered, but the bright-green scenery makes up for the difficult cycling conditions. The Pamir Mountains are majestic with some peaks still holding snow from last winter. Water is plentiful for filtering, as the small markets, known as magazines, do not carry it. People drink river and stream water, and as we filter they look at us and wonder what we are doing. None of the markets have any refrigeration so all drinks are warm.

Unfortunately we are both still sick. I can't seem to shake my cold and neither of us can get over diarrhea. We filter and sterilize water, clean up with sanitizer lotion, and avoid meat, but we still can't figure this out. We have taken antibiotics, but those don't seem to help. We recently heard that giardia is a persistent parasite that lives in soil, food, and water and is common in countries such as Tajikistan and affects those who drink untreated water. It is an illness that appears to go away but returns, sometimes often.

Afghanistan is always in view with Afghans waving and yelling greetings to us as we ride. The Tajiks are also friendly. Miles are slow but rewarding. One afternoon the wind increased, and we noticed a haze appearing behind us. We were soon engulfed in a sand storm that roared up the valley. At this point we were wondering how we could camp in this massive valley of windblown sand. As we cycled into the next village there was a large building that looked like it could be a hotel, and it was. With great relief we moved out of the sand and into a $7 hotel room. Also located on the property was a restaurant where we enjoyed a fine soup dinner and a few glasses of warm beer. We met a policeman from Dushanbe who was visiting his uncle who happened to be the proprietor of the hotel and restaurant. The policeman spoke English, so we enjoyed talking about Tajikistan. We were told that sandstorms are a common occurrence in the fall and announce cooler weather coming. Along the way we met a New Zealand couple cycling from Melbourne, Australia to Ireland and are in their eleventh month. A few hours later we were at the border between Tajikistan and Afghanistan. Between the borders is an island on the Pamir River where every Saturday there is a bazaar featuring Tajik, Afghan, and Pakistan products. We were excited about this, and after parking our bikes and handing our passports to the guard at the bridge gate we walked to this island. Unfortunately, the bazaar was not being held this day. We were standing next to the Afghan border when a few military people approached us. For some reason I was turned around and said something to an officer who I mistakenly called a Tajik. From the look on his face, I immediately regretted saying that as he turned angry. Jocelyn gave me that, "Dad, what are you saying?" look. I apologized and we walked back over the bridge to Tajikistan.

In the next village we were finally able to find a simple rice lunch and also five two-liter bottles of water. No matter how the river, stream, or fountain water is filtered and sterilized, it still tastes bad. Now we crave bottled water. After lunch I asked where the toilet was. The waitress pointed across the street to a school where I wandered, looking, before asking again in a market. I was pointed the same way and figured that the toilet was in the school. After more wandering, I noticed kids (male and female) exiting a cave-like room. I entered and was immediately taken aback by the foul smell in the room with about a dozen holes occupied by squatting males and females. From the look on the floor, the kids didn't always use the holes. I sheepishly tiptoed around the filth and found a vacant hole and urinated. Upon exiting, I was emotionally upset after witnessing this school bathroom and how the Tajik schoolkids live. I did not see any toilet paper or wash sink. Once again I was reminded of our comfortable life in America.

We continued climbing through the valley and passed our old record of 8,050 feet and hit over 9,000 feet. We are slowly building our legs and acclimatizing our bodies to altitude. We do rest more and drinks lots of water whether we are thirsty or not. Late in the afternoon, we were thinking of where to camp when Jocelyn spotted a homestay sign in front of a small farm. A family of five lives on this farm where there is an extra room. At least we thought it was an extra room. We liked the family and land so decided to stay. Right next door are the remains of a 3rd century B.C. fort. After *chai* and snacks, the kids took us on a tour of this interesting fortress. When we returned, our host had cooked a delicious vegetable meal. After the meal, Jocelyn showed them pictures of our family and our trip. We then said goodnight and settled onto a large sleeping platform. While walking to the outside toilet, I noticed the family huddled together on the ground. They slept outside, giving up the family bedroom for a few dollars.

We stayed with this family in Tajikistan on their farm. After dinner we shared with them our family pictures.

The next day we continued on our bikes to the town of Langar. We had heard from other cyclists that the route up to Khargush Pass is steep, sandy, and narrow and that there are taxis available to take backpackers and cyclists up toward the pass at various levels. We found a taxi who agreed to take us up to the military police border post where our Pamir Highway permit was checked. Our driver drove us to the military post within 4,000 feet of the pass. We arrived at night, thinking that we would pitch our tent near the post, but instead we were welcomed into the post's building where we were warmly greeted by the military police. This building did not have electricity, and the heat was provided by a cow-chip-burning stove. They served us snacks, *chai*, and a delicious vegetable noodle soup. When we started yawning, they placed mats and pillows in the adjoining room and said goodnight. As I often say, this adventure is all about the people you meet. We never expected to spend the night with the military police. They were kind and curious about America.

The next morning we rode and pushed our bikes through the 14,200-foot pass. It was a long struggle through the mostly rocky and sandy road. Along the way, we met another Swiss cyclist, Michael, who was going our way and have met other places. After the pass, it was mostly a downhill but precarious ride until close to sunset when we set up camp.

Meeting our Swiss friend Michael while riding through the Pamir Mountains, Tajikistan.

After thirteen hours in the tent we warmed enough to continue and soon joined the Pamir Highway and once again a paved road. We continued on M41 through the small village of Alicar and had lunch with our Canadian cyclist friends, Nick and Virginia, who we met in Dushanbe. We cycled out of town and set up camp on another chilly night. The days and nights are cold and we are glad to have our Sierra Design minus 39F sleeping bags.

One of our all-time favorite rides was the following day as we rode 65 miles to the town of Murgab. The stark mountain scenery, way above the tree line, was striking, the climbing easy, and the quiet road addicting through the on and off snow flurries. In the afternoon, we arrived in Murgab and had a day's rest in this little town that looked like a frontier Alaskan town.

The first morning in Murgab it was snowing harder with a biting wind. We met the Swiss cyclist, Michael, along with Nick and Virginia, who arrived the day after us, and we all decided to stay an extra night in the only hotel in town. Along the Pamirs we have observed downed power poles and there is no power in Murgab. The hotel does have a small generator that is run two hours a day to heat water. That's what we were told anyway, because we didn't get any hot water in the showers. The locals charge their cell phones here for a small fee while the generator operates. There is a bazaar/market composed of long rows of shipping containers that was interesting to stroll through. There was also a restaurant next door to the hotel where the locals went to drink and the place was always packed.

From the last few weeks of cycling, it is pretty apparent that the Tajiks have a tough life. I had read that over 85% of the people live at poverty level, and with 90% of the country above 10,000 feet it is a hard life. But I am happy to say that we have lived among many Tajiks, and they all seem happy with their life. They don't have much — few cars and no powered farm equipment – but they are always smiling. As we cycle through villages, the kids run alongside us laughing and smiling.

Jocelyn's Instagram Posts:
Septermber 27, 2014, Tajikistan.

There isn't anything like camping across the river from Afghanistan. I woke up early in the morning having to pee, and I spied four fellows watching from under a tree. Afterwards, we exchanged waves and hellos.

Camping in Tajikistan across the river from Afghanistan.

The highlight of our stay in the Wakhan Valley was getting to interact with the people of Afghanistan! Waving, hooting, and hollering happened. During this conversation, the leader waved fiercely with his crop knife and I yelled over, wanting to exchange transportation with him. He then laughed even more violently!

Septermber 28, 2014

Early morning pushing up to a very high pass. In two hours we traveled only six km. The rock mixed with heavy thick sand and the amount of weight I'm carrying made for the worst day of our tour. Since being sick for the past week before this, I was already much weaker than I've ever been, so pushing a fully-loaded bike uphill was by far the hardest and most mentally upsetting challenge I've ever faced. Never have I been so proud and felt so ashamed for being so weak. There is a lesson to be understood in everything. Just got to listen, push on, and keep moving forward, and I now know exactly who I am and what I'm made of. Even if most everything flushes through my system with no benefits, I still am made of a lot. This pass was just at 14,212 feet with Pakistan and Afghanistan snow-covered mountains in the distance. The day's temperature consistently stayed at 35°F, so I decided it was probably time to put my hiking boots on as I've been wearing my sandals since Istanbul.

Septermber 29, 2014

And then at the peak of the tallest most difficult mountain pass I've ever cycled/pushed my bike up, there was a moment of pure satisfaction, silence, and awe. The challenges we face daily are little particles constructing our beings into this greatness that might never be fully known or written, but what we do with it and how we perceive the now is ultimately satisfied into a continuous cycle of growth.

The struggles make us stronger. The satisfaction and calmness of knowing you've accomplished something so grand is awe-inspiring. It's so crazy where I have been and what I have seen. It takes a lot of silence and recollection with peace to fully grasp my everyday life.

I just like cycling to new places and seeing new things. In a way I'm fearless, simply because I've switched out of the normal routine of life and everyone else knows it. Now I live for what's around the next bend, the purest water source, a simple hug from a stranger, or the hellos from around the world. They make up what is real and important. Of course, I'm human and miss my family, my dog, my friends, oh gosh, I miss my friends. Sure the normality of life seems pleasant, but when I'm deeply sick and barely able to sit on my bike saddle, it is a strain. I am grateful knowing the importance of living out my dreams is the ultimate happiness in my life. Say I'm selfish, because I am. This is what I want to do and I'll do it just like Nike always told me to.

Septermber 30, 2014

By way of hitch-biking we were able to make it to our 21st country, Kyrgyzstan, when I began to puke even more and had to lie down frequently to the point I couldn't ride the dirt/rock/sand roads anymore and had to get to Osh to go to the hospital. The first and probably only truck we'd see we got a ride with and it happened to be going to Osh as well. It took twelve hours and just 230 miles later to arrive in Osh. Let that length of time and short miles soak in for a second. Wink!

New friends from South Africa we met along a very isolated road. They gave us ice cold beer!

Jocelyn with new friends in a small Tajik village.

Murghab, Tajikistan with our Canadian friends Nick and Virginia along with our Swiss friend Michael.

Kyrgyzstan

"It is by riding a bicycle that you learn the contours of a country best, since you have to sweat up the hills and coast down them. Thus you remember them as they actually are, while in a motor car, only a high hill impresses you, and you have no such accurate remembrance of country you have driven through as you gain by riding a bicycle."

—Ernest Hemingway

Mike:

We left Murgab and spent the next few days cycling and camping toward the Tajik border before getting a ride to Kyrgyzstan as told in the beginning of this book. We continued driving on the increasingly degrading road to the Kyrgyzstan border. Upon arrival at a miserable duty station high in the frigid and windy mountains, we were told to unload our bikes and gear during a truck inspection. I talked with the driver, and since we were both headed to Osh he agreed to drive us at a negotiated price. Our bikes and gear in the open truck back were completely covered in dirt. After reloading the bikes, our passports were stamped into this free country and we departed the border. It was a miserable seven-hour ride into the Kyrgyzstan Mountains until we reached the city of Osh in the dark and rain. We were dropped off onto the street where our filthy bikes and panniers were soon muddy from the rain. We were wet, cold, dirty, and miserable as we walked the crowded streets with our bikes while looking for a hotel. It is times like this when I think, *What the heck are we doing?* After asking several people, we found a hotel. As we unloaded our panniers to carry them to the room, the hotel clerks stared at our mess until one of them helped us as we must have looked pretty pathetic. I locked the bikes downstairs and that was it for the day. We were so happy to be somewhere safe and warm and to have a bed.

The next day we washed the panniers, helmets, and trunk bags in the shower and dried them on the floor by setting them on our tent tarp. We gave almost all of our clothes to the hotel clerk for washing and washed our bikes. We visited the closed China consulate and a few travel agents inquiring about a China visa. The China consulate was closed for a holiday and this seems to be a recurring theme with us. We were told that China visas can only be obtained from the northern city of Bishkek, which is a twelve-hour van ride or twelve-plus days on our bikes. We found an English-speaking agent, Svetlana, who offered to help us obtain the visas without us having to travel to Bishkek, as her daughter flies to Bishkek a few days a week and could deliver our applications. Also thanks to Svetlana, we moved into an apartment while waiting for our visas.

We visited a hospital near our apartment to investigate Jocelyn's continuing medical issues. We wandered through the various hospital buildings not knowing where to go until we met the hospital's neurologist, Dr. Nurbek, who immediately came to our help and spoke English fairly well. He guided us to two doctors, one who diagnosed that Jocelyn had an ear infection and an internist for her stomach pain and weakness. He also drove us to another hospital where he liked one of the doctors better than at his hospital. After these three consultations (consultation fees: $3), he took us to a pharmacy, helped us get the proper medications ($25), and wrote down in English the correct dosages. We hope this sends Jocelyn on the road to recovery. These next two weeks in a completely furnished apartment may be a blessing since we can rest and recuperate for our China and Southeast Asia journeys. We are anxious to see what China has in store for us.

We spent many days exploring Osh with and without our bikes. Our apartment was centrally located and completely furnished, including cabled Internet and at $15 a day was cheaper and more comfortable than a hotel. There were many restaurants nearby, but we enjoyed cooking. Across the street were vegetable and fruit stands. Next door was a market that was convenient for our cooking needs. Our go-to meal was a large pot of vegetable soup. We talked, or tried to, with the neighbors, watched the kids play in the dirt lot out back, and fed the local stray dogs sausages that we bought just for them.

On October 17, 2014, Jocelyn and I celebrated her 24th birthday in Osh, Kyrgyzstan. Her 21st birthday was on the road in Texas, and her 22nd in New Zealand. During our time in Osh, we have met several touring cyclists of which many we have met before. Nick and Virginia, who we last saw in the Pamir Mountains, Tajikistan, are here in Osh after cycling to the China border and finding it closed for a holiday and getting a ride to Osh. Plus, we revisited several friends who we had met in Dushanbe, Tajikistan. It is indeed a small world. That evening, we all met at a local German restaurant for dinner. Svetlana, our China connection, appeared with flowers for Jocelyn and the best gift of all — our passports with China visas! We have waited three weeks for this moment. Also stamped in our passport was the required Kyrgyzstan immigration registration stamp. Now we can successfully exit Kyrgyzstan and enter China! The thirty-day visas cost $400 each and are one of the highest we paid. It is much easier and cheaper to get a sixty-day China visa while in the U.S.

Jocelyn spent the last few weeks learning basic Chinese phrases along with planning an interesting route to take advantage of many areas we wish to visit with our allocated thirty days. She is feeling much better thanks to the medication, and we are both feeling better from the long rest. We will take a few train rides through the Gobi Desert since we only have thirty days.

Jocelyn's Instagram Post:

October 18, 2014

Everything seems so surreal. I was so sick . . . I lost like fifteen pounds in a week and yet my 24th birthday was pretty rad. I had a few friends to celebrate with at dinner, a few beers, and two women gave me ravishing flowers! We also got our passports back with a Chinese visa inside, and we will be heading to Kashgar, China in two days!

China

Mike:

Bicycles are not allowed to cross the Chinese border and are not allowed in the area known as 'No man's land' — from the border to the first major city of Kashgar, China. We were told that there are sometimes taxis available at the border that can be hired for transit to Kashgar. We decided to take a bus instead of taking that chance. We left our apartment in Osh for a precarious ride to the bus station. We cycled our way through back unpaved roads and walked our bikes through a crowded Sunday bazaar. Jocelyn navigated through the narrow stall alleys, and we eventually found our way across the river to an unfinished old Soviet Union bus station. This was an adventure in itself and was a precursor of what was to follow. Once at the station, we prepared our bikes for the scheduled 7:00 P.M. departure on a Chinese sleeper bus that finally left at 9:00 P.M. — right on time. This part of the world does not run on schedules. The bunks were somewhat comfortable, but it felt like I was on a hospital gurney all night. We reached the snow-covered Kyrgyzstan border at 5:00 A.M. Since the border didn't open until 9:00 A.M., we had a long wait onboard. We exited the bus a few times, waking the driver each time, for a call to nature, trying to be discrete between trucks. There were hundreds of vehicles, mostly trucks, massed at the border on this Monday morning as this border is closed on weekends. When the border opened, our driver precariously drove off-road bypassing most trucks before cutting back in line. We continued through four checkout posts and did not see any border taxis, so the bus was a smart move.

Soon, the first China customs checkpoint appeared, and we were required to exit the bus along with all our belongings including our bikes and all panniers. The panniers were sent through X-ray plus all bags were hand searched. The guards took a real interest in our camera and computer and scanned through the picture files of both. Occasionally we heard,

"No!" and assumed they didn't like a picture, but we were not asked to delete any. A British traveler that we met onboard had a map of China that included Taiwan. A Chinese woman border guard looked at his map and noticed Taiwan and shouted, "No!" At this, she picked up scissors and was going to cut Taiwan off the map, but Alan convinced her not to. Instead, she took a black marker and covered Taiwan! This was so funny because she was extremely serious.

One hundred miles later we reached the official Customs and Immigration Station. So what did we do? We once again emptied the entire bus and went through another more detailed inspection. In addition, the bus was driven through three large garages, each with a different type of scanning X-ray. This stop was three hours, whereas the first was about half that. At this second stop we received our passport entry stamps. From there it was another two hours to the first major city of Kashgar where we were dropped off in a dark dirt field. The streets were crowded with electric motorbikes that silently whizzed around. We had many near collisions with these darting silent hazards as we navigated our way to Kashgar Old Town Youth Hostel. In large cities we prefer staying in the old town sections, which are much more interesting.

We had met a Romanian girl on the bus who took a cab to the same hostel, and the three of us went exploring and found an intriguing food bazaar for dinner. It seems like everything imaginable especially with meat was offered. We settled for a simple but delicious vegetable noodle soup where we were able to select the ingredients while our Romanian friend was excited at finding lung. At this point we thought it was 9:00 P.M., but the next day we realized we were two hours late as all of China is on Beijing time. What a rude awakening it was when we woke up thinking it was 8:00 A.M. when it was really 10:00 A.M. We attempted to find train tickets for the desert ride to Urumqi. Even though we never did find where they were sold, we had fun exploring this new country that is fascinating and frustrating at the same time. Chinese transportation tickets are difficult to purchase unless you or someone with you speaks Chinese. As in Osh, Kyrgyzstan, we found an English-speaking travel agent. Musa was a tremendous help in purchasing our train tickets.

The night before we left Kashgar, my intestinal illness reappeared with a roar. After so many antibiotics, we believe the Giardia parasites are still dormant inside our intestines and surfaces at the worst times. The vomiting, diarrhea, and nausea is wearing on me. We slowly worked our way to the train station where our bikes and most of our panniers were packaged for a follow-up freight train. We were unaware that our bikes would travel separately, and since we were planning three train trips with the final stop at Chengdu, we had them freighted through to Chengdu and hoped they would arrive at the end of the week. Without Musa at our side, who knows where they would have been sent. We figured the three train trips should be enough so that when we start cycling our thirty-day visa would last until entry into Vietnam. Little did we know that we would use each of those thirty days. The Gobi Desert ride from Kashgar to Urumqi took 25 hours and did provide me with lots of sleep as we were in a two-berth soft (enclosed) sleeper. Near the Urumqi train station we found a decent hotel, which again provided me with much needed rest. Crackers and watered down noodles was all I could stomach. We did manage to explore parts of Urumqi but stayed close to the hotel.

After two nights we were back onboard a train to our second stop of Lanzhou. This time our berth was a four-berth soft (enclosed) sleeper that we shared with two others. While waiting for the train in the terminal, Jocelyn painted her toenails. This attracted quite a crowd of male onlookers who stood and stared as she painted and buffed them. I wonder what they were thinking. While this was happening, I looked up and saw our Swiss cycling friend Michael. We have caught up with him many times. He also has a thirty-day visa. There is no way to cycle across China in that little time, so most cyclists use trains for part of the journey. Other cyclists ride their thirty days and exit the country. We hear that visa extensions are easy to get and require five days of waiting, but we do not want to spend any more time waiting for visas.

We had originally planned to spend two extra days in Lanzhou so that we could travel to the Tibetan Plateau and Grasslands and tour the Labrang Tibetan Monastery, which is in China but also is known as 'historical' Tibet. We had checked with the bus station for the four-hour drive but couldn't figure it out, and because of inclement weather, sometimes the pass is closed due to snow as it was the day before. While discussing options with the English-speaking hotel manager, another guest mentioned that he and his friends were considering renting a van and driver the next day to travel there and if we were interested the cost would be split seven ways. We immediately said yes, and the next morning we drove with five new friends from Malaysia. It was raining until we climbed the Tibetan Plateau to about 10,000 feet and arrived in LaBrang, China. This part of Tibet, also called 'The Roof of the World' due to the immense size of the plateau, is open, but the Tibet area south of the Himalayas also known as 'political Tibet' is closed to tourists and requires a special permit and guide similar to Iran. Tibet is a former independent nation, whereas the plateau and highlands were always part of China. Tibet became part of China in 1965.

We spent Tuesday night at a hotel in Labrang and toured the thought-provoking Labrang Tibetan Monastery Wednesday. We were in awe as we took a guided tour by an English-speaking monk. The monastery was first established in 1709 and is one of the six major monasteries of Tibetan Buddhism. The richly-ornamented buildings are splendid and magnificent. Labrang Monastery is not only a religious center but also an art museum. It was interesting to observe the monks in their daily religious practice. The entire monastery is surrounded by a circuit of large prayer wheels that the locals walk each day while spinning the wheels by hand. We followed part of the circuit and fit right in with the locals. After touring the monastery we all drove back to Lanzhou.

Revolving prayer wheels that surround Labrang Tibetan Monastery, China.

The next day we boarded the train to Chengdu and were in an eight-person hard sleeper, an open compartment with four bunk beds on each side. The train station in Lanzhou was recently the scene of a knife yielding activist attack that killed many people. Our bags were sent through X-ray, and my enclosed large pocket knife was found. At this, the three guards were going to confiscate my knife but I asked them not to. They then wrapped my knife in plastic, and after several wraps of duct tape, they handed it to me and said, "No use!" When I answered, "Okay," they posed for pictures with me with their cell phones. In our three train rides, we went from the best compartment to the worst. In the hard sleeper, there were smokers and heavy drinkers. We tried to keep a small area to ourselves, but it was difficult as there were so many people coming and going. We carried a bucket of KFC chicken onboard. Our compartment mates ate chicken feet and other strange parts and stared at us while we ate our KFC. On arrival at Chengdu we crossed our fingers and found our bikes after an intense search between several buildings. While reassembling them on the street, we attracted quite a crowd of staring Chinese. We smiled and said, "Hi," but they just stared and it was a bit unnerving. In China, people on the street just stop and stare at us. We try to be friendly and talk, but they just stare. So we walked down the street to finish assembling our bikes and they followed us. We quickly got everything together and finally rode off into the extremely crowded street. Jocelyn had a hostel mapped on her phone that took a long time to find through all the crowds. I lost Jocelyn several times in large groups of other bikes and mopeds. I finally saw her waiting in front of Lazy Bones Hostel. We checked in and were right on time for a Halloween party where we were given masks and food.

The next morning we toured the Chengdu Giant Panda Breeding Center and were fascinated with our first panda bears. We hadn't realized that there were so many varieties and sizes of pandas. Of course, the highlight was the panda nursery where we both wanted to take one home. We met several new friends at the hostel who we joined for a walking and subway tour of Chengdu. One night we found a Mexican restaurant, and the next day we spent a Sunday afternoon in a People's Park. All parks in China are called People's Park where large groups of people exercise while others sing karaoke right next to each other. We then visited the Chengdu Seafood Market for lunch and were surprised at the assortment of live seafood available for purchase. If it lives in the ocean, it was here. It was disturbing to see large live sea turtles in tiny tanks and hundreds of fish crammed into small tanks. The assortment of eels and snakes were interesting and they were skinned alive. After that, we headed across the street to a giant meat market, but after seeing dogs and cats hanging on racks at the entrance, we immediately left.

After four weeks off our bikes (three weeks in Osh, Kyrgyzstan and one week training in China), we were finally back on the saddle. It felt great to cycle again, although working our way out of Chengdu was a bit challenging due to all the traffic. Many of the intersections had six roads leading into them, which were enormously confusing and a bit intimidating to enter. As usual, Jocelyn shined with her excellent navigation skills, and a few hours later we were finally out of the city. Although it was busy, we enjoyed this interesting ride and watching the people and traffic. We were in awe of what a Chinese bicycle can carry. It is unbelievable to see how many products can be piled on a bicycle and still be peddled, and we thought *we* carried a big load! We met a cycling couple from France headed our way and shared lunch with them. The four of us had our fill of fried rice and steamed vegetables for about $4 total. After lunch we continued cycling together for several miles before they branched off to the west and we continued south to the city of Pengshan where we decided to get a hotel for the night.

The following day we rode to Leshan, home of the largest stone Buddha in the world. We found a hotel, and the entire staff and others carried our bikes and gear up four flights to our room. We had an enjoyable time with the friendly and fun staff. For dinner we sampled the street food. It was too spicy for me, but Jocelyn certainly enjoyed it. Each day is a new adventure in China as we never know what is going to happen. We are in the land of 'No English', so it does get interesting and fun, especially when both us and the Chinese start laughing.

Our hotel had a large gaming area full of Mahjong tables. I have never played this Chinese game, but it sure looked intriguing. There are also groups of men playing cards with cigarettes hanging from their mouths. It seems so '70s America. But it is disturbing that cigarettes are dropped on the floor, which makes quite a smelly mess.

We had cycled to the Grand Buddha the day before, but there wasn't a safe place to leave our bikes so we taxied back to the attraction. Along with the stone Buddha, there are many smaller Buddhas and several working temples spread over many acres. The Giant Buddha is 233 feet tall, the shoulders are ninety feet wide, and the smallest toenail is large enough to easily accommodate a seated person. The Buddha, carved from a cliff face, was started by a monk during the Tang Dynasty in 713 and completed by a successor in 803. The ears are made of wood and the head is covered with a thousand curls. The Buddha faces the union of three famous rivers.

We enjoyed a fascinating look inside Buddhism, which complemented our previous trip to the Labrang Tibetan Monastery. Once again we felt like we were exploring a museum with so many interesting and beautiful pieces of art. Fortunately, there were no photography restrictions as there were in Labrang. Since we didn't return to our hotel until late afternoon, we decided to spend another night in Leshan.

We had an early start from Leshan, and after a few hours started climbing into the Emei Mountains heading south to Kunming. The climbing was tedious through the traffic. Our goal for the day was the town of Ebian, but as the rain and darkness increased we started looking for a place to pitch our tent even though it is illegal for foreigners to camp in China. On the right side of the road was a wide, deep drainage ditch that led to a steep slope and on the other was a cliff. We thought about putting our tent up in the courtyard of the occasional house but soon a small town appeared. We inquired at a small restaurant if there was a nearby hotel, and we were led to another restaurant where they had rooms available upstairs. The price was right at $8, so we locked our bikes in the kitchen and sat down to a delicious noodle dinner. We soon retired to our beds even though we were still wet from the rain and perspiration. The next morning we rode into a huge river gorge and began our wavering mountain ride in the rain. The traffic finally lightened and the rain stopped as we reached another small village. Many people came out to meet us as we sat and ate a soup lunch. There must have been fifty people watching us eat. They stared at us in shock when we brushed our teeth. We felt like celebrities. When we left the crowd, we passed a guy selling live catfish out of his tarp-covered truck bed full of water and fish. He was so proud of his business and smiled when we took a picture. There was a long line of people as he netted fish for customers. After another few hours we were weary of the constant up and down, so we inquired at another restaurant about rooms. There just happened to be rooms upstairs so we spent the night.

Last year, I read a book about an American couple cycling in China who wrote about these unofficial hotels. Twice during their ride the police came to their door in the middle of the night and made them leave because they were foreigners and were not staying at an officially registered and legal hotel. They are cheap at $8-$10 per night so we will take our chances. They only provide a bed and sometimes a shared bathroom. We do like cheap accommodations.

We attracted quite a crowd as we ate lunch in this Chinese mountain village.

The day started misty again so we donned our rain gear. This makes cycling uncomfortable because while climbing we sweat inside and then during the downhill you get cold from being so wet inside. On a typical day we will don/doff our rain gear up to dozens of times. The scenery through this gorge is beautiful as we passed many high waterfalls and small villages. The villagers are always a hoot as they act like they have never seen foreigners before. We wonder how many cyclists have ridden this road less traveled. The mountainside terrace farming is fascinating, as they utilize even the steepest parts of the mountains.

Once again it was a long day and it was time to find a place to sleep as it was getting dark. We talked with several people with our pocket translator and point-it book trying to find accommodations. We asked at one house where we could camp, and the man looked shocked as he put his hands near his ears and growled. It took us a while to figure out that he was probably warning us of bears. Finally there was a group gathered at a store. We asked about a room and they all pointed up a steep hill. One of them made a phone call and a lady who rents a room in her house came down to meet us. We locked our bicycles in the store and climbed up a steep hill to find a decent room, although it was cold and there was no heat. She cooked breakfast in the morning and then we were on our way.

It was raining again and we wondered if the sun ever shines here. After reaching 7,000 feet, the mud was flowing on the steep climb and we were not able to ride. After a few miles of pushing our bikes uphill in the mud, a truck appeared and gave us a ride over the 9,200-foot pass. We cycled to the city of Ganlou in the hopes of finding a bus ride to Kunming, as our time is running short and we still need visas. There were no buses going that way and what often happens is that someone who speaks English steps up to help. He found a van and driver for us and we drove over another mountain range. Thirty miles and five hours later we arrived late in the city of Xichang.

Taking a break in a small Chinese village.

Jocelyn is still having fun as she negotiates the mud and clay!

Since our time was short, we took a bus to Kunming, arrived there at 11:00 P.M., and found Cloudland Hostel after riding an hour in the dark.

The next three days were spent in a flurry of activity finding consulates and applying for our Vietnam and Thailand visas. We had to jump through a few last minute hoops for the Thai visa as the consulate is only open from 9:00-11:30 and is busy. But we successfully obtained both visas so our consulate visits on this portion of our world tour is complete! Our Laos visas will be obtained on arrival at the border. Thailand does offer a visa on arrival when entering overland, but it is only for fifteen days, which isn't enough time for us. We are excited to ride our final 200 miles south to Vietnam. Our China visas expire in five days, and once again we are on a schedule, which we dislike.

We have ridden long hours in the last four days because our China visas expire tomorrow. The last three days have been in the mountains of Southeast Asia, and it is everything we had pictured it to be — muddy mountain roads and lush tropical plants. We have ridden and walked the sometimes steep roads through many villages. We do have to walk at times as the mud literally flows and the tires just spin. On one day we met three Chinese cyclists on tour. We followed them to the next town where after a long climb we arrived at a hotel at 10:00 P.M. This hotel was not government licensed and the proprietor took our passports to the police station who said it was okay for us to stay. It is scary when people leave with our passports. It was late when we finally left with our new friends to find dinner. After several stops most restaurants were closed because the cooked rice was gone. We tried one more place and found it open.

Today we had to stop every few miles and wash our bikes with river water or use our favorite tool, chopsticks, to dig the mud out from the tires and fenders and also the derailleurs and brakes. When clogged with mud neither will work; in fact the wheels will not roll at all. We spent over twelve hours on the road for the next two days riding until dark and camping. Camping was a bit scary as the jungle comes alive at night with birds, insects, and critters. The wind blowing through the banana groves became a bit unnerving.

We arrived at the border town of Hekou, China and splurged on a hotel. The shower and sink became a mud bath as we cleaned everything after four days on the road. We rode our bikes to a car wash where two guys washed our bikes for free. Of course a crowd soon gathered to watch. We found an auto parts store where I purchased a few cans of spray cleaner and sprayed our gears, chains, and rims. Around back was a hose and we sprayed the accumulated gunk off. Once we lubed the chain, the bikes were ready and we returned to the hotel with new-looking bikes.

Jocelyn's Instagram Posts:

October 28, 2014

We have entered China! I immediately feel transported to an exotic place filled with wonderment and strange imagery. We traveled by rental van with five Malaysian guys to Labrang, China and visited one of the largest Buddhist monasteries in the world, Labrang Monastery. I am very grateful to get to experience this intensely religious historical Tibet. We walked the streets with many monks and bought Tibetan prayer flags that represent the elements; blue for heaven, white for air, red for fire, green for water, and yellow for earth. In Tibetan, they are known as *Dar Cho*: *dar* meaning to increase life, fortune, and health, and *cho* meaning all sentient beings. Timothy Clark describes the flags as, "Blessings spoken on the breath of nature. Just as a drop of water can permeate the ocean, prayers dissolved in the wind extend to fill all of space."

November 4, 2014

Rolled on through a bunch of rice paddies. Today was a glorious day. I finally feel myself again and I charged the entire day. I couldn't control myself from keeping my fast pace and had to stop several times to wait on my dad. I am resorting back to my useful productivity of the pushup game (while waiting for Dad, I do pushups on the side of the road). So happy to be strong again and thankful I have gained back the weight I lost while being sick. I am actually grateful for a month off the bicycle touring.

We went to visit the Leshan Giant Buddha and Mt Emei World Heritage site today. It was a magical walk through a Chinese rainforest with many stones of Chinese mantras, several Ying-Yang worked into the stone or painted upon the rock. Within, there are several temples dating back to the Tang Dynasty (618-907) with many elegant statues and Dashi Buddha made of bronze. There are also several towers and thousands of stairs. There is also the largest stone Buddha in the world at over 200 feet.

November 17, 2014

On the road to Vietnam. After 340 miles in 4 days, I am exhausted after many days of mountain climbing and mud — always mud. At first it was fun and much better than rock or sand, but when you stop or slow down, the mud builds up in the fenders and the wheels won't turn. It was terrible. The road from Pingbian to Hekou was all under construction and very dirty, so I am needing a shower and a cold beer.

On the muddy road to Vietnam.

Vietnam

Mike:

We arrived at the confusing Chinese border exit. After a long search, we were directed inside and waved over by a border guard. We handed him our passports, which he studied closely, so long in fact that I was getting worried that something was wrong and I immediately thought about our Tajikistan exit. But he looked at us, smiled, and said, "Close, very close." This was day thirty of our thirty-day visa. I had read other biking blogs where cyclists have been detained and fined up to hundreds of dollars if their visa is expired. With a sigh of relief we exited and easily entered Vietnam. There was a hotel right up the street and the price was right so we got a room. We exchanged our currency and enjoyed lunch of a popular noodle dish around the world — *Pho*. Over lunch we discussed our train trips and bus trip. If we had not used this public transportation, it would have been a different story on exit. As I have said before, our visa could have been extended but it would have required a minimum wait of five business days in a major city. After lunch we explored stores and open markets. "This is going to be a fun country," I said.

Good Morning, Vietnam! We climbed west to the French colonial mountain town of Sa Pa, which is known as one of the most beautiful areas of Vietnam. This 24-mile continuous climb from Lao Cai took us six hours even though the altitude is only 4,900 feet. The ride was fun as we encountered small villages, roadside vegetable stands, and many people walking their water buffaloes and pigs. The rain sprinkled lightly and near the town a heavy fog set in. The ride was absolutely breathtaking as we viewed the terraced farms and small villages while the courteous drivers gave us a wide berth. Once in town, we were escorted by a hotel manager to his hotel. It was clean and had an excellent place to store our bikes. There are many activities in this area so we will take tomorrow off for an all-day hiking tour of the surrounding areas.

On our way to Sa Pa, Vietnam. Jocelyn entered this picture in a bike and beard contest.

We boarded a van and drove to an area overlooking a large, deep valley containing several villages. The trail down to the villages was steep and full of mud. There were six of us and we each had an escort of two Vietnamese girls who took me by each arm and guided me through the mud. I did slip a few times but they caught me. My shoes were continually being sucked into the mud, so the day was quite a mess. We finally reached the valley floor, walked to the villages, and bought a few souvenirs. We watched as the villagers went about their routines. It was a long hike across the valley floor before one last village and the van ride back to town.

We had such a good time in Sa Pa that we decided to stay another night. Sa Pa is a large town with a small-town atmosphere and plenty to do. It would be easy to spend a week here. The people are friendly and most speak some English, and many are fluent so it is easy to get around this French colonial town. The weather is odd as each day goes through four seasons: cool spring in the morning, sunny summer in the noon time, cloudy autumn in the afternoon, and cold winter at night. This weather pattern is quite fascinating.

A typical Vietnamese town.

This morning we had a leisurely breakfast at our favorite eating establishment on the lake, followed by an interesting and fun visit to the Sa Pa town market/bazaar. We enjoy exploring bazaars wherever we have been. Today we bought enough souvenirs, including several shirts, to mail a box home. A few days ago we received an email from Andee showing the package that we sent from Tajikistan about two months ago. To be honest, I never thought that the package would arrive, but it did and all in one piece. It was hard enough in Dushanbe, where no English was spoken, just to find the post office. It must have been sent on a slow boat. We requested air travel on this latest box from Vietnam. We did try to mail from China several items we bought, but they were rejected due to political reasons. These items included souvenirs from the Tibetan monastery we visited and several maps and other items with Tibetan language. These items were all forbidden even by DHL.

We were out the door by 8:00 A.M. on a rainy Saturday morning with the intention of climbing over the upcoming mountain pass early, as we had heard it was a tough climb over the broken-down road. But Jocelyn's bike had other plans for us. The rear tire had a puncture and the tube was quickly replaced. For some unknown reason, when we tried to reinstall the wheel we discovered that the rear derailleur was broken so we could not set the chain. The hotel manager directed us to a person who works on bikes. This 'bike mechanic' said the derailleur was broken and replaced Jocelyn's Shimano Deore XT with a used Chinese Shimano Altus from a rental bike. The replaced derailleur shifted but skipped. The bike mechanic adjusted it but the shifting was questionable, and with the upcoming climb it didn't seem like it would work. At 11:30 we finally had breakfast and discussed our options. The bike mechanic called Hanoi, and the original Deore XT part was available and could be sent to Sa Pa or we could take a five-hour bus ride to Hanoi. This would change our plans in Laos, so we decided against that and didn't want to wait in Sa Pa. The hotel manager said he could arrange a bus ride over the steeper mountains toward Laos and we could exit the bus wherever we wanted. We decided on that option and the bus left at 7:00 P.M.

We were immediately uncomfortable on this sleeper bus when our bikes and panniers were tied to the bus's roof in the rain. The driver was impatient and rushed everything, but I was persistent in making sure everything was tied down properly. The bus itself was a mess and loaded with people. Jocelyn and I shared a side by side top berth of which the outside railing was not attached. The outside berth was dangerous as the speeding bus swerved from side to side. I had to hold on or be thrown down to the floor where people were lying in the aisle. At each stop more people were crammed on the floor and forced to sit. This being a Vietnamese bus, it was designed for short people so there was little room. I had a 'death grip' on the side to not fall out.

A few hours later the bus stopped and the driver yelled out that this was the eating break. All the floor people were slow to get up and he yelled at them to hurry so that the berth people could leave. Next to the restaurant was an empty lot where both males and females rushed to relieve themselves. Jocelyn and I said, "No way!" and went inside to use the water closet (WC). It was despicable, so I went to the outside lot while Jocelyn used the toilet. The food looked disgusting so we passed and returned to the bus. A few more hours passed with us climbing over unpaved roads and around rock slides. By 2:00 A.M., we were fed up and figured a disaster may soon happen and told the driver to stop as we wanted off. He obliged and was probably glad to get rid of us. We exited the bus, loaded our bikes, and continued down a dark, muddy road in who knows where. At 5:00 A.M., we were exhausted and thought about pitching the tent for rest when we passed what we thought was a hospital. To our pleasant surprise, it was a large hotel that was open. Vietnam is funny this way as there are huge hotels seemingly in the middle of nowhere open for business. The receptionist was sleeping behind the counter on a bed covered with a mosquito net. I woke her and handed over our passports for a room. This was a good way to end such a hectic day and a scary, long fifty-mile bus ride. That day, workers spent several hours preparing the hotel for a wedding. When the wedding party and guests arrived, we figured they would be there most of the night. Thirty minutes after they arrived they were all gone and the decorations removed. We don't know what that was about.

After a rest from the crazy bus ride, we were on the road again with the idea of reaching Laos later in the week. We started climbing immediately and passed through many small villages. The big bonus was that the sun was out and the temperature was in the 80s as we were so tired of the cold. At the end of the day we cycled into a larger town and found a guesthouse for the night. We immediately named it the 'No' guesthouse, as everything we asked for or that we used the point-it-book for was answered, "No."

We also witnessed the most disturbing thing we have ever seen. As we were walking our panniers past the open kitchen, a man had a gas-fueled torch and was torching an animal that at first appeared to be a child. This stopped us dead in our tracks, but it turned out to be a monkey. In fact, there were three monkeys in the process of hair removal, one being torched, one in hot water, and the third being scraped with a knife. Our curiosity was peaked, so we took pictures. This is the real world where everything is eaten. We have seen some strange things on this trip, but this tops it. Sometimes reality is sad. We have also seen raw meat sitting outside for sale throughout Asia. Animals are killed, butchered, and sold right on the street with no refrigeration.

In this part of Vietnam, communication is non-existent except for "Hello" and "Bye, bye." The locals don't understand pictures with our point-it-book either. It is difficult to order food without meat. Most touring cyclists ride to Hanoi and east to the beaches. As usual, we take the roads less traveled and have been rewarded with beautiful jungle mountains, small roads and villages, and friendly people.

Jocelyn:

One moment I was running up and down the restaurant hotel with all our gear, and the next I was running up to my dad crying my eyes out. I saw these feet, little and cute, clinched behind a large man. I heard piercing screams. It was a kid. I swore it was! And then the men in the kitchen invited me in . . . It wasn't a child, but a monkey being scorched to death with another monkey in the corner screaming in shackles. We watched for only a moment. We left quickly and sat in front of the kitchen drinking a pint of beer and crying. My dad even showed some emotion. The owners asked if we wanted food but we refused.

After walking several blocks, we found a place that would serve us *Pho* without meat. The water they used to boil our noodles in was later used to wash all four of their kids in front of us. After all, we were sitting in their home with a hallway with three bunks, a small kitchen, and a large table.

Laos

Mike:

Our ride to Laos involved a large climb to the Vietnam/Laos border crossing at Tay Trang. The first several miles were flat and fast before the first mountain climb. The fog finally burned off as the climbing started while walking the steeper parts. By 2:00 P.M., we were at the border and checked out. I noticed other people exiting Vietnam with *dongs* (Vietnam currency) inserted into their passports. The border officer motioned to me about the cash, but I just ignored him as I figured it was some sort of bribe, and he stamped both our passports and we exited. The Laos entry point was several miles away. Laos is visa on arrival, and we already had downloaded, completed, and printed our visa applications and glued the pictures. The border officer was impressed that we had that done. We paid $35 each for the visas plus a small $1 processing fee. The transaction was simple and efficient. I don't know why more countries don't do it this way.

We continued riding into Laos and found a guesthouse in a small village. We met two other touring-cyclist couples at the next-door restaurant. It is such a small world, as we had not seen other tourists since Sa Pa, Vietnam.

After today, we decided Laos has the most hills of any country we have ridden in. But the reward is a beautiful ride. There are numerous temples with fine-looking Buddhas. We brake for temples!

This morning we ate at the same restaurant as last night because of the Western breakfast menu. We each had fried eggs with potatoes and a banana pancake including a papaya shake. We spent the entire day riding along a river where for once the road stayed at about the same elevation. In our experience, most of the river roads we have cycled will climb sometimes several thousand feet. It turned out to be one of our favorite rides as we followed the windy river through tiny villages. Kids were in school and they always ran to greet us.

Overlooking the mountains in Laos.

We took a two-day boat trip upriver to Thailand on the Mekong River. Our bikes are loaded on the top to the right.

It was also a good day to meet other touring cyclists, as we encountered a group of five (three Canadians and two Czechs), and after that a Japanese cyclist. They were all headed to Vietnam and had nothing but good things to say about Laos.

Jocelyn's rear derailleur that she had installed (the used Shimano Altus from Sa Pa) has been chattering with the chain jumping gears. She removed three links and that seems to have fixed it, although it is still quite noisy. We hope it lasts another month.

We arrived in the touristy town of Luang Prabang from Oudomxay, Laos. We usually try to avoid towns like this, but after hearing the praises from so many cyclists about the Mekong River cruises we decided to investigate a river cruise to Thailand. The Mekong River slow boats travel north or south, and originally we wanted to head south to Vientiane, Laos, which is a border city with Thailand, for our next country entry. But due to low water levels, the boats are not cruising south this season. Instead, we will backtrack and head northwest to the Laos border city of Huay Xai and enter Thailand from there. The Mekong cruise takes two days to navigate about 300 miles and requires a one-night guesthouse stay in the town of Pakbeng.

We have met many touring cyclists from around the world in the last several days. It has been fun comparing notes and routes. Yesterday we rode with five others and had a group of seven until we turned off for lunch. We had a regular peloton going as we cruised up and down the hilly road toward Luang Prabang. Soon after lunch we were passed by a dozen roadies on a supported bicycle tour of Laos. We can go for weeks without seeing other cyclists, so this was a real treat for us. Several of the roadies 'slowed down' and talked with Jocelyn.

One evening we were looking for a camping spot when I spotted a truck with two tents atop it near a river. We investigated and found a French family of four from New Caledonia (a South Pacific island north of New Zealand) that have spent the last ten years driving a Toyota Land Cruiser around the world. They invited us to camp near them, and we swapped stories of our tours between a truck and bicycles as we all have the common goal of exploring the world.

In Luang Prabang we made reservations for a slow boat to Thailand. They are called slow boats because that's what they are, and there are also fast boats which are small with no room for bikes. Two days ago we met several other touring cyclists and enjoyed beer and 'Tales from the road' with them at a bar. Our group represented seven countries!

The next day we toured the ancient capital of Luang Prabang in Northern Laos, which lies in a valley at the merging of the Mekong and Nam Khan rivers. Inhabited for thousands of years, it was the royal capital of the country until 1975. It's known for its many Buddhist temples. It is also a United Nations Educational, Scientific, and Cultural Organization (UNESCO) World Heritage Site.

We boarded the slow boat to Huay Xai, Laos on Thursday and quickly settled in for our nine-hour trip to Pakbeng. It was fun and relaxing to just sit onboard and watch the world go by on the Mekong River. We brought a large box of red wine and an assortment of food, so we quickly settled in and enjoyed the early morning mist as we slowly glided on the Mekong. There are luxury cruises available complete with staterooms and gourmet dining, but I can't imagine this trip without traveling with the locals. We watched elephants and people bathing, people crossing the river with rafts full of goods, kids playing in the water, many riverside villages, and an occasional resort. We stopped a few times as people disembarked with loads of goods from shopping trips. Pakbeng is the midpoint, and all passengers must find a guesthouse for the night. We unloaded all our gear and bikes and settled on the first one we came upon. At $7 per night ($8 with the air-conditioner remote), it was clean and we immediately met another cycling couple across the street at an Indian restaurant. Eric and Amaya have been cycling around the world since 2006 and have cycled through almost 100 countries. Some people sell everything to finance their ongoing adventure that seemingly never ends.

Friday morning, we once again boarded on a different boat and left for Huay Xai on another nine-hour cruise. This part of the river widened at times and then narrowed with surging water. The captain expertly navigated the vessel through the rapids. We arrived close to sunset, unloaded our bikes, and decided to enter Thailand without spending the night in Huay Xai since we were meeting fellow cyclists in the town of Chiang Khong. This took a bit of finagling with transportation to the Laos exit point on the Friendship Bridge. We arrived at the bridge and learned that walkers or bicycles are not allowed to cross. We exited Laos and had to pay for a bus across to the Thailand border. What a racket for the bus company, and we had to take everything off again along with our front wheels. On the other side we entered our 25th country, and since it was dark and late we hired a *tuk tuk* (taxi) to take us into town. Along with our website, fatherdaughtercyclingadventures.com we have been posting on crazyguyonabike.com which is an interesting and popular website where touring bicyclists around the world post their journals. A few days ago I received an email from another cycling couple, Bruce and Andrea, from Portland, Oregon stating that they were staying at the Ban Rimtaling guesthouse in Chiang Khong. Jocelyn directed the driver, and by the time we unloaded everything it was late and we were exhausted from the last two days. Fortunately there was a restaurant on the premises, so we settled in for a delicious Thai meal. Bruce and Andrea arrived and we enjoyed a few beers and conversation about Thailand. Bruce and Andrea have been coming here for many years to bicycle throughout Southeast Asia with Thailand being their favorite. In fact, we later reconnected with Bruce and Andrea who hosted us in their Portland, Oregon home as we cycled down the West Coast of the U.S. in 2015. Bruce and Andrea are back in Thailand with their bicycles as I write this.

Jocelyn's Instagram Posts:

November 27, 2014

The downhills I've been on the past two days as we entered Laos through mountain passes have been killer, and they get me so hyped :). The uphills, yuckkkkk, I've walked some, but it's so gorgeous that I don't even care!

I'm thankful for my life and my views. Two years ago today I was in Sydney, Australia. Now I'm in Laos. And two years and two months ago I had never been outside of the USA. Here I am, cycling around the world and the thing I'm most passionate about — I'm with my papa. Of course, I always miss my Momster and bro, and they support me with my dreams. They tell me they're okay with me not getting a degree at this time. I'll get a degree, for myself, just to say, "Yeah, I got some degree." They understand now what living is, at least what living is to me. So much love for you all and I'm wishing my friends in the States a fantastic Thanksgiving.

November 30, 2014

While riding along the most epic river road, we came across a large market. *Sa-bai-dee* (hello in Lao) is shouted out everywhere and I shout back as it's become one of my favorite hellos in another language. It's too fun to say. Anyway, the large market is in front of this school in session, and kids are screaming hellos and such out the windows. I couldn't help but think it must be so hard to focus while such a large market is being held right outside the classrooms.

Then, I see a group of maybe twenty kids running in a perfect line around an imaginary track field. It was inspiring and their strides looked on point! To the right of this area I notice these two dragons with seven heads each and I must stop. I walk up what seems to be a stairway to a temple, but it leads to nothing. Confused, but amazed at Laos and the people, I find the culture is mesmerizing. And the women, the most beautiful I've ever laid my eyes upon.

December 2, 2014

Thinking; The essence of living in the present moment, the Now, is focusing the mind here and take attention away from thinking about past or future. The present moment is all there ever is to experience life directly. Past and future are only concepts of our mind and therefore are good for learning from the past or conceptual planning when it is useful, but after this there is no need for them. Especially not to dwell in them and get stuck there in the mind by constantly thinking loops.

Thailand

"It is not down in any map; true places never are."
—Herman Melville

Mike:

The next day we toured Chiang Khong on our empty bikes. Along the way we stopped at our first Thai temple and rode a few miles up and down the Mekong. What we like is that the temples, as in Laos, are open to the public without admission fees. That afternoon we met Bruce and Andrea for a walking tour. We found a bike museum maintained by a gentleman who at one time held the record for bicycling around the world in 106 days. He also raced internationally and has quite a collection of interesting bicycles. That evening we ate at a Mexican restaurant. We had a fun evening with new friends.

We began our ride toward Bangkok. Sunday was our first mostly flat day in months, and it was a welcome change. The riding was easy and enjoyable. We can't say enough good things about bicycling in Thailand as the drivers are the most courteous of our entire trip. The roads are in excellent condition even in the mountain pass areas. The people are friendly; the food is excellent, and the beer is always cold. Speaking of beer, it is ice cold and served with a glass of ice. Jocelyn has a list of the top five vegetarian Thai meals listed on her phone. She shows this to the cook, and we are told if it is available.

We continued south through many forests. Yesterday, at our midafternoon beer break, we met a Swiss couple. Bea and Peter also are headed to Bangkok and are also stopping for their midafternoon beer break. This seems to be an occurrence of many cyclists and helps us continue for the long afternoon. We followed them to a hotel and enjoyed dinner together. The next morning, after breakfast, we all took to the road again and Jocelyn picked a good spot for lunch as the owner spoke excellent

English and French. We were soon joined by a dozen Thai roadies and had a fun time talking with them.

Camping in a Tibetan Monastery, Thailand. We free camped in several monasteries. This was a very peaceful night. We awoke to monks chanting at 3 a.m.

After spending another night with Bea and Peter in Tak, we continued south along cane fields and banana plantations. We have one more week before we reach Bangkok, and we are spending the extra time cycling south. The last few days have been easy as the road is flat and the wind has switched from the south to the north so we have a strong tailwind. We have not camped in Thailand due to the mosquitoes and snakes. It seems as though no one camps here because of that and the inexpensive, clean rooms. In the evenings the mosquitoes appear with a roar.

In Thailand people drive on the left side of the road. It took me a few days getting used to and I endured many, "Dad, you are on the wrong side again," comments. The drivers are almost too courteous and will pass cautiously. There is little car honking in Thailand, unlike China where drivers honk at everything. Chinese drivers honk excessively. They honk to let you know they are behind you, if the driver in front is too slow, if they are passing, and if they are in the oncoming lane they honk to let oncoming traffic know they are there. It is excessive and at first it drove me nuts at their rudeness. They will not slow down. At first I thought the vehicle horns were tied to the accelerator and if the vehicle slows down the horn activates. A fellow cyclist living in Chengdu said it best: "If there was road rage like in other countries, the population of China would be half."

Along the way we stopped to visit the ancient city of Ayutthaya, which was the capital of Thailand until 417 years ago. The city was founded in 1350 when Thailand's northern neighbors forced the government to move. The city is full of ancient temple ruins and only 48 miles from Bangkok.

Since we were a few days ahead of schedule, we headed south away from Bangkok to explore more of Thailand. The riding is simply great through the coconut, papaya, and banana plantations. There are fruit stands everywhere and we stop several times daily for our papaya fix. There are times we are required to be on a highway to find the smaller road connections, but that is fine with us. Jocelyn is doing a great job at keeping us off the major roads. We have also met a few more cycling tourists.

Today we found the beach, our first since the Black Sea in Georgia. We swam in the Gulf of Thailand at the end of today's ride and stayed in a bungalow on Cha Beach. That night we had our best Thai food yet: shrimp and broccoli, stir-fried vegetables, and a spicy scallop dish.

On Sunday we started our return trip north to Bangkok by way of a different and scenic country road to the west and then north. The riding was easy with small hills and a light headwind. Jocelyn's rear derailleur that was replaced in Vietnam finally broke for good. She modified her drive train into a fixed gear and we continued. On the first night it was getting late, so we decided to stay at a Buddhist Temple. It was so quiet and peaceful as the monks welcomed us into a prayer room with a large Buddha. We had heard that cyclists sometimes stay in these temples, and we thought it was great as it is free and the karma soothing. Throughout the evening, night, and morning, we were mesmerized by the chanting at prayer times. When we left early the next morning they gave us food and sent us on our way.

Another temple closer to Bangkok was full of aggressive dogs that kept us up most of the night. All dogs are not neutered, which causes their aggressive behavior, and there was one 'chief' male dog that deeply growled at the others. Our tent was safely enclosed in a fenced area so the dogs couldn't get to it. When we first pitched our tent, the chief dog peed on it followed by the others. At that point, the monks directed us to this fenced area. After eating at a market, we returned to our tent and were given food, which we saved for breakfast. There were also three funeral ceremonies close to our tent, and that made for a long evening along with the howling dogs. As the monks chant, the dogs howl. I think we did manage to nap a few hours. Monks rise at 4:00 A.M. to start their prayer service.

Jocelyn mapped a route to Bangkok since we had heard that it is a difficult city to bicycle into, even more so than Istanbul. But the Thai drivers are much more courteous and the traffic flowed smoothly. We were soon in the city and found the Swana Bangkok Hotel in old town Bangkok where our Swiss cyclists friends Beatrice and Peter are staying. We spent one night there before cycling two hours to the other side of Bangkok and another warmshowers host the next day. Our host greeted us and gave us the key to a three-story apartment. It was empty so we camped inside. About a half mile away there were plenty of stores and restaurants. We visited several bike shops until we found one that had bike boxes available. Two bike mechanics helped us disassemble and box our bikes. They also arranged for a *tuk tuk* to transport us back to our apartment.

Back at the apartment, we were soon lost in thought as the realty hit home — our bikes were boxed so the cycling was done. We were somewhat bummed about this on Christmas Eve and were missing our family as we settled in for three nights. Jocelyn's friend Rachel, who works in Cambodia as a cook, soon appeared after a ten-hour bus ride. The three of us celebrated with a fine Christmas Eve Thai meal.

Christmas Day morning found us cleaning out all of our panniers and getting rid of unneeded things now instead of at home. Many bicyclists stay at this warmshowers location, so we left lots of stuff. The afternoon found us at the giant MBK Bangkok Mall for Christmas Day tattoos and also a bit of partying. We accomplished everything for a memorable Christmas celebration. The next day we continued sightseeing Bangkok through the excellent Metro and Skytrain public transportation systems. We were in shock while using the subway as the Thai people are so courteous and actually stand in line to board the subway train. In most countries of the world, people shove and push their way onboard.

Two days later Rachel hopped on a bus for her return to Cambodia and we found a ride to our next warmshowers host near the airport. We were the first to stay in Joe and Noi's beautiful home only a few miles away from Suvarnabhumi Airport. They treated us to our last Thai meal at a Buddhist Temple restaurant and we tried many of the foods we have never attempted and were pleased with the selections made by Joe and Noi. Seems hard to believe, but just a short 11 ½ months ago we started in Marrakech, Morocco and are now in Bangkok, Thailand after almost 8,000 cycling miles.

Jocelyn's Instagram Posts:

December 5, 2014

We took a ride from Laos across the new Friendship Bridge to Chiang Khong, Thailand because it is forbidden by bicycle or foot and everyone has to take an official bus. So we missed a chance to get a proper welcome to Thailand and a border crossing photo. We got a suggestion to come here by two other fellow American cycle tourists, Andrea and Bruce from Oregon, who have been here for a few days after cycling down from Burma! We stayed in an epic bungalow, right on the Mekong River with new friends and cold beers. What can be better? Oh, ya, and to die for green curry.

December 6, 2014

Tonight we met Alan Gate, the world record holder for cycling around the world in 106 days. That is 24,900 miles! I met him while he was sitting on the ground of his own bar/cycling museum drinking beer. We took shots together, and I thought he was an interesting man.

December 19, 2014

The other day we rode to one of the most famous temples in Thailand, Wat Bang Pra. I bought an offering of flowers, incense, candles, and cigarettes for 100 Thai *bahts* equal to three dollars for the purpose of receiving a *Sak Yant* tattoo. When I researched this sacred tattoo, I thought it was to be done by a long needle attached to a bamboo stick. Well, I sadly found out that those *Sak Yant* tattoos are only allowed for Thai men. If I knew it was done by a gun, I might have not made such a detour, but I sat in a room with twenty or so other people waiting my turn to receive this magical tattoo. The monk sits in a meditation state, and one by one everyone takes turns holding the person's skin tight until it's your turn.

The monk doesn't use gloves, and he doesn't change out the needles, so it's a major risk. But I bowed and the monk granted me with *"Hah Taew"* tattoo, which represents 5 *yants* or magical spells. *Yants* are accompanied with chants or *Khatas,* and the sounds are pronounced over and over to invoke a state of the mind where the mind can create magical spells. They are chanted 108 times before entering the high level of  meditation. Each one will be done individually, and the following magical spells have been cast to do as described below.

1. The first row prevents unjust punishment and leans in your favor when the area is gray, cleans out unwanted spirits, and protects the place you live in.
2. The second row reverses and protects against bad horoscope constellations and bad fortune.
3. The third row protects you from the use of black magic and anyone who tries to put a curse on you.
4. The fourth row energizes your good luck, success, and fortune in your future ambitions and lifestyle.
5. The fifth row is to gain charisma and attraction to the opposite sex. It is also a boost to the fourth row.

The origin of the *Hah Taew* is magic power born from the four elements, fire, water, air, and earth.

December 20, 2014

We made it to the beach on the Gulf of Thailand. Some huge parties are going down tonight, and we are staying at a small bungalow on the beach for $45 a night. We decided to take our first break day in Thailand here. But huge parties, bringing in huge stereos, and the barbecues are out, and people are arriving on this Thai holiday. This isn't even the touristy spot, so I am excited for tonight with the local people, haha. This is the first time we have seen the sea since July!

December 23, 2014

Don't you ever feel like going home, passing every old house, seeing everyone? Today brought a realization ever so fast to me. I think about wandering down my old street, right to the beach, with my surfboard in my hand and a beer in the other hand. I go for a quick paddle out, things change, but really nothing ever changes. It's no longer home to me. Home is change, and I'll try to adapt to that while I am home for the next few months and will hope everything turns out okay. Don't get me wrong; I miss my family, friends, dog, and bedroom, but I'm different. It is like everyone else has changed. I don't know where to belong, perhaps on the road, I belong. Damn! This ride is over.

We have finished this segment of our around the world tour. We rode a total of 8,000 miles (13,000 km), in just over eleven months, with two of those months sitting and waiting for visas. This number is our calculated bicycle miles, since we have taken an assortment of other means of transportation. In total, including our U.S. Southern Tier and tour around the South Island of New Zealand, we have 12,000 miles (19,000 km), so logistically we are almost halfway around the world!

December 26, 2014 For Christmas in Bangkok we hung out at a tattoo shop, Malakor Tattoo, with Bear, who is this huge man with dark-black hair that was so long he wrapped his hair around his neck like a scarf. All three of us got tattoos, and my friend Rachel and I got a 'same same' *Sak Yant* tattoo. I got *Bpaaet Thit*, which represents protection in the eight directions of the universe. My dad got the world with a bicycle on his right calf, and Rachel got the peaceful Buddha, and our 'same same' tattoo represents Tiger strength such as "The eye of the tiger."

Ray Ray and I then took my dad home and decided to go out for one more drink. Of course it turned into a night we'd always remember with no photos to prove of it. We were walking down the street and heard a band playing that sounded rather good, so we decided to investigate! Turned out that this band was on a roof of an abandoned building. So we had to climb up four flights of stairs, walked in, and went straight to the stage like we owned the place. It was packed and everyone noticed the White girls. Instantly we met the owner of the Playboy Thailand and all the Playboy Bunnies. They knew we had crashed the party and wanted us to stay. We pretty much raged till about 4:00 A.M.. I stole a mannequin from the mannequin store next to our apartment and slept next to mosquito coils and woke up in such a fog with a smile on our faces. I don't know if anyone will ever believe us, but that party was the best party I've ever been to on Christmas!

Mike:

All of a sudden it was our day to fly home! Noi arranged for a truck to take us and our bikes to the airport, and we checked in at the Southern China Airlines counter. We had all of our panniers and trunk bags enclosed in four large zippered plastic bags along with our two bike boxes. We were allocated two bags apiece and paid a total of $300 for the two additional items. The flight to Guangzhou, China (near Hong Kong) was on time, and on arrival we waited a few hours to board our Southern China Airbus 380 for the flight to Los Angeles International. We knew we were back in China when a bar waitress loudly said, "YOU PAY NOW!" immediately when ordering two beers.

The flight to LAX on the largest commercial aircraft in the world, Airbus 380 with 506 passengers, was pleasant with plenty of room. I have traveled on this aircraft a few times with my Antarctic adventures while flying to New Zealand. After arriving in Los Angeles, we were required to retrieve our luggage and go through customs and then recheck the bags through Delta to Orlando, Florida. This went well as the LAX International terminal has a transfer service to domestic airlines. I have read many blogs where people arriving back to the U.S. recheck their bags and are required to pay again. We were expecting to pay another $600 ($150 x 4), as Delta only allows one checked bag for domestic economy. But everything transferred successfully! This was a real bonus as our flight home from Bangkok was only $700 each along with $150 each for excess luggage. This was quite a deal — thanks to Jocelyn's research.

We were met at Orlando International by Andee and my son Cary after 16,000 flying miles and 33 hours. We had not seen them since June in Turkey. After lots of hugs and tears, we loaded our truck with the bikes and gear and soon were home in Cape Canaveral where we were greeted by a large "Welcome Home" banner dressing the house and of course Jocelyn's dog Yaki. It was two days after Christmas and time to start celebrating! Out of the last 39 months I have only been home for five months between my Antarctic positions and bicycle touring. I am ready to become a husband and father again.

Washington, U.S. to Honduras, Central America and Calgary, Canada to Nova Scotia, Canada and South to Florida

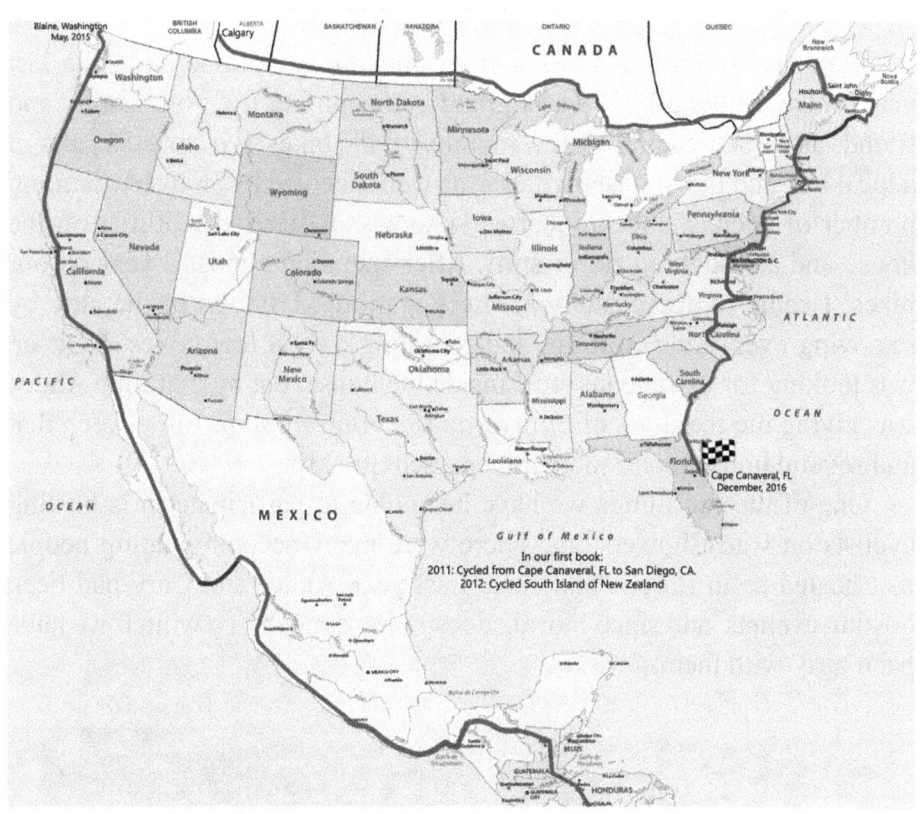

Starting our next ride

We arrived home in Florida from our tour of Europe and Asia last year on December 30th. It was a grand homecoming from our family and friends as we settled in for a few months off the bikes. We hosted a party at a local bar, and our slideshow/talk was well received by an overwhelming number of friends. Jocelyn started school and I started working on the house and also getting rid of stuff. After spending almost a year on our bikes, I came to appreciate that 'Less is more.' I started in the attic by removing everything, sorting, and returning only a few boxes. Next up was looking for extraneous stuff inside the house, but by that time Andee was giving me that look of *Stay away from our/my stuff.* In-between that and several house repair jobs, time passed quickly.

One of the fun things we have been able to participate in is hosting cyclists on warmshowers.org. There were many accommodating people that hosted us in Europe and Asia. Last year, Andee and Cary had been hosting cyclists, and since Florida doesn't have much of a winter, we have been busy with them.

After eleven months of riding from Morocco to Bangkok, Thailand we flew home for a few months before continuing down the west coast of North and South America.

But I was always reminded of the road as Jocelyn would update me almost daily on where our new bicycle touring friends from around the world were. We both missed being out there, and it seemed my house had hold of me. These past few months with our family have been special, but we do have more of this wonderful world to explore with our bicycles.

Jocelyn:

May 25, 2015

Dad and I are setting up camp for the night at Eisenhower State Park in Kansas. I cycled through here in April, 2012 with my friend Rachel, and it was so dry back then that it reminded her of South Africa. Due to all the rain, especially last night, the ground is saturated with water and green. I am excited to test our new tent, the REI Quarter Dome 3.

May 27, 2015

Just had a wonderful time with our close family friends (Susan and Richard from Rockledge, Florida) out here in Limon, CO! We had an amazing dinner, grilled chicken and veggies with Amish potato salad and coleslaw! Oh, and I can't forget the grilled peaches! It poured again all night on our tent and got down into the low 40s!

May 31, 2015

The past few days we toured in Colorado and met up with some awesome friends. Thanks, Carol, for coming out and having a few beers at O'Furrys, my old watering hole in the Springs! And thanks to Blake for showing us around downtown Denver and having me over for the night! Miss you both already. I also visited with my friends Zack and Chelsi and met some of my dad's buddies from the ice. William is a traveling doctor who lives in Boulder, and we stayed with him. I also got to meet the owner of University Cycles in Boulder, Doug, who gave us a tour of his amazingly huge bike shop!

June 4-5, 2015

My mother has joined our tour and will be driving along while we ride. Today we are touring the Seattle area and taking the ferry across Puget Sound to Port Angeles. I gave my dad and Nicole a tour of the Girl Scout camp, St. Albans, where I worked for the past two summers as a lifeguard and counselor. We did some serious hiking and then found our way to Mom's dear friend Janice's home in Olympia for the night. The next day we went to Peter G. Schmidt Elementary, where thanks to another one of Mom's friends, Denise, we had lunch! My father and I showed over 1,300 pictures of our first leg of this world tour. It was so awesome to be inspiring over 200 kids! The best part was having a 4th grader come up to me and say she was going to go ride her bike once she got home!

On our ride from Washington to California we were joined by Jocelyn's friend Nicole who rode with us and my wife Andrea and son Cary who drove our truck and set up camps along the way.

Mike:

June 8, 2015

After a cross-country trip with our bikes atop our truck, we are ready to ride again. We spent a week camping and staying with friends from Florida to Washington. When we arrived in Seattle we picked up Andee at the airport and stayed with her sister-in-law, Beth, in Blaine, Washington. Jocelyn and I, along with Jocelyn's friend Nicole, started riding from Peace Arch, south of the Canadian border, through Bellingham Bay to a scenic state park in Bay View, Washington. Andee and her brother Greg, who joined us for several days, arrived ahead of time and set up camp with the barbeque ready for burgers. It was fun being catered to. We pitched our tents after a long, satisfying first day back.

Starting our next ride

We reached Whidbey Island and met our gracious hosts, Bob and Sue. Andee knows Sue from high school days in Anaheim, CA. We were warmly welcomed into their beautiful home and enjoyed an excellent meal. For the next several days we continued south, exited Whidbey Island by ferry to Port Townsend on the Northern Peninsula, and found a rail trail to Sequin Bay where we had another beautiful bayside campsite. Andee explored the area during the day while we cycled. She visited small shops, lighthouses, and libraries, and did all the shopping for dinner and breakfasts. Jocelyn's friend Nicole has quickly become quite the touring cyclist. Before this trip she had never cycled more than thirty miles in Florida. Now, with the many hills, we are averaging over fifty miles per day and Nicole is keeping up with Jocelyn while I tag along sometimes way behind.

After Sequin Bay we rode to Port Angeles on the Strait of Juan de Fuca where we enjoyed a portside lunch before our climb into the Olympic Mountains and Olympic National Park. It was a grand ride among the trees past several lakes and our destination of Lake Crescent for the night. I feel like there is more oxygen in the air, and the smells are amazing.

The following day we continued riding west through the Olympic Forest to Kalaloch Campground on the Pacific Coast. We were back on the beach and loving the huge trees right along the coastline. Once again Andee scored a beautiful campsite where we marveled to the crashing surf all night. Each night we also have a camp fire, something that would not happen this time of the year in Florida or if we were alone with our bikes. It is a bit cool in the mornings, but that helps us get started strong.

Saturday morning found us up earlier than all the other campers — maybe because it was so cold on the coast. Andee prepared us an excellent spaghetti noodle *Pho* (Vietnamese soup) that fueled us to get on the road. We had a long day of seventy miles of hills, and once again she scored us an excellent campground on the banks of the Hoquiam River.

A few days later we crossed Astoria Bridge into Oregon. The wind was howling across the Columbia River and kept pushing us sideways. We stayed at a beachside county park that Jocelyn had previously stayed in while riding the Transamerica Bike Route from Virginia Beach to San Francisco and then north to Washington. Now she is riding south along the coast, which is more popular since the water is to your right and not across the road. It was time for a family side trip, so we loaded the bikes onto the truck and drove inland to visit relatives and friends in Portland, Oregon.

We had a fun time spending the night with Bruce and Andrea, who we met in Thailand last year. They live in an over one hundred year old house that is full of artifacts from their many years of exploring Southeast Asia by bike. In fact, their home is a museum. Following our stay with them, we spent three nights at my brother-in-law's and his wife's house in Hillsboro, Oregon. Cam and Cece drove us to several popular breweries and wineries and cooked many delicious meals. It was fun catching up with them since I had never been in Oregon. We repacked the bikes on the truck and returned to the coast and started riding again. It was a bright, sunny day, and after 25 miles we called it a day at Beverly Beach State Park six miles north of Newport, Oregon. Along the way we were treated to a whale sighting within easy viewing from the road.

We spent two nights in Florence Beach enjoying a vacation home that Jocelyn's friend Terry and his wife Kim manage. We drove to Eugene on a day off to explore that part of Oregon. Terry and Kim were quite the hosts and treated us to a wonderful, large steamer pot full of all kinds of seafood. We last ate like this on the Spanish coast during our European ride in 2014. Jocelyn and Nicole rode the beach on Terry's fat-tire Surly bicycles. We rode out of Florence and continued south to the town of North Bend, north of Coos Bay. Camping seemed sparse so Andee and Jocelyn drove ahead and looked at potential campsites. The few that did have space did not take tents. There have been several campgrounds like this and I have yet to figure out why. We were near a KOA in North Bend, so instead of riding on we quit early in the day and stayed at their campground. We continued south through fog, drizzle, and wind, rode over the Rogue River, and found a camp in Gold Beach, Oregon after thirty miles. A few days later found us in Crescent Beach, California where we camped among the redwoods.

We climbed into the Redwood National Park and were in awe with the incredibly large trees. This continued most of the day with a few times back down to the coast followed by climbing back into the redwood forest. Andee drove ahead and found an awesome campsite at Prairie Creek Redwoods State Park. In fact, she scored the last tent spot. The ranger did say however that California State Parks will not turn away camping hikers or bikers as long as there is no vehicle. In the evening, we attended an interesting ranger presentation about the early redwood logging days.

Starting our next ride

In 1800, redwood forests covered about two million acres. As the gold fever in the mid-1800s subsided, redwood fever replaced it and the trees soon fell to determined logging. In the 1920s, California preserved some key groves with the help of some rich and influential people. Congress created Redwood National Park in 1968 to save the world's tallest trees. This park system protects the nearly 40,000 acres that remain. These "old growth" trees can be 2,000 years old and stand nearly 380 feet. There are second growth trees that are planted and harvested eighty years later.

The next morning we continued south through the redwoods and stopped in the coastal town of Trinidad for an excellent seafood lunch and a wine tasting at the local Moonstone Winery. After that, Jocelyn found us a few small narrow roads that ran along bayside cliffs and more importantly avoided the busy Highway 101. In Arcata we spent two nights with a couple, Paul and Diana, who Andee met through a high school friend. Jocelyn had stayed with Paul and Diana on her ride north two years ago. On Thursday, July 2nd, we had one of our best rides ever through Humboldt County and the Avenue of the Giants. This scenic road runs parallel to US 101 and takes you through some of the tallest redwoods in the state. The ride was breathtaking as we looked skyward for the tops of these giant trees. I'll list it as one of our favorite rides so far in our world trip.

Andee began having a difficult time with finding camping spots as this is the 4th of July weekend. The next available campground Giant Redwoods Camp, Myers, California, put us at 73 miles for the day. It was exhausting with the hilly conditions but satisfying. Right next to the camp we met Andee at Riverbend Winery and enjoyed a tasting before settling into our camp. The next day we continued through the mountains toward the coast. Andee called and visited several campsites, but all were booked. She even called motels, but nothing was available. Previously we had talked with a ranger and were told that all state parks have 'hiker and biker' spots available at $5 each and you will not be turned away. We looked at Standish-Hickey State Park in Leggett, the last campground before a large mountain pass the next day. We inquired about parking a car, of which they didn't like, but gave us a buffer spot anyway. These spots normally are not used but held in reserve in case someone needs to move their camp. The next day we rode over the Leggett Pass at 1,900 feet, back to the coast, and continued south to Fort Bragg. It was foggy again and the temperature dropped from 100°F to 50°F in the fog. Since it was the 4th

of July, there was no camping or rooms available anywhere. Andee talked to a guy who worked in the North Coast Brewing Company who offered us his yard for camping. We took him up on his most generous offer and he let us use the bottom floor of his 1920s house. Right down the street from his house is the North Coast Brewing Company Restaurant where we enjoyed a fine meal with a fireworks show, so it turned out to be a good 4th celebration night.

The following day, while climbing, I heard a loud pop from my bike and found that my rear hub drive side flange was cracked in half. Andee picked me up while Jocelyn and Nicole continued riding on their own for a tedious 57 miles to a beachside campground.

Jocelyn and Nicole continued to ride the beautiful Northern California coastline. With my bike on the truck rack, Andee and I searched for a bike shop to replace my cracked hub. None of the shops had spare hubs, and it appeared that it would be easier and quicker to order a new wheel and have it sent overnight. I decided to go that route and ordered a new wheel from a local bike shop. It arrived the next day, and I was back on the road with Jocelyn and Nicole. My new wheel's rim and hub were a few quality steps below my original one, so I mailed my old wheel to my sister Tish's house in San Diego and asked that my brother-in-law Jim take it to a bike shop to install a better hub and use my rim that was installed in Istanbul, Turkey last year.

My son Cary flew into San Francisco to join us for a few weeks. We had heard that road work on the main road leading to the Golden Gate Bridge would close part of the main road and the bridge starting the next day, so we loaded up the bikes and drove closer. Unfortunately, I had suffered from a flu bug the last few days and wasn't well enough to bicycle across the famous Golden Gate Bridge. After riding across the bridge, Jocelyn and Nicole found Andee and me at Half Moon Bay State Campground on Francis Beach. I had another rough night sleeping but still rode to the town of Aptos a few miles south of Santa Cruz. We enjoyed watching the surfers at Steamer Lane before arriving at our host's home for the night. Andee's dear friend Teri lives here with her husband Brad. We had another good stay with friends. It is always a pleasure to rest in a house after a week of camping.

We left Aptos and spent a few days riding to Monterey where we took a break day to visit the world famous Monterey Aquarium. This fascinating

Starting our next ride

and well done aquarium showcases all the undersea eco-systems in California's coastal area and beyond. We decided not to ride the narrow Highway 1 down the coast because of the busy summer vehicle traffic and instead opted for the interior valley drive to San Luis Obispo where my niece Makani works.

We had a pleasing day strolling through downtown Morro Bay with my niece Makani. Morro Bay is a small and touristy but not too crowded beach town in front of the massive Morro Rock that juts out of Morro Bay. After a portside lunch we checked into a motel room before an afternoon wine tasting. It is days like this that make bicycle touring so entertaining by pausing to explore an area.

The following morning we packed everything and returned to Makani's townhouse in San Luis Obispo where Jocelyn and Nicole spent the night. We were soon riding by Pismo Beach, another blast from the past from when I was a kid, as my family would spend summer Sundays on the shore. The afternoon found us at Andee's cousin Pam's house in Santa Maria where we enjoyed family hospitality.

We soon returned to the coast and met Andee at El Capitan State Beach where we were able to score a hiker/biker campsite on a cliff overlooking the beautiful Pacific. We hiked down to the beach and explored the tide pools before a dazzling cliff-side sunset.

We arrived in my hometown of Oxnard, California after a wet ride and met my sister Tish from San Diego. We enjoyed two nights with the six of us staying in a large suite at the Embassy Suites in Mandalay Bay Beach. We had a great time visiting, reminiscing about our childhood with Tish, and swimming in the ocean. All too soon it was time to say goodbye, as Andee, Cary, and Nicole drove east in our truck for Florida and Tish south to San Diego. Thank you to Andee and Cary for adding more fun to our adventure. Also thanks to Nicole, our cycling companion of 1,600 kick-ass miles. Nicole started the ride with a bang and never slowed down. Jocelyn also enjoyed having a partner that could keep up with her.

Once again, Jocelyn and I were on our own and had a windy ride down the Pacific Coast. Several times in the succeeding days I would see a white truck riding nearby and think, *There's Andee*, either on her way to shop for dinner, bring us lunch, do laundry, or find our next campsite. She had the hardest job in the last six weeks as we just rode our bikes and she did the rest. I drove with her for two days while waiting for my new wheel. The biking was much easier than the logistics role of the trip. We will miss her and Cary.

Since I grew up in Oxnard, I have been south along this coastline countless times by car, and witnessing everything by bicycle was a vastly different experience for me. The coastal area is filled with long hills that we rode with pleasure. The wind stopped and the sun emerged near Santa Monica. Jocelyn found a twenty-mile bike path on the numerous beaches we passed, including the always interesting Venice Beach where I let my video record the unique collection of people and activities.

As we neared Los Angeles International Airport we could hear the planes departing directly overhead, but because of the thick fog we couldn't see them. We were soon in Redondo Beach at a friend's house. Nansea and Pete used to live in Cocoa Beach, Florida but two years ago moved in with Nansea's parents Esther and John. Jocelyn went to school with Nansea's and Pete's daughter Aja. We were warmly greeted by them and were served an excellent dinner with enjoyable conversation. Today was a long and satisfying ride from Oxnard.

The next morning we enjoyed an excellent pancake and fresh fruit breakfast thanks to Nansea and Esther. We discussed different paths to Long Beach, trying to avoid the busy San Pedro area along with the oil refineries in Torrance and Wilmington. Esther called the local bike shop who suggested taking Pacific Coast Highway to Long Beach and then dropping down to the waterfront on a bike path. Esther was one of our biggest followers throughout our trip and left many comments on our website. We followed this route, and except for a few busy trucking areas where containers were being transported off ships, the path turned out well. We continued along the beach on the excellent bike path to Huntington Beach where we stayed two nights with my brother-in-law Jeff and my nephew Perry. We had a lot of fun, especially when we met with another brother-in-law Chip for breakfasts at the popular Sugar Shack in downtown Huntington Beach. Jocelyn enjoyed spending time with her two uncles and a cousin.

After two nights we were riding along bike paths down the Pacific Coast Highway (PCH) and the many Southern California beaches. Our goal of Carlsbad was about seventy miles away, and since we didn't leave until 11:00 A.M., it was a challenge through the hot, crowded summer day. I had always wondered how cyclists get south to San Diego through the

Starting our next ride

massive Camp Pendleton Marine Base area, because the only other road is Interstate 5, a major freeway. It was simple as we cycled south and showed our IDs to the Marine sentry at the north gate. It was fun riding through the sprawling base. We soon entered the cities of Oceanside and Carlsbad. We found our warmshowers host's home and were immediately welcomed with their family to a barbecued tri-tip dinner. It is wonderful and sometimes surprising how some hosts welcome us as family. This family was comfortable to be around and told us to grab an empty plate and fill it. We slept soundly in their extra room.

The next day we rode south to Torrey Pines Glider Port where we enjoyed a front-row seat lunch for all the flying activities. We rode through La Jolla and enjoyed happy hour at La Jolla Brewing Company. We finally reached my sister Tish and brother-in law Jim's home in Pacific Beach, San Diego. We finished our southern tier bike ride here in 2011. We have ridden about 1,800 miles from Blaine, Washington and were greeted by another large welcoming banner on their garage. Andee, Cary, and Nicole arrived home in Cape Canaveral, Florida within the hour. They traveled over 2,000 miles and us around 200 miles, but we took a day off.

We spent eleven days in San Diego preparing for our Latin American ride. A bike shop installed a better hub on my original wheel and I swapped that with the new wheel that was installed in Northern California. Jocelyn trained back to Orange County for several days to visit friends, while I enjoyed many days visiting with Tish and Jim as it is not often that we are together. I also stripped down and cleaned both bikes and sorted through my panniers one more time. It seems as though I do this task too often, but as touring cyclists we are always looking to purge excess weight.

Jocelyn's Instagram Posts:

June 8, 2015

After spending the night in Bellingham with Aunt Beth, we began our ride at a nice park just south of the Canadian border along the Puget Sound. We all took pictures and loaded them on Instagram and Snapchat. My mom sent her pictures to Facebook, and Dad waited patiently. Uncle Greg and Mom headed south to find a place to camp while we rode 52 miles right to our campsite where they were waiting with cold beers and dinner. Uncle Greg and Mom slept in the truck, while we were cozy in the tents. We strolled along the rocky beach and enjoyed a beautiful sunset about 9:20 P.M.

June 9, 2015

Mom and Greg went touring while we made our way to Deception Pass today. It was awesome! We continued south down Whidbey Island, and it was a long day riding for all of us. I started to think about my "ex" a bit because she is from Whidbey, so my ride turned a bit emotional. I guess after all these years and miles I have ridden, I still can't help feeling the true love I shared with her. We spent the night at another friend of Mom's, Susan's lovely home. My Uncle Greg came and hung out with us for our first two days, and I'm so grateful and happy he was there. I love this Pacific Northwest state.

June 28-30, 2015

This is the 3rd time I have entered California by bicycle! We had good nights camping in Oregon, and now we are heading through the forests. Nicole is gaining strength and charging up and down the hills. People ask us how fast, and I think we average about 10 mph! Mom has taken many pictures of our team riding among the trees, and we camped in Prairie Creek on the 30th. I am loving this life, the freedom to ride, and heading south with my dad and best friend, Mackin!

July 7, 2015

This past week we have camped in some unusual places due to the 4th of July holidays. WOW! I am looking forward to some break days when my brother Cary arrives in San Francisco. Because it's all about the food, duh! Lol. We cycled into Petaluma KOA for two days with the first night interrupted by a touring bus full of college kids playing their late night shenanigans. Nicole, Mom, and I are going into San Francisco tomorrow to pick up my brother and to get lost in the city for a bit!!!

July 9, 2015

Today, Nicole and I biked across the Golden Gate Bridge — my second time! We were headed south to Half Moon Bay to spend the night and visit with another cheerleading friend of my mom's, Laura! She has the connections in this state! I am sorry that my dad didn't feel well enough to venture across this epic bridge, but I know that my mom kept him busy chattering about her interests. Cary took some beautiful pictures with his iPad and some video that is part of our story now!

July 12, 2015

Decided to take a break day and dedicate it to the famous Monterey Bay Aquarium! We enjoyed the town, wine tasting, viewing the sea critters and marine environment, and dinner at this fancy hotel. Oh, I got a new phone! What a memorable day.

I cannot say enough about how proud I am of my best friend Nicole Mackin for taking pedaling to a whole new level. Bike touring has changed my life forever, and without my bicycle I wouldn't have seen the places I have ridden through these past five years. I wouldn't have met the friends I have made nor would I have inspired these new dreams and goals. She has experienced this very special form of traveling now, and I'm excited to see where she'll be off to next. With that being said, we went ahead and got another matching tattoo of our bike gear and bike grease.

Those who wish to control their own lives and move beyond existence as mere clients and consumers - those people ride a bike.

~Wolfgang Sachs

July 18, 2015

My five billion star hotel-like campsite this night was the best that camping life offers! The fresh air and freedom to pitch your tent wherever camping is allowed is an intense feeling. We located our gear right on the cliffs of the Pacific Ocean looking down into the deep-blue water. We are grateful for the best spot this trip!! Nicole, Mom, and I slept in my three-person tent. It was pretty cozy! At around 6:00 A.M., my mom woke me up with the camera capture sound on her phone. She had a big smile on her face as she has always enjoyed taking creepy stalker sleeping photos of me. I will miss her soon as she and my two partners will be heading east to return to Florida for the school year.

July 19-21, 2015

Today we rode into my dad's hometown of Oxnard, Ventura County, to honor his parents at their final resting site. We cycled in during a minor rainfall and found my mother, brother, and Aunti Tish waiting for us. Of course, we shared greetings, tears, hugs, and flowers for the gravesites. I will always remember this day with the pictures we took, the memories we retold, and the good food we ate back at the resort in Mandalay Bay, Oxnard.

Time to separate!

July 21, 2015

Yesterday we happened to stop at one of my grandparents' favorite places to rest and eat while driving through Malibu, California. I pushed my dad all the way through Venice Beach, and we rode till dusk to my friend Nansea and Peter's house. We had a lovely dinner, with good beers and giant belly laughs. It was so nice to reconnect with them. I know I can count on them, and that's what makes them very dear friends to me.

July 24, 2015

We are in San Diego, relaxing with my Aunti Tish, Uncle Jim and family, reorganizing our gear, getting our bikes tuned up, and having my last IPAs. Next stop is biking into Mexico, so that is exciting and I'm anxious, but I'm more excited to be with family and friends for a bit longer. I'm really enjoying my godparents and their cool home in Pacific Beach. We really like "benching" which is happy hour in their neighborhood. One of my cousins, David, is stationed in the area with the Navy and he came by to visit. On the 30th I had some much-needed dread maintenance done. Jami's Braids and Dreads in San Diego locked my links in for the next leg of my tour.

> *"We start with our family, we may stray as life goes on but we all end up with our family - appreciate them!"*
>
> –Catherine Pulsifer

Jocelyn:

July 31, 2015

I cannot believe this worked out; at the last minute I hopped the Amtrack train back up to Huntington Beach to see a couple more friends that I missed when I cycled through. All thanks to Nansea for being so generous, loving, and helpful in all ways. My friend Diane had a layover in LAX from New Zealand, so we managed to pick her up and hang out in the 'one and only' (haha) Venice Beach. Best part of the day, my childhood friend Aja, Nansea's daughter, came by to hang out for a bit.

My Uncle Jeff and Cousin Perry also entertained me for a few nights, and they always make me feel welcome in their home. I can't forget to mention I hung out with a good friend, Alex, too. She inspires me with her perseverance and positivity as she always moves forward. It was nice to reconnect with her once again. At times I have fallen hard for old friends; she is one of them. Her soul is so divine; she is a goddess and an inspiration.

August 4, 2015

Tomorrow we start our next leg of our bike tour heading south into Mexico. We will be cycling down the Baja coastline and are a bit nervous to travel through Tijuana and Ensenada. There are many people who have shared their thoughts about the dangers and difficulty as this is a desert peninsula! Please think happy thoughts for us as we have cycled down many crappy roads. My bike feels and might be twenty pounds heavier because I filled my ten-pound water pouch and decided to carry a fly-fishing rod set, which was inspired by my Uncle Jim! And of course, my aunt added lots of unnecessary food, which we are now grateful for.

Mexico

Mike:

Last year I was concerned about riding through Morocco. The same can be said about Mexico, maybe even more so. Family and friends said, "Don't bike through Mexico as the drug cartel will kidnap you." Jim and Tish drove us 25 miles to the border as the non-freeway riding alternative is confusing and lengthy. We soon entered Mexico and were directed to immigration for our six month *tourista* card at a cost of $22. All of a sudden we exited immigration and were navigating the busy and narrow Tijuana road to the coast. I can't remember breathing a sigh of relief until we were out of town after a long, steep climb. Mexico Highway 1 led to the scenic toll road with an excellent shoulder, and we immediately saw large "No Bicycle" signs. I have driven the free road several times many years ago while in the navy and did not want to cycle it due to the heavy truck traffic and no shoulder. We were soon busted by rifle toting *federales* who whistled us off the road. "*No bicicletas.*" After talking with them, we asked if hitchhiking was allowed. "*Si, si,*" they replied. Jocelyn stuck out her thumb and many California pick-up trucks passed without stopping, but we couldn't understand why. Finally a truck stopped and Jocelyn ran to it, opened the door, and was asked, "Where are you headed?" in English. Victor was headed to Ensenada and warmly welcomed us and our bikes. He drove us the 40 miles to Ensenada and dropped us off at the port where we were once again legal on our bikes.

We found one of my old favorite bars, Hussong's, where we enjoyed two beers. Next door we ate at the *Taqueria* where I last had a 'bean cone' 36 years ago. At that time, my fiancée Andee and I, along with Tish and several of Andee's brothers, drove here before our wedding for an early celebration.

We met a new friend Ryu where we enjoyed tacos and beer in a very hot Baja desert.

The Pyramid of the Sun in Teotihuacan, Mexico.

Celebrating Mexico Independence Day in Mexico City.

Fun times during the celebration in Mexico City.

We rode south of Ensenada and stayed at a hotel on Estero Beach. We figured out why so many California trucks passed us without stopping. One of the *federales* holding his rifle stayed with us the entire time to make sure we didn't try to escape up the road on our bikes. I know I wouldn't stop and pick up a hitchhiker with an armed *federale* standing nearby!

We left Estero Beach and headed south into the morning traffic. Soon, we were on a more deserted Mexico 1 and continued through the interior since there is not a coastal road. In the afternoon the climbing began, and we spent several hours in the backed-up traffic. It was a hard day, especially with the 110°F heat. Most of the hilly roads do not have shoulders so the riding was difficult. Later in the afternoon we entered a recently paved road complete with shoulders and made our way to the small town of San Vicente where we found a small motel thanks to the directions of the town's police department.

The next morning we continued south where the traffic built again. A kind gentleman, Gabino from San Quintin, pulled over and said he is a warmshowers host and that he and his family would like to host us. In the last two years he has hosted 182 people. Even though San Quintin was over fifty miles away, we biked hard to his lovely and comfortable home. His wife Lupita and daughter Fanny made us feel welcome with a meal and a safe place to sleep.

We left San Quintin with a good tailwind under a cloudy sky. Soon we were riding near the coast and finally enjoying less traffic and a cool temperature drop from 110° to 90°F. We turned inland into the mountains and found enjoyable climbing since we used the mostly empty lane. We climbed into the town of El Rosario where we spent the night in preparation for a long stretch in the desert.

After four days in Baja we reached the midway point through the desert in the town of Guerrero Negro. It's been a long, hot, and sometimes tedious ride as most of the terrain is like a roller coaster. We ride hard because there are limited services. The road has numerous Mexican military inspection road blocks with an occasional military Humvee driving by. We feel quite safe as we are waved through.

Our warmshowers host in San Quintin gave us a list of ranches that have water and sometimes food available. That list was helpful as we were able to ration our water consumption. Fortunately most of the ranches were open, even though most looked abandoned and closed. A stop and friendly yell of "*Hola*" usually brought someone out. A few even had cold *cervezas* in ice boxes. We have not seen any evidence of power or generators.

We encountered a third 'road angel' in the last few days. The first was the gentleman who gave us a ride to Ensenada after the *federales* told us no bicycles were allowed, and then Gabino who invited us to his home in San Quintin, and the third was a kind and generous Mexican family who stopped and offered us water. Our ten-liter bag was down to just two bottles left when they pulled over as we were transferring water to our bike bottles. They were on their way to Cabo and gave us four bottles of water, two Gatorades, and a bag of apples and peaches. We gorged ourselves on the cool, refreshing fruit as we profusely thanked them. Their kindness and generosity was so uplifting during this difficult time. The camping has been difficult as we try and hide near sunset. Camping in the desert is in fine dirt, sand, and lots of thorny plants. Last night we camped in the dirt surrounded by animal poop and did not sleep well as the donkeys, dogs, and coyotes howled all night. I asked myself if I can continue to do this for another year, but this morning it was all okay again.

"Where do the Mexicans get their money?" We have rarely seen a bank, and the three ATMs we have seen usually have extremely long lines. We guess they drive to nearby larger towns when they need cash. We were running short on *pesos* but fortunately found a bank and ATM in Guerrero Negro.

After eight riding days in Baha we decided to take a break. What do touring cyclists do on their day off? We stripped the bikes and toured the area. It was a fun day as Jocelyn wanted to go fly fishing. Her Uncle Jim in San Diego had assembled a small box containing a collapsible pole with reel along with an assortment of flies. We rode toward the beach on another bright, sunny day and found a good spot for her first attempt. Although there were no bites, Jocelyn did practice casting. We toured the town and went back to our motel for a relaxing afternoon of reading and napping. We went to bed early and planned to leave before the heat set in.

While loading my bike, I noticed that a rear rack had broken loose from the frame from a sheared bolt. Jocelyn stayed at the motel while I cycled to an auto mechanic shop. I received instant help from several workers, and the piece of remaining bolt was drilled with a tiny bit, a tap being inserted, and the bolt successfully backed out. I did have a few spare bolts that were too long, so the mechanic cut the length and reinstalled the rack.

We didn't get on the road until 11:00 A.M., which was late and hot but we persevered in the 115°F heat along with swarms of flies as we rode to the next town of Vizcaino. The flies must like my sunblock as they swarm around me and like to fly into my helmet. Jocelyn is carrying 22 extra pounds of water and me eight. The water we drink is hot but wet, and we couldn't survive without it. We stopped at the first hotel in town and were rewarded with our first air conditioning in Mexico!

After a delicious breakfast of oatmeal and fruit we started early to beat the heat. The friendliness of Mexicans is quite apparent in restaurants. When a customer walks inside they say, "Buenos Dias," to everyone present. At one point we rode into a thunderstorm and received about nine cooling drops of rain, although it is still not as hot as when we rode through the Iranian deserts last summer. At that time it was 130°F and Jocelyn was completely covered. After several hours we entered the town of San Ignacio and found delicious fish and shrimp tacos. There was also a hotel, and after negotiating with the manager we reached a decent price. We never pay full price when we are the only customers. That afternoon we stripped our bikes and took a cycling tour of Mission San Ignacio and the town. San Ignacio is situated on a river containing water (the first river water we have seen in Baja) and is a genuine oasis in the desert. We thought we were back in Thailand while riding along the lush river full of tropical plants and trees.

Today we continued in what we call the '3H' club – as in heat, hills, and headwinds. The day stretched on as we headed east, and when we noticed the Gulf of California we imagined we would soon have a break. Another three hours of riding through a gigantic never-ending canyon brought us to the coast. We endured the bright sun all day and were glad we carried an extra four-liter bottle of water as we drank over sixteen liters between the two of us. It was our most demanding riding day since our start in Washington, and we quickly settled down in a Santa Rosalia hotel. The beach had two trash dumps and a mineral plant next to it, so we decided not to take the plunge. Today was one of those days you wonder, "What the heck are we doing here?"

We again left early with the hopes of beating the heat. In this kind of weather we are like robots as we go through the motions. After a few hours we sighted our first *cabana*-lined beach and made a long downhill detour to swim in the flat, inviting, turquoise water. We were immediately disappointed as we stepped into the hot water — not refreshing — but it was wet. There were a few restaurants on the beach but none open as we are 'off-season' in Mexico. Several more miles down the road we found an open cafe with cold *cervezas* and fish tacos. We also found a fellow cyclist, Yru from Japan, heading south. He had been sitting there for some time trying to cool down. Soon we were joined by a fellow American IT consultant, Kirk, who was working a job nearby. We had a good visit with both of them but the flies and heat were overwhelming. When it came time to leave, Kirk paid the entire bill. We enjoy meeting fellow travelers and adventurers such as Yru and Kirk.

    We continued south with the idea of camping on a deserted beach when we saw Playa Buena Ventura that advertised "Open" on a sign. Most of the beach restaurants and markets are closed until the season begins mid-October. We met the owners Mark and Olivia who have worked this property for a challenging sixteen years. I say challenging because the property is without electricity or water. Mark manages several weekly trips to nearby Loreto for expensive generator gas and water. They welcomed us with cold beer in frosted glasses along with one of the best hamburgers we have every enjoyed. After a refreshing shower we pitched our tent a few feet from the water's edge. Their big guard dog slept outside our tent the entire night

    Two days later we arrived in Loreto, a fishing town on the Gulf of California, and found a bungalow across from the beach. The proprietor was a friendly American lady who spent 41 years living and working on a charter fishing boat with her husband. She told us, "We had a wonderful and adventurous 41 years in Loreto." She recommended a bar down the street, Augies, for dinner. At Augies, we were immediately welcomed by many '*gringo*' fishermen with free *cervezas* and Augie himself at his 'world famous' bar. Loreto is home to 19,000 people including over 2,000 *gringos*. We were told that the gulf fishing is superb. We had a fun time at Augie's half-price happy hour with *cervezas* and fish tacos. Throughout our time in Mexico we have consumed loads of fish no matter if fried or breaded in tacos, sautéed, or grilled. Every bit of it has been fresh and excellent. Another one of our favorites is fresh tortillas whether corn or flour. Whenever we ride by women baking tortillas on an open grill, we stop and enjoy them warm. Add avocados and our diet is set. We always carry avocados, tortillas, and tuna and will enjoy a simple breakfast, lunch, or dinner of sliced avocado on tortillas. Sometimes we find peanut butter and add that to the taste.

The next morning we cycled to the Loreto bus station and inquired about a ride to the next city of Ciudad Constitucion as we longed for a break from the heat. We were soon on a bus and enjoying the air conditioning for the seventy mile, 1 ½ hour ride. After another two days riding and camping we arrived in La Paz where we settled into a room after making reservations at the Baja Ferry office for the eighteen-hour ferry from La Paz to Mazatlán on mainland Mexico. We were excited to be here after cycling 907 miles, the length of Baja California, as it has been a real challenge with the heat and terrain.

We spent three nights in La Paz waiting for the ferry by exploring the town, taking morning swims in the bay, and spending an afternoon snorkeling with whale sharks. We hired a boat, guide, and captain and spent several hours searching for the humongous fish and then swimming amongst them with masks, snorkels, and fins. It was scary at first but we were soon into a rhythm of swimming with sharks from eighteen to thirty feet. Swimming with the whale sharks has been one of the most exciting but serenest things we have done. I was surprised at how calming this experience was as we watched the behemoths slowly cruise the water in search of plankton. We also enjoyed a particular beach bar where we chatted with many Americans living and working in La Paz. Once again we were ahead of the tourist season, so the town was quite mellow. It is little breaks like this that make us appreciate all the demanding work to bicycle the world.

On ferry day we rode thirteen miles to Baja Ferry on another sun-filled and pretty day. After two hours of windy hilly terrain we arrived at the ferry, and after a few of our panniers were searched we proceeded onboard where we stripped our bikes and locked them to a bulkhead. The workout began as we moved our gear up several flights of narrow stairways and checked in with reception for our cabin key. We decided to rent a cabin including bathroom at an additional cost of about $60. The alternative was sitting in an airline seat for eighteen hours. The bikes cost an additional $12 each. The total cost came to under $100.

Above our cabin was a large 'lido' deck with seating, music, and a bar. We enjoyed being at sea and met a fellow traveler from Germany. Matt has been riding his motorcycle through the Americas since March, and he also intends to ride to Ushuaia, Argentina. Our ticket included dinner and breakfast. Dinner was served in a small dining room with the chow (slop) line opening at 7:30 P.M. and promptly shutting down at 8:00 P.M. The food was filling, but the best part was the bottle of fine Mexican wine we brought onboard. After dinner we enjoyed a few more hours on deck watching the full moon. Matt did not have a cabin, so we invited him into our four-berth cabin for the night.

We all slept well with the gentle roll of the ferry. The sunrise was beautiful and signaled another great day of adventure. Breakfast slop was served in a crowded dining room promptly at 8:00 A.M. and ended at 8:30 A.M.

We arrived in Mazatlán after a 250 mile ferry ride. After a lengthy and tedious departure from the ferry we saw Matt flagging us over to a cafe for cooling fresh-squeezed lemonade. We also met a fellow traveler, Peter from San Francisco and England, who was also on the ferry. Peter is hiking through Mexico. Matt left on his motorcycle to the cooling mountains, and we continued south to a hotel. After checking in we saw Peter walking past the beach in front of our hotel, invited him to our room, and offered him the floor, which he graciously accepted.

The next morning we parted ways with Peter hiking off to explore more of Mazatlán and us riding south. The change from Baja was astounding as we were completely soaked through with sweat before even getting on our bikes. Once outside of Mazatlán the green tropical terrain was beautiful and was a big change from the deserts of Baja. We spent most of the day on shoulderless Mexico 15 free road. The buses drove close to us, but most truckers and cars were respectful with some space. After sweating buckets we called it a day in our third town with the name of El Rosario. In this town, founded in the mid 1650s, we found a decent hotel for $13. The further south we travel the cheaper it is. We found Mexico 15's toll road, and it is much safer with its wide shoulder and less traffic than the free Mexico 15. We have cycled on many toll roads around the world and always get waved through.

After several days of riding we entered the small fishing town of San Blas where we immediately headed to the beach for a delicious fish lunch. The port of San Blas was founded in 1768 and soon became the most important shipyard on the Pacific Coast. Spanish ships would set sail from here en route to the exploration of Alaska and California. With over twenty miles of beaches, San Blas also has the longest surfing wave in the world at Las Islitas, but unfortunately it was not breaking this time of year.

We were in search of a long rest so we settled on the excellent Hotel Garza Canela. The staff was attentive and we enjoyed complimentary desert with our dinner and a complimentary breakfast as the staff were interested in our adventure. Once again we were the only guests and a little negotiation rewarded us with a good price.

We were soon climbing along the coast with our goal of Puerto Vallarta in two days. After several hours we stopped for *cervezas* in a hilltop cafe. I asked the shopkeeper if there were any hotels nearby, and he pointed to his building which had seven attached bungalows on a bluff overlooking the ocean. We were quickly sold on the $12 for a simple room in a no-name village. What's funny is that as I was communicating in Spanish he finally responded, "Do you speak English?" At that he spoke excellent English. I guess I need more practice.

A five minute walk away was a sandy beach where we enjoyed a refreshing swim and late lunch in a beach restaurant. The next day we continued south through the hills, many small towns, and increasing traffic as we neared the major tourist city of Puerto Vallarta. While searching through the many beachside 'resorts and spas' costing upwards of $180 per night we cycled closer to central downtown inland from the tourist resorts. Jocelyn spotted a hotel sign advertising 269 *pesos* each, so I crossed six lanes of traffic on foot and found a small hotel with a pool for exactly that. At $30 per night we decided to take a break day.

After two nights in Puerto Vallarta we walked our bikes through many bumpy cobblestone roads until we were on the outskirts of town. Back on a paved road, we immediately started climbing along the coast with scenic views of Puerto Vallarta. The climbing was easier this day as the traffic was much lighter on this Saturday morning. The thunderstorms started early but by now we are used to getting soaked every day. We do enjoy the cooling effect but not the lightning, so we occasionally pulled over to wait out the closer strikes. The climbing grew more difficult and after eight hours and only thirty miles we reached a small town hotel in a downpour where we quickly settled in and collapsed in bed. There are times when we don't bother eating because we are exhausted. The temperature was a pleasant 60°F. We would have camped if it wasn't raining so hard.

It rained all night but by morning the sun was shining. We spent another full day riding and put another 64 miles under our belt. We exited on a dirt road and rode west a few miles where we were rewarded with the small beach town of Perula and a beautiful Playa (beach) Dorada. We also crossed into our fifth Mexican State of Jalisco.

We settled on the Hotel Playa Dorada located right on the beach. It stormed all night and into the morning. We were exhausted and didn't get up until after 9:00 A.M., which is very unusual for us. That is when my sister Tish notified Andee at home in Florida that Hurricane Linda was off the coast of Mexico. We found out about Linda when Jocelyn Skyped Andee in the morning. Jocelyn researched this storm and we decided to stay in Perula at least one more night. Hotel Dorada was a bit expensive for our taste so we walked with our bikes in the rain and found a family-run hotel for $13. It was smaller and not as fancy but there were many friendly locals staying there. Soon we were facing the strong storm bands as they came ashore.

The following morning was clear and we were quickly on the road. A few hours later Jocelyn had a tire wobble that we investigated and found a rear tire bulge near the rim. It looked as though the tire was coming apart on the sidewall from probably repeated travel on rocky roads which cut into the sidewall. Fortunately, we carry two spare foldable Schwalbe Mondial touring tires. She replaced her tire and continued. Soon the thunderstorms were heavily upon us and we looked at our options of continuing to the next big town, about ten miles over a large hill, or turning right and looking for a place near the beach. Since the sky was dark and visibility low, we chose the two mile route to La Manzanilla Beach and found a bungalow. After negotiating the price with the senorita in the pouring rain, she motioned to bring our bikes inside. The bikes were full of mud as we rolled them onto the clean tile floor. She retrieved a mop to clean the floor but I stopped her and took the mop and we cleaned up our mess.

A few hours earlier, I also developed a wobble on my rear tire and discovered a tire failure similar to Jocelyn's. The next morning I changed my rear tire with our second spare. We were disappointed to have only 11,000 miles on these tires before they failed. Last year we rode many miles off-road from Morocco to Southeast Asia on these tires, and in Mexico some of the rocky roads have been tough. It's funny though that we have carried two spares for over 15,000 miles the last few years and all of a sudden we use both spares within a few hours of each other.

We left La Manzanilla Beach and headed to Manzanillo in our sixth Mexican State of Colima. We rode another scenic coastline and found a cheap hotel. After much discussion we decided to ride a bus 340 miles to Acapulco. We have a warmshowers host in Acapulco lined up that will store our bikes while we bus to Mexico City for Mexico's Independence Day on September 16th. Saving the estimated 10 days it would take us to cycle from Manzanillo to Acapulco will get us to Mexico City in time for this major holiday. The next day, after a nineteen hour bus ride, we arrived at our host's cliff-side condo, stored our bikes, and hopped on a bus to Mexico City. Mexico City is one of many side trips we have planned. In situations like this we will bus on the side trip to save time. Cycling to Mexico City and back to Acapulco would take about eleven days. We want to explore the world and not just bicycle it.

We arrived in Mexico City to massive soccer match crowds. After the five hour bus ride we boarded the metro for the historical district of Mexico, or so we thought anyway. We were wrong and ended up at the soccer stadium. The crowds were insane and we returned by metro to the bus station and hailed a taxi. Our goal was the central historical district and Cathedral Metropolitana. We finally arrived and looked for a place to stay. The crowds were also insane here with Independence Day pre-parties. While wandering around the square we spotted Mexico City Hostel right around the corner from the cathedral. We were surprised that they had one room left and we paid for three nights. That evening we walked the streets and enjoyed the pre-celebrations and many well-lighted artistic signs exclaiming, "Viva Mexico: 1810 – 2015."

The next day we took a tour to the ancient Aztec City of Teotihuacan. Teotihuacan was a pre-Columbian Mesoamerican city located thirty miles northeast of modern-day Mexico City. It is known today as the site of many of the most architecturally significant Mesoamerican pyramids built in the pre-Columbian Americas. Apart from the pyramids, Teotihuacan is also anthropologically significant for its complex, multi-family residential compounds and the Avenue of the Dead. The city is thought to have been established around 100 BC, with major monuments continuously under construction until about AD 250. The residential compounds have many remarkable unrestored original painted murals created over two thousand years ago. We climbed the two major pyramids: Pyramid of the Moon at 145 feet tall and the larger Pyramid of the Sun with a base of 738 feet, a height of 213 feet, and the third largest pyramid in the world. We were fascinated as we climbed the exceedingly steep stones. We read that the surfaces were this steep in order for the severed sacrificial heads to roll all the way to the ground from the top. If the head did not reach the bottom, the sacrifice didn't count. Our tour included many historical buildings including cathedrals and temples. When the Spanish arrived most temples were destroyed and the Spanish cathedrals built on top. Next to our hostel is Cathedral Metropolitana, the largest in Mexico City. We spent a few hours exploring this impressive classic monument. There are many glass windows looking down into excavated areas below the cathedral floor to view the remains of the Aztec Temple that was destroyed and used as the foundation of this cathedral.

Mexico City's 205th Independence Day found us in a sea of humanity with the largest fireworks show we have ever witnessed along with a huge military parade the following day. The increasing crowds were sometimes overwhelming with pushing, and the central square seemed like it was under bombardment. After three days of exploring the historical city we took a ten-mile taxi ride to our next warmshowers host. We stayed with Santiago two nights and enjoyed his bicycle touring stories along with his and his friend Mariana's excellent fish cooking skills. They had both cycled through South America to Ushuaia, Argentina two years ago.

We also enjoyed touring the Palace of the Arts, the National Museum of Anthropology, and the University of Mexico. The museum contains hundreds of statue pieces and carvings depicting the history of all regions of Mexico. After a fun and informative week in Mexico City we returned to Acapulco and our bikes.

Sunday morning we headed south out of Acapulco. Outside of the city is a large steep climb of three miles. We rode some, walked some, and rested in shady areas on this hot day. Mexico City, at over 7,000 feet, was much cooler. It was at times a struggle since we haven't been on our bikes for a week.

To the south of Acapulco are miles of flat beaches. I had to wonder, "Are we still in Mexico?" Flat, straight roads can be boring, but once in a while they are a blessing along with a fine tailwind. This tourist area is similar to Italy as there aren't any public beaches. Instead there are beach clubs and resorts. We enjoyed a seafood lunch at one of the beach clubs and then continued south where late in the day we found a family hotel. We had looked at a few others but they were way overpriced and touristy. We like being with the locals and the Mar Azul Hotel a block from the beach was our stop for the night. We swam in the ocean and enjoyed watching the horses and dogs run around on the beach. A small fishing fleet charged ashore onto the beach, and we watched the fish being unloaded and sorted.

The next two days we continued south and stayed in the towns of Cruz Grande and Cuajinicuilata. The riding continues to be hot over 110°F. We take many breaks for shade, water, fruit, and Gatorade. Combined with the hills, it is challenging but we persevere. After three days in the mountains we arrived at a warmshowers host in Puerto Escondido. This small fishing town is known as Mexico's Pipeline (as in surfing Banzai Pipeline, Hawaii). Jim is an American who has lived and worked in Puerto Escondido for many years. The next day we went to Zicatela Beach, which is home to Mexico's Pipeline. The surf was too large and was breaking fast, so we tied our rental longboard on top of a taxi and took a fifteen-minute ride to La Punta Beach, which is a smaller and slower left-point break. We spent a few hours taking turns with this board before the weather started deteriorating due to Tropical Storm Marty. It rained hard all night, but by mid-morning Marty had moved north and we headed south. We had a late lunch at a beach shack restaurant on Playa Blanco. Since it was getting late we pitched our tent on the beach and quickly fell asleep while listening to the surf and falling coconuts. I woke up once and the tide was within ten feet of us. It looked like high tide so I went back to sleep.

The next morning we were up with the sunrise, heated noodle soup, and were on our way off the beach and back riding through mountains. We continued over the low coastal mountains with the major port city of Salina Cruz on our mind. It turned out to be a long and hard day through the heat and hills. In fact, it was my most difficult day so far in Mexico. The reason why we pushed so hard was that we wanted to head east to the Gulf of Mexico and then continue south to the Maya ruins of Palenque. From there we will enter Guatemala from inland instead of on the Pacific Coast. We arrived in Salina Cruz on the Gulf of Tehuantepec late in the afternoon. We rode through the central district, biked through a parade, and found a hotel. We spotted a Burger King nearby and decided to take a break from our typical Mexican fare. It was quite good and tasted just like America's.

Jocelyn and her riding companion Spumoni contemplating the magic of an ancient Maya temple in Palenque, Mexico.

After five days we arrived on the Gulf of Mexico in Coatzacoalcos, a major port city in the southern part of the Mexican State of Veracruz, on the Coatzacoalcos River. Coatzacoalcos comes from an indigenous word meaning "Site of the Snake" or "Where the snake hides." Across from us and to the northeast is our home State of Florida and south at six-hundred miles is Cancun. We met two touring cyclists headed to Cancun and then flying to Cuba before returning to Mexico. We thought of this too as we would be entering Cuba from Mexico and thereby bypassing American travel regulations to Cuba. It was tempting, but we passed. The Gulf of Mexico is beautiful with good waves. We found a hotel across the street and tried to find a surfboard — but to no avail.

We cycled out of Coatzacoalcos on a Monday morning and spent the first three hours on hills. For the next five hours the road was totally flat. We were excited as our miles for the day were 74. A few days ago, as we rode through the major city of Villahermosa during a busy lunch hour, I was hit on my left rear pannier by a minivan bus while on an overpass.

I hit the guardrail, bounced off that, and did quite a wobble trying not to fall and get hit by another vehicle. A similar situation happened last year in Spain when a truck's whoosh of air threw me against the guard rail. Fortunately there was a guardrail, since on many roads they are non-existent, especially on overpasses. Thankfully the cars behind the van managed to avoid me. In the scheme of things, we have been fortunate on the road as we try to stay out of high traffic areas, but sometimes they are unavoidable.

Four days after the Gulf of Mexico we entered the town of Palenque, Mexico and the nearby ancient Maya city of Palenque. We attained our thirteenth state of Chiapas, a southern Mexican state bordering Guatemala. The mountainous highlands and dense rainforests are dotted with Maya archaeological sites and Spanish colonial towns. After eleven days of cycling from Puerto Escondido we were ready for a day off the saddle to explore Palenque.

Palenque is a Maya city in Southern Mexico that flourished in the seventh century. The ruins date from 226 BC to 900 AD. By 2005 over 1,500 buildings were discovered in one square mile of jungle. It was interesting that the city was designed and constructed according to the stars. At night the architects reflected the sky with a layer of water and set the buildings accordingly. The commoners built the structures by carrying rocks over the mountain from the other side. Eventually the city was abandoned when the Maya moved to the Yucatan because crops could not be grown in the soil anymore, possibly because they burned live trees that caused black acid to accumulate in the soil. We spent the entire day exploring this captivating period of history.

We had a late start from Palenque due to a computer problem that my son Cary helped fix while talking with him through Skype. Skype works well and Jocelyn talks with her mom whenever we have Wi-Fi. We also had a few bicycle issues that we worked through. As a result, we didn't get on the road until 11:00 A.M. Outside of town the growling of howler monkeys took over the otherwise quiet road. Between them and all the birds sometimes we couldn't even think. The day was a delight with a few long, steep jungle climbs along with grand vistas as we rode through the mountains toward Guatemala. The day was late as we gained 56 miles and the town of Tenosique. It was also one of my favorite rides in Mexico.

Jocelyn:

August 5, 2015

On the first hill through Tijuana to the coast, we both had to walk and nearly passed out from the unbearable heat. Taking more than a week off was very comfortable, but now I have two weeks of damn pain and mental setbacks to overcome. After being chased off the toll road by the *federales* (Mexico's federal police) with guns, we had to be babysat while I tried to hitchhike. Many people passed us up . . . maybe because of the men with guns? Eventually we met a man, Victor, who graciously picked us up in his tiny truck, and the three of us rode together to Ensenada where the free road begins. Right away we visited the extremely famous bar since 1892, Hussong's Cantina. "*Dos cervezas por favor!!!*" My dad used to drink in this dive over 40 years ago. Then we ate next door at the *Taquería* and enjoyed fish and *carne tacos* and *conos de frijol* (bean cones), which is my newfound favorite food. These beans don't compare to anything else I've ever had.

August 9, 2015

Sometimes I imagine myself on a motorcycle, where I can just go and go, and then I realize I'm pedaling and all my force is pushing me forward to another place. It's pretty cool what the body can do even if I'm semi-out-of-shape. I'm able to cycle in such diverse climates and terrain, and I'm still alive. Thanks to all the drivers out there looking out for my life and other fellow cyclists!

August 12, 2015

It's unreal how we were welcomed into such a nice place the other day. It was hot (Duh! It's the desert.) and I ate too many *huevos rancheros* at noon. This unexpected ranchero showed up after two very long hill climbs (just about 3,000 feet), and we ran in to chug water and drink the shade. The senorita saw me lying down on a bench and invited me into her outside bed *cabana* area. There were five beds of sorts and two hammocks. She said, "Sleep, dear. You look hot." So, I did, and an hour later we left and rode another 50 miles. Without that siesta, I wouldn't have made it to the next water opportunity, and I wouldn't have made it halfway through Baja California where I am now, Guerrero Negro. Tomorrow we start on the next half of the desert, Baja Sur, and I certainly can't wait!

August 19, 2015

During the hottest part of the day, noon to 3-ish we try to find cover and luckily found a cafe that was actually open and met another crazy cyclist, Ryu, from Japan. He is cycling to the Yucatan Peninsula and then flying to Cuba to cycle tour, and he also thinks it is too hot. He took a photo of us as we left to look for the next water hole. I gave him my extra pair of riding gloves because the crazy guy didn't have any and half his handlebars didn't even have tape on them! We are now on the Gulf Road and it is very green on this side.

Today we had a very hard time climbing massive hills with high grades, and the heat was once again unbearable. We happened to cycle into this strip of beach that looked deserted. But it wasn't and we were lucky again! A Wisconsin man and his Mexican wife own the entire property, at least 3km of beach and 15km of the mountains. They fought for this land and have had a hard time fixing it up. It is called Playa Buenaventura :) and so we got to be friendly and had a party in their bar. Grubbed out on Mark's famous burgers and swapped stories of our lives, giggling the entire time while the one fan worked magic on us. It was an unforgettable experience to literally go from crying to cheers-ing with friends. Even though this ride through Baja has been the toughest, the people we have met make all the pain worth it.

August 25, 2015

Just seeing a whale is not a big deal, but I caught sight of a beautiful one from our place watching the sunset in La Paz. When I'm on a break from my bicycle for two or more days, I start to create even wilder dreams. As the whale was breaching, I started to realize that my clothing of choice isn't fashionable when you wear it every day. Now I think that I'm totally cool, but others push their noses up, and I can tell they think I am homeless!

We rented a boat and were fortunate to find several whale sharks offshore from La Paz with our two guides since we got out early. Our guide filmed me with my "spirit" animal, and I was able to swim fluidly through the water for minutes with this gentle creature. It was like the smoothest dance I've ever experienced. She was kind, soulful, and turned to look me in the eyes before she dove into the deep, blue water and I lost her. This was one of the most beautiful encounters that I am thankful for the Espiritu Baja Tours! On Thursday, the 27th, we shall set sail on the Baja Ferry to the mainland.

September 7, 2015

I really like Mexico for many reasons. I saw this sign on a business: *'Abarrotes Jocelyn'* and thought that it was interesting to find a Mexican grocery store with my name! We had to stop and have a Victoria *cerveza* that was delicious and chilled.

September 12, 2015

We stayed last night in Acapulco in my friend's beautiful apartment. Our goal has been to stash our bikes and gear so that we can travel by bus to Mexico City for their Independence Day celebrations on the 16th. Last night I decided that I will live here for a little bit someday! This city is gorgeous with so much going on around it. This morning we transformed into backpackers and jumped on the first bus, and upon arrival in Mexico City five hours later followed a large group heading to the arena for a big *futbol* game. Oops, that took us on a train in the opposite direction, but it was fun! Tomorrow we will visit the Pyramid of the Sun, one of the largest structures in the ancient Aztec city of Teotihuacan, and the third largest pyramid in the world.

September 15, 2015

I've never been in another country for their Independence Day celebrations, so when I heard the date, I pushed us to make sure we could get to the capital of Mexico. It's only fitting that we happened to walk by the Angel of Independence that I think is one of the most beautiful I have ever seen. Dad and I wandered through the crowds and found a cool place to sit, a terrace bar where we had drinks while watching the parade that included mostly all military groups.

September 20, 2015

We are finally back to riding, and as usual we faced a serious hill climb to get a wonderful view looking south out of Acapulco. We often get asked questions about our bikes, and today I said it weighs way too much. Considering I barely use anything in the front two panniers, which holds food for four days for both of us, two stoves, gas, pots, pans, knifes, bowls, utensils, and I carry winter clothes that I haven't even used yet. But everything just might be necessary at some point. I got pretty upset walking up this hill because walking is more painful and more tiring! I think my bike and gear weighs a bit over fifty kilos. I yelled at the air, screaming hurtful things to no one in particular. When I get this crazy, I am surprised that my dad still wants to stick around. I know I am too old to have a tantrum like this, but sometimes when I get frustrated I can't help but kick rocks and carry on like a child.

September 26, 2015

We made it to Puerto Escondido, and I finally got a three-hour surf session at Zicatela Beach known as the Mexican Pipeline. The waves were small but very powerful and fast, which makes it tough to paddle in a wave with a rented, waterlogged longboard. It was stupidly crowded, and I haven't surfed in more than five months since my last bicycle accident. Now my shoulder is really sore, but that's totally worth it! I trash talked at a local *nino,* because this grom was ridiculous, cutting every surfer off by forcing them to back out of the wave. I simply explained that the next time he tries yelling at me to not drop in on him, I will drop in on him and my board will hit him in the face. He let me catch the next point break and it was epic. I also got asked by a local fisherman if I wanted to go fishing. When I said, "No," he asked if I smoked cigarettes and I said, "No," so he asked if I smoked weed and I said, "NO." Then he laughed and said, "Okay, you just drink beer!" "*Si.*" Anyways... now we're waiting out this tropical depression hitting us right now and hoping to get back in the water tomorrow!

September 27, 2015

The last two days I've watched many different types of hummingbirds, and this quote I just found is fitting:

> "Legends say that hummingbirds float free of time, carrying our hopes for love, joy and celebration. Hummingbirds open our eyes to the wonder of the world and inspire us to open our hearts to loved ones and friends. Like a hummingbird, we aspire to hover and to savor each moment as it passes, embrace all that life has to offer and to celebrate the joy of every day. The hummingbird's delicate grace reminds us that life is rich, beauty is everywhere, every personal connection has meaning and that laughter is life's sweetest creation."
>
> –Papyrus

October 4, 2015

We enjoyed our first *cocofrio* (coconut drink with milk and water) off the side of the road. I thought after halfway through the drink, "Omg, watch us get sick, but it's so good!" The ice was homemade, and the lady went behind the counter to mix water, not from a sealed bottle, in our cups. Let's hope nothing happens! We reached the Gulf of Mexico, too! Now we will bike to Palenque (Maya ruins) and then into Guatemala, en route for Tikal National Park (more Maya ruins) for my birthday! So, for my special day I'd love to see an anteater. We are close to our next country, Guatemala, and I think we can carry a bottle of tequila and cans of Fresca, plus ice, for a small sum.

October 8, 2015

Yesterday we made it to the town of Palenque after we rode for 11 straight days from Puerto Escondido. We actually arrived earlier than previously thought! So today we took a break day to visit Palenque and the Mayan ruins in the State of Chiapas. This place has a distinct tranquility within the walls, trees, and steps that tell long lost stories of the true Mayan culture. It was absolutely fascinating to walk around, though we couldn't see all 1,400 structures that have been reported and documented in this national park and World Heritage Site. Visiting here was one of the best decisions I made in our route planning!

Walking through the jungle of Palenque you can find ancient homes begging to tell you their story. Lizards run back and forth, while howler monkeys throw themselves around the trees, and the distant waterfalls serenade your every step. This is a place I will long to return to again.

Even though there are centuries between Egyptian and Mayan civilization construction of pyramids, how is it that they are very similar? It's wild to see a stone-carved image of a dragon on the walkway in the Palace here at Palenque ruins, the same image I have seen several times cycling through China and Southeast Asia. Why is there a cross carved out to make a window (baffling the Spanish when they arrived)? The answer just might be within the stars. Astrology and agriculture are very well connected, obviously, so maybe the specific alignment and structure of their cities just came from studying the stars for years. Could this specific alignment of pyramids be a connection to Orion's belt? And yet... maybe we are all truly connected!

Honduras, Central America to Chile, South America

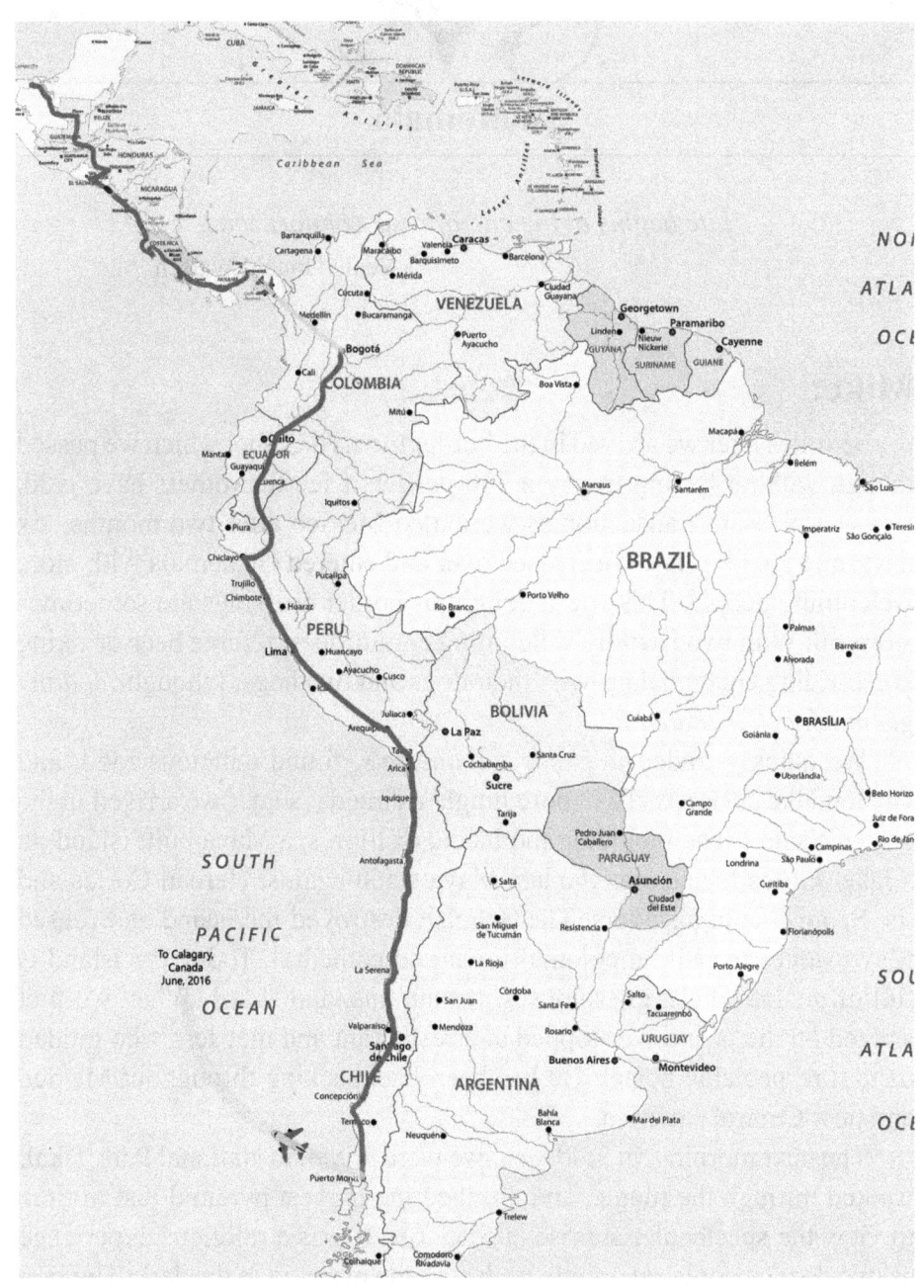

Guatemala

"Life begins at the end of your comfort zone."
 –Neale Donald Walsch

Mike:

35 miles later we arrived in the border town El Ceibo, which we passed though without having to pay a 330 *peso* exit fee that others have paid. It was a pleasant transaction as we exited Mexico after two months, six days, and 2,434 miles. We crossed over and entered Guatemala with more welcoming people. This was a delight as border crossings are sometimes stressful. With two friendly welcoming committees of three beer-drinking horse-riding Guatemalans with their dogs and two hogs, I thought, *It don't get much better than this!*

We quickly traded in *pesos* for *quetzals*, found delicious food, and Guatemalan *cervezas*. Two more jungle riding days later we arrived in the city of Santa Elena including the Island of Flores, a Maya built island on a lake. Flores Island was the last Maya stand against Hernan Cortes and the Spanish conquistadors. The Spanish destroyed the island and reused Maya stones to build a colonial town and cathedral. Today the island is full of quaint hotels, guesthouses, restaurants, and shops. When we first arrived on the island we stopped at a restaurant and met Jess who guided us to a respectable hostel. He has been backpacking throughout Mexico and now Central America.

The next morning, at 3:00 A.M., we were driven to National Park Tikal, walked through the jungle, and climbed the highest pyramid just in time to view the spectacular sunrise at 5:55 A.M. It was a religious experience as two dozen people sat quietly high atop the pyramid in the dark. The rain forest became alive with howler monkeys and many other animals noisily greeting the new day. We swapped a day of riding for a day of hiking.

Tikal is the ruins of an ancient city found in a rainforest in Guatemala. It is one of the largest archaeological sites and urban centers of the pre-Columbian Maya civilization. Tikal was the capital of a conquest state that became one of the most powerful kingdoms of the ancient Maya. Though monumental architecture at the site dates back as far as the fourth century BC, Tikal reached its height from 200 to 900 AD. The ruins lie among the tropical rainforests of Northern Guatemala that formed the cradle of lowland Maya civilization. The commoners that constructed the temples and palaces worked 360 days straight to the end of the year and then had five days off. After that five day rest, it was work for another 360 days. We witnessed many Guatemalan highlanders performing a ceremony to bless their upcoming corn crop. There were several groups burning offerings, dancing, smoking, drinking, and chanting. Watching these ceremonies was inspiring as the locals have practiced this custom for centuries.

We enjoyed several meals and adventures with Jess including a boat tour where we witnessed many huge, wild iguanas. After this ride we visited a small island and found a 'restaurant' that was recommended for fish. Aunty expertly fried three lake fish. We haven't had any better fish than at this shack that had three tables. Jess continued his travels while we headed south toward Honduras. The days were slow due to rain. Guatemala is green for a reason, as it is indeed a tropical rainforest. The shouldered road has been pleasant. The truck and bus drivers are more courteous and we get many good honks. We haven't seen any military road patrols as in Mexico but feel quite safe.

The picturesque mountains were riveting as we admired the oversized tropical plants and listened to unseen animals lurking roadside. We passed many small villages while looking for a hotel or guesthouse but found none. Darkness comes early now. Jocelyn had previously written in Spanish words to the effect of who we are and that we are looking for a safe place to stay for the night. We spotted a house with a large, covered front porch and she bravely went to the door and read it to the senora. She called her husband who must have said okay because she motioned to put our tent and bikes on the porch. We were soon the news of the town as people walked by to see the two *gringos* setting up camp. The family of five that we stayed with were friendly and let us use their inside bathroom. I walked to a nearby store for food and drink. At 7:30 P.M. we said, "*Buenos noches,*" (good night) and were soon asleep.

The next morning we rose with the sun, and after saying, "*Muchas gracias,*" to our hosts, we were on our way. It was Jocelyn's 25th birthday. Her mom had given me a card, which I presented at our breakfast *palapa* (an open-sided dwelling with a thatched roof of dried palm fronds). Soon we were in the popular sailboat cruising destination of Rio Dulce, which means Sweet River. It is part of a lake system that leads 24 miles away to the Atlantic Ocean. The river has many marinas and is packed with sailboats this time of year as it is one of the best hurricane holes in this part of the world. Most sailboats stay here for the entire hurricane season.

Last night Jocelyn had found 'according to trip advisor' the best local fish restaurant. It was a boat ride away and it was excellent as we enjoyed her birthday meal, including a variety or fish and shellfish cooked in coconut milk. After dinner we enjoyed a sunset cruise back to the marina. At a lunch spot that day we ate in Jocelyn's Restaurant. The restaurant was named 'Jocelyn'. While there we met an American rancher from Utah who moved here years ago and bought a marina and another ranch. Today he works his cattle business and enjoys living in Guatemala.

We celebrated Jocelyn's 25th birthday at 'Restaurant Jocelyn' in Guatemala.

We finally left Rio Dulce after two nights and climbed deeper into the Guatemalan Mountains. I say finally because it could be one of those kinds of places where a cyclist could get stuck for several days. Some sailors spend months here during hurricane season. Everything is here in one place — marina, hotel with pool, great internet, restaurant, and bar, plus most of the people speak English. A bonus is the friendly and safe town directly up from the marina. I have a history of sailing experience, and at one point after high school I wanted to sail around the world. I had found an old wooden sailboat and showed my parents. After that, my 'sails' were wisely deflated. My wife Andee and I sailed in the Bahamas on a charter sailboat with four neighbors in 1981. Andee and I then spent three months sailing down the East Coast of the U.S. from Massachusetts to Port Canaveral on a 46-foot catamaran. After that we moved back to California for my college schooling, and we crewed/raced on several sailboats. Anyway, during the two days in Rio Dulce I reminisced about that and maybe more sailing in the future. Life is all about exploring the world with whatever vehicle is right for you.

Yesterday, while riding at point, a dog was startled and stared at me while she walked out onto the road. I thought, *Oh no!* when all of a sudden a truck sped by and ran over her. We have been chased by dogs countless times, and this is the one thing we fear, a dog chasing us and getting hit. That is why we stop when a dog starts chasing us as they always stop because the chase is over. I watched as this dog was run over without the driver even slowing. I was devastated as the last time I saw this happen was when my dog Sunny from many years ago was run over in front of our house in Florida. The dog didn't even whimper and Jocelyn pulled her off the road. I called her Guatemala and will always remember the look she gave me. This quieted us the rest of the day.

Jocelyn:

October 11, 2015

We are entering our 27th country, Guatemala, and on October 17th I will turn 25 years old. It's hard to believe that in 4 years I have cycled across 25 states and now 27 countries.

October 12, 2015

Today we hiked very early in the darkness to the top of a Mayan temple in Tikal, where I experienced the most majestic sunrise. I've never walked through the jungle at 4:00 A.M., and I've never sat in silence with over 30 cliché "backpackers". It was a spiritual awakening. As the sun rose, so did the animals and we were listening intently trying to understand their chatter.

Tikal is one of the largest Mayan cities and archeological sites in Mesoamerica. It has over 4,000 structures and according to our tour guide, Tikal might have over 10,000 structures as there is an entire city below the findings of today. Of course there are many theories and we all want to believe something, but one thing is for sure; the spiritual freedom I witnessed today by the Mayan descendants made the entire place become even more alive! This is what we tour for, to experience the cultures all around us and share smiles that are given and received.

> *"We are not myths of the past, ruins in the jungle or zoos. We are people and we want to be respected, not to be victims of intolerance and racism."*
>
> –Rigoberta Menchú, 1992

October 15, 2015

It's been pouring down rain the entire day. I appreciate the rain, but I don't appreciate my rain gear. It isn't breathable and I literally took an all-day sweat shower. The beauty of slow traveling on a bicycle is that you magically find unique places you had no clue about. This place is one of a kind. Included on this very large property is a hostel/hotel, tree houses, a local Macaw, hundreds of hammocks, a large kitchen with margaritas, semi-good WiFi, a fresh water spring that flows into a lagoon where you can swim with some turtles. Also, there is a Mayan Pyramid less than half a mile away. It isn't uncovered and it's gloriously tall! There are horses and many mosquitoes, and there is this jungle shower that reuses the water the kitchen uses! Eco-friendly!

October 17, 2015

I thought it'd be fun to go hike up the pyramid by myself after it's been raining for 2 days straight. Well... not so much, the mosquitoes are rampant, and I slipped like 5 times and the actual trail is way too steep! Today my birthday wish didn't happen; no big deal. Time to keep riding!

Honduras

"To travel is to discover that everyone is wrong about other countries."

–Aldous Huxley

Mike:

After four days of mountain and valley riding we cycled into our 28th country of Honduras. It was one of our biggest challenges yet to cross the Sierras Del Espiritu Santo Mountains. We easily exited Guatemala after paying $2.50 each and then entered Honduras at a cost of $3 each. A few miles from the border we stopped at a lookout, and as I surveyed this mountainous country with all its peaks I wondered how I was going to cycle through this land. I was totally overwhelmed by what I saw. It is moments like this that make you feel so vulnerable. As we walked away, I told Jocelyn, "It looks like I'll be walking a lot." While riding from the border, a kind man stopped and told us about his family-operated hotel in the Maya ruins (Copan Ruinas) town of Copan. We easily found Hotel Mar Jenny and felt right at home with this warm English speaking family. Whenever anyone approaches us and suggests a place to go or stay, we will usually investigate it, as I like enterprising people who are not just waiting for customers to come in the door. After we settled in, we were offered a horseback tour of the town. We anticipated exploring Copan Ruinas and decided to take a day off to explore the ruins by horse.

The next day, horses were delivered to the hotel, and we had a fun and adventurous three-hour horseback ride around town and through the hills above the Maya ruins. We then spent the afternoon exploring Copan Ruinas Archeological Park on foot. Copán is an archaeological site of the Maya Civilization located in Western Honduras, not far from the border with Guatemala. It was the capital city of the kingdom from the 5th to 9th centuries AD.

Honduras Achieved!

Jocelyn's cousin Kate lives in Honduras. This day we hiked to a waterfall. We were standing in Honduras but El Salvador is shown to the left of the falls.

One of many falls during a slippery mountain ride to El Salvador.

We left Copan and headed toward Santa Rosa de Copan. We figured it would take a few days and Jocelyn had mapped out a dirt road that looked interesting. Once we arrived at the dirt road turnoff we paused and questioned it. A local kept saying, "*No, no... peligroso,*" (dangerous), so we talked it over and decided to listen to the local knowledge. We knew it would be a steep up and down dirt road but wasn't sure he was talking about that or maybe the people that live along there. Honduras is one of the poorest countries in the world, and we have been warned several times to be careful. So far we have had mixed reactions from people seeing us. Our bikes probably carry more than a lot of people in poor countries even own. Except for dodging many huge potholes, the road was fine and the mountain and valley views were scenic. We were also told to never camp in the wild because it was not safe, but to camp near a house was okay. Others have said not to camp at all. We made it to the town of La Entrada the first night.

That night, Jocelyn was sick with an intestinal bug. The previous day for lunch we ate street food which is usually pretty good. She ate the chicken while I had the beans and salad, so we think it might be food poisoning from the chicken, which I did not eat. When I'm hot and tired with much more roadwork ahead, I don't like eating much, which isn't always a good thing. She was up on the toilet most of the night. We decided to head out anyway with the goal of Santa Rosa de Copan another 35 miles. With about fifteen miles to go, Jocelyn was struggling so I put out my thumb and surprisingly a pickup almost immediately stopped and we loaded our bikes in the bed. We were soon on the outskirts of town where he was turning off. Back on the bikes, we climbed up and down through this hilly city and found a cheap hotel. After several hours in bed, Jocelyn felt well enough to explore the city a little. We were caught in a large flooding thunderstorm that lasted a few hours. In-between the torrential rain we walked through town. We returned to the hotel by taxi with a driver who wanted double the fare. We gave him his quoted price but then he said it was for one. We have encountered this problem around the world. Usually we ask a price and confirm that the price is for two but sometimes we forget. The driver was angry with us and stormed off.

It is sad to see how dogs around the world are treated. In La Entrada we had eaten at a Chinese restaurant and were served an enormous portion of shrimp fried rice. We took the box of leftovers back to the hotel to have for breakfast, but since Jocelyn was sick, she couldn't eat. I went in search of dogs to feed. I saw one who was approaching me but turned around when he saw three girls. At that, he jumped around and wagged his tail like he knew them. All three immediately picked up rocks and started throwing them at him. We have seen this in countries all over the world, adults and children throwing rocks at dogs like it is a game. This is disheartening to witness. I ended up dumping the leftovers on the side, but I'm sure it fed a lonely pooch.

Jocelyn was feeling better, so after a morning rest we toured the world-famous cigar making factory, Fabrica de Tabacos La Flor de Copan, which makes cigars from Central American tobaccos. The company employs 650 people. It takes about three years of curing before the tobacco is ready and the cigar is rolled. It was a fascinating tour, watching the entire process from the curing of the leaves, mixing different flavors, rolling the cigars, and the packaging.

Both of us were sick last night but we decided to continue anyway. It turned out to be an exhausting day and we needed almost eight hours to get thirty miles to the next town of Gracias. In many towns, there are welcoming signs sometimes several miles from the actual town. Gracias is the case here. Many miles and climbs later (after the sign), we were finally in a town. When you are sick, this can be demoralizing. Jocelyn spotted a hostel on the left and we immediately stopped. Jardin Cafe and Hostel is exactly what we wanted with a restaurant, large and comfortable rooms, and at a price of $8 per person. The manager spoke excellent English. The historical downtown district is only five blocks away or ten *lempiras* (*limps*) apiece (about $.50) on a *tuk tuk* (semi-enclosed, mechanized, three-wheeled rickshaw).

This morning I was feeling better, but Jocelyn slept in because she was up most of the night. We decided to take a day off, and we traveled to town on a *tuk tuk* for a breakfast of pancakes. We hiked to the 1864 Fortaleza San Cristobal. This fort was inspired by forts of the Spanish colonies and constructed with stones and adobe. It is interesting that the fort's towers look like they belong in the Middle Ages of Europe. Last year we cycled by many medieval forts and castles. However, the entire building was designed in the neoclassic style with geometric figures.

The funniest thing we saw was a sign that read that in 1539 Don Pedro Alvarodo ordered the foundation of the city of "Gracias a Dios". After a difficult trip of looking for a suitable place he found this place and exclaimed, "Thank God (*Gracias a Dios*) we have found flat land!" We have not seen any flat land in Honduras. That is what makes this country so compelling.

Before we reached Gracias, we had a quick 1,700-foot drop and noticed our brakes were not up to par. They were replaced in Istanbul, Turkey last year, so it was time. We replaced all the pads and performed other routine maintenance.

The next day Jocelyn was still sick. Last year Jocelyn had similar symptoms while in Tajikistan. Traveling through foreign countries leaves us exposed to many disabling gut-wrenching bacteria/parasites/viruses. Jocelyn's cousin Kate manages medical clinics (through a charity organization) in the Honduran municipality of Colomoncagua. Jocelyn messaged Kate about this illness and Kate checked with doctor friends who suspect she has a parasite of some sort. Kate then sent Jocelyn a list of recommended medicines. While cycling out of Gracias we stopped at a pharmacy that had all the medications on Jocelyn's list. Continuing through town, we passed the bus station and decided on a bus ride to La Esperanza where we would meet Kate. The bus ride was an adventure in itself and the forty miles took two hours. The driver would not leave until the van was full inside and out. Outside there were people on the roof and a few standing on the running board. My niece Kate joined us in La Esperanza and we had a fun Halloween evening walking through town enjoying delicious food and the local culture. Halloween is not celebrated here, but the next two days, November 1 & 2 "All Souls Day and All Saints Days" are, so there were many ongoing celebrations and events. The next day we rode our bikes to her friend's house for storage while we bused to her town of Colomoncagua, an indigenous word meaning hills, mountains, and water. The almost four-hour, thirty-mile van ride over a cratered and rutted road into the mountains near El Salvador was another adventure. Kate manages the area's medical clinics and rents a room in a house where we were welcomed to stay in an empty bedroom. We attended a work meeting with her on Sunday and then enjoyed a late lunch with several of her Honduran co-workers. Her current project is conducting a census of all the families in the remote areas and encouraging them to visit the clinics for medical care because many of them walk across the border and receive their health care from El Salvador.

Monday morning we met with fifteen census takers that she hired for the project and rode by truck near the border. We stood in the small pickup bed grasping anything we could to hang on, but I soon felt that I would be thrown out of the truck on the bouncy dirt roads. When the truck stopped I jumped out and moved to the inside passenger. We have seen pickup beds packed with people on the roads. But we were off road on a four-wheel-drive truck. We split into teams of two and spent the day using a rough hand-drawn map to find these remote homes. We climbed through the dirt and rocky jungle paths in the rain and managed to find eleven occupied crude houses. Unfortunately there were kids everywhere, as most don't attend school after a certain age. There is an elementary school to grade six, but after that, nothing, unless they can find a way to live closer to the city. Most families need their kids at home to help with the chores. The experience was humbling, observing how others live with little or no chance for the kids. After the exhausting day we recovered at a local store that operates a small restaurant in the back.

Jocelyn's medication was working and whatever it was inside her seems to have been knocked out or gone dormant. Yesterday we visited a few clinics with Kate and delivered five water filters and medical supplies that Kate had ordered to the local elementary school. The following day we hiked to a waterfall right on the Honduras/El Salvador border. The waterfall is in a beautiful jungle setting with a river separating the two countries.

We left Colomoncagua by van and returned to La Esperanza. After another almost four-hour van ride we arrived and found a hotel. A few weeks ago while eating an ear of corn, a front tooth, with a previous root canal and crown, became loose. Today we visited a dentist who removed it and re-cemented the post to the root for $4.

Our health is back to 100%, and that is good because of Jocelyn's difficult but inspiring planned route to El Salvador. We retrieved our bikes and continued riding into the mountains. The ride and road was adventure cycling at its finest as Jocelyn found the road less traveled — dirt, rocks, and ruts. On the first day we crossed a few mountain ranges to find the small town of Marcala, Honduras. The climbing was fun but the descents were difficult in trying to keep our speed down while negotiating the slippery road. In fact, our descents took longer than our climbs. It took all day to reach Marcala only 25 miles from La Esperanza.

Jocelyn:

October 23, 2015

We went on a three-hour scenic tour of Copan Ruins, Honduras by horse and galloped down the stone streets on a busy Friday morning, (Never have I ever ridden a horse through a town before or up a mountain.), crossed a few streams and muddy roads, met a local Mayan tribe — the Chortís, visited the ruins of a fertility hospital in the jungle on the hillside, and rode back down with my four-legged amigo. We also visited the Ruins of Copan National Park, toured the tunnels, and became even more fascinated by the Mayan Civilization. At one turn, we were all galloping and laughing when I heard my dad howling. I turned and saw Dad sitting like halfway off the horse, on its side. I laughed even louder but slowed my horse down so that his horse slowed down and he didn't actually fall. I won't ever forget his face though. Haha!

October 25, 2015

Yesterday we "beasted" up some nice climbs and I was so proud of my father. Of course the beautiful lush countryside was stunning, but I didn't get a good enough photo to fully represent it so I'm hoping my father did! Unfortunately, yesterday for lunch I knew something was iffy and sure enough, four hours later the "shit hit the fan" and I haven't stopped going yet. Every 20 minutes it's like a race to find a bush or perhaps a real toilet. Today I tried pushing the next 25 miles to Santa Rosa de Copan, but after refusing to eat or drink anything I slowly made it 10 miles and gave up. Food poisoning and bike touring don't mix well. We luckily bike-hitched and got a ride with a guy from Santa Rosa. Hoping I can feel better by tomorrow or the next day.

October 28, 2015

A lot of people traveling have a purpose or reason behind their journeys. Lately, I've been trying to figure out what mine is. When someone asks me this, I usually say, "I'm living out my dreams, dude!" But is that a good enough reason? I don't get much recognition, and I believe it's because my purpose isn't enough for people. But do I care? A little bit, actually. And that's partially because I feel too much at times — but who am I kidding? — most of the time. People might think one thing and that's fine, and they'll never know the reality of this adventure or they might, if they decide to purchase our next book. I'm just hoping that one day living out my dreams will pay off so that I can help other people live out their own dreams! For now, I'll stick my tongue out to the nonbelievers and ride on.

Nov. 4, 2015

For the last few days we've been out on the *frontera* of El Salvador in and around Colomoncagua, Honduras. We are staying with my cousin Kate who works for the charity Shoulder to Shoulder Organization. One of her current projects is going to every home in the jungle and filling out a family health survey. Dad and I were able to join her and go out in the field for an entire day. Her staff is comprised of hard workers and literally hike all over the surrounding mountains to find all 24,000 families. Though they just call it "walking", it was tough and I give them all the props. Believe it or not, we are enjoying a "nice" ride back into town in the back of a pickup truck. It's so fun and a bit dangerous but totally the norm.

El Salvador

Mike:

The next day would prove even more difficult because of heavy rain the night before and continuing into the afternoon. Climbing once again was much easier than the unstable descents with multiple falls on the slippery clay mud. On the descents, we had to keep both hands on our brakes because a momentary release of one would project us into an unsafe speed through the rocks and ruts. The occasional car or motorbike beeped us good honks. After another twenty miles we reached the border exit station for Honduras. We were directed to the El Salvador border several miles further down the mountain where once again there was no stamp to enter. The border police told us our stamp into Guatemala was good for ninety days through Nicaragua. As we left the border station the guards watched us and shook their heads. We were twelve days in Guatemala, sixteen in Honduras, so we have another 62 days to travel through El Salvador and Nicaragua, as these countries are included in the Central America visa time of ninety days.

At this point it was getting toward dark, and we continued on the extremely rough road with more walking than cycling as we dropped about 3,000 feet to a small town. We were at the point of camping in the mud when we spotted a motel. The motel had a garage and we were able to roll our filthy bikes inside and forget about them. There was an outside restaurant on premises where we stuffed ourselves since we had only snacked on peanut butter and crackers during the day. The senorita was very happy and talkative as she cooked many delicious *pupusas* for us. A *pupusa* is a traditional Salvadoran dish made of a thick, handmade corn tortilla filled with a variety of meats, beans, or vegetables and then cooked. We were surprised that El Salvador currency is $USD. Fortunately, they took Honduran *lempiras* and we were given change in $USD.

We took our time getting back on the road and washed our bikes' gears, chains, and rims as we prepared for a larger descent. After another ten miles of mud the road turned paved. The next three days we rode over a few more mountain ranges to the city of San Miguel which sits at the base of Volcano San Miguel. We spent the night in a San Miguel American Hotel Comfort Inn surrounded by several layers of coiled razor wire and three armed patrolling guards.

Several people have told us to stay off the roads on Sunday afternoons as that is known as 'drunk day' in Central America. Unfortunately, from what we have seen, we do agree. The further south in Central America we head, the rows of coiled razor wire increases along with the number of shotgun-toting guards. It seems intimidating, but the guards are friendly whenever we say, "*Hola,*" or, "*Buenas,*" to them. We wonder how this kind of security would be received in America. It is a bit alarming, but we take it in stride and do our thing. Traveling through poor countries on a bicycle is eye opening. I believe that given the opportunity, everyone should spend time in an impoverished country. We have cycled through some of the poorest countries in the world in Central Asia and Central America. It is a humbling experience and makes one appreciate what you have at home. It is heartwarming to see that people, especially kids, seem happy everywhere. Almost everyone has cell phones and satellite dishes, even the shacks on the side of rivers that are nearing the stage of falling into the water.

As we cycled into the port town of La Union we tried to find a downtown hotel that Jocelyn located on Google. After asking about a dozen people we finally found it. One always has to ask many people because everyone gives a different answer. No one ever says, "I don't know," because they would be embarrassed. I enjoyed the afternoon sitting on the street next to an older senor, talking with the locals and sharing a few beers. It's funny how they all take double looks, and I knew what they were thinking, *Hey, there's a gringo in town!* We have nothing but good things to say about the Latinos we have met. Many people walk up to us to shake our hands and say with a smile, "Welcome to El Salvador." At this cheap downtown hotel the manager watched us leave at night for ice cream. When we returned he smiled while he closed and locked the heavy metal gate topped with three rows of coiled razor wire.

Jocelyn:
November 8, 2015

Yesterday we climbed to 6,400 feet, took on the rock, gravel, sand, and dirt clay to get here while in the pouring down rain. We made it to our 29th country with two crashes and no injuries! We shared many smiles, smelled the pine trees, and arrived soaked to the bone in El Salvador!

We were only in El Salvador for less than a week, but every day I had *papusas*! One day we had them for breakfast, lunch, and dinner.

I connected with this company that had another connection on a boat ride from La Union to Nicaragua. I thought that'd be an interesting experience, so I convinced my dad to ride there. It took forever to find the hotel where we were supposed to meet this man to hook us up with a boat. After we cooked dinner outside on the stairwell, the guy arrived and talked us through the process of getting across on this small boat. We had to go to their "customs" and then convince a boat to take us. So we did just that, but the boat left five hours after it was supposed to embark. We had our bikes lifted into the boats. Luckily, we planned ahead and had some warm beer to enjoy on our voyage across the sea. We actually stopped at several islands, delivering goods to the locals. I jumped off to help transport these goods. All in all, the three-hour slow-boat ride was epic. Even though they couldn't dock on the Nicaragua side, we were able to carry our bikes above our heads as we trudged through waist-high water.

During this time, my Facebook got shut down and my mother freaked out about the fraud once again.

As we were celebrating our crossover into Nicaragua, a call came on my phone. The owner tried to get me on the phone, but I was so scared and couldn't understand what she was saying. The next day, I realized my cousin Kate had called me wondering if we were still alive and well. My mom was freaked, and so were we, once we found the internet connection. It's all about the adventure — right?!

Nicaragua

"Nothing compares to the simple pleasure of riding a bike."
–John F. Kennedy

Mike:

It's hard to believe that last year we flew to Morocco and cycled through our third country and now we have entered our thirtieth. We cycled to La Reunion Harbor for a small boat ride across the Gulf of Foseca to Nicaragua. We found the La Union Immigration Office, and checked out of El Salvador after only three days and 82 miles from the Honduras border to La Reunion. We waited at the city dock until 11:45 when we and our bikes were carted along the low tide mud to our boat. The captain walked alongside us with a 75 HP outboard over his shoulder. By the way, a 75 HP outboard weighs in at 330 pounds! Shortly after noon, we were underway for the thirty-mile 3 ½-hour trip. It was a fun ride that we shared with seven German and Swiss backpackers along with several locals. We also carried supplies to one of the many El Salvador volcanic islands. A few hours later we were in Nicaragua where the boat captain dropped us off in the water close to the beach even though there was a small pier a few hundred feet away. We then waded ashore with our bicycles and panniers over our heads as the rain started. Next to the beach was the immigration office where we were stamped into Nicaragua after a lengthy and confusing process. We were not pleased with the 'immigration officers' who seemed to be there to pocket extra dollars. We refused to pay extra and were somewhat detained along with the backpackers. After fifteen minutes we were told, "Go." We cycled about 1,000 feet into the gulf-side village of Potosi and stopped at a hostel. The seven backpackers arrived shortly after us. We slept like a rock until 5:00 A.M. when the jungle came alive with a multitude of bird sounds.

Our first two hours of riding south from Potosi was on a dirt road. After that, there was a newly-paved road that led us to our beach destination of Aposentillo after an eleven-mile ride on pavers and rock. We found a hostel full of surfers from around the world named Joe's Place. Joe warmly welcomed us with a room on the bottom floor so that we could roll our bikes in. Joe is a fellow traveler who circumnavigated the world on his sailboat. He now owns this cool hostel close to the world-famous break called "The Boom". Dinnertime was fun as the food is served family style — plentiful and excellent. Surfers from Australia, New Zealand, Canada, U.S., England, and Norway were staying here, some as long as a month already. We had a great time swapping surfing stories, and they were all fascinated by our bike trip. Four of the guys had driven a car from California and could not believe that we rode our bikes here. The next morning, we were on the beach early to check out the wave action. Joe offered us longboards, but the waves were way too fast and heavy, so we opted for body surfing. We were heavily pounded to the ground but did manage some barrel time.

A new sport for us — volcano boarding in Nicaragua.

On a biking day off we hiked up Volcano Conception on the Island of Ometepe, Lake Nicaragua.

We left Joe's Place and can't say enough about the hospitality, food, and friendly atmosphere. As in many hostels around the world, this hostel operates on the honor system. Whenever you take an item, whether it is food, drinks, or miscellaneous items, you itemize this on your sign in sheet and pay when you check out. We were soon in the colonial city of Leon. Leon is popular with backpackers, and it was difficult finding a room. We finally found a new hostel with room for our bikes. After cleaning up, we headed to the main square and cathedral for an excellent dinner and local entertainment.

The next morning, several of us from the hostel rode a bus to the beach. The driver would not leave until all standing space was taken. We stood and were cramped as he drove off. He stopped at several places where even more people were loaded. With the temperature over 95°F, we were sweating and dripping over the seated passengers. They didn't like that, but what the heck were we to do. After 45 minutes, we made it twelve miles to the beach outside of Leon. We settled into a beach bar/

cabana hangout, rented a board, and surfed. Lunch of a whole fish was excellent. The waves were fun, the board was crap (but who cares), the beer was cold, and the sand was so hot we had to run across the black sand beach. We have noticed that the less we surf the harder it is to paddle out as our 'surfing arms' are weak. The best part of the day was hanging out with our new friends from Nicaragua, Israel, Texas, and Australia.

We took another 'day off' to try a sport new to us — volcano surfing/boarding. We spent the afternoon hiking to the top of Volcano Cerra Negro, an active volcano in the Cordillera de los Maribios Mmountain Range in Nicaragua ten miles outside of Leon. It is the youngest volcano in Central America, having first appeared in April 1850 with the last eruption in 1999. We each carried a toboggan-like board on our back for the one-hour 2,500 foot climb. The view was astounding as we stood in awe atop Volcan Cerra Negro and caught the sight of five Nicaraguan volcanos lined up from the north to south. This scene is sewn onto the Nicaraguan flag. We were soon sitting on our boards and swiftly descending the steep volcano. I flipped once because I was afraid of my speed and dug my heels into the loose black gravel while attempting to slow down. As I flipped, I remembered our guide saying, "Do not dig your heels in the gravel." I feel the same way on my bike during a steep downhill and overuse my brakes. We were wearing coveralls, gloves, and goggles, so we had some protection. Volcano boarding was one of the coolest things we have done. We finished the day with new friends along with wings and beer. Several days later we were still cleaning volcano sand from our bodies.

Our next objective was a surf resort in Miramar Beach that Jocelyn had heard about from a friend in Leon. We arrived there in the late afternoon and found the Puerto Sandino Surf Resort owned and operated by two Americans. Even though there were no rooms available, they invited us to camp on the patio. The resort is a surfing camp with several rooms, a pool, and a large upstairs open living and dining area located right on the beach with five breaks within walking distance. We were warmly welcomed by all and joined in the family-style dinner. There weren't any flying bugs so we slept on the upstairs living-room furniture. I was thinking that if I were younger this would be a great place to live and operate a surf camp.

The next morning everyone was up and surfing by 6:00 A.M. We walked the beach, had breakfast, and were back on the road at 8:00 A.M. The next two days were spent on unpaved hilly beach roads before turning inland and passing through Managua, the capital of Nicaragua, on the way to Granada. Granada is a city on the shores of Lake Nicaragua. Founded in 1524, it is home to multiple Spanish colonial landmarks that have survived repeated pirate invasions. The city's main plaza, Central Park, is dominated by the colorful, neoclassical facade of the Cathedral of Granada, originally dating to 1583. The Centro Cultural Convent, San Francisco, nearby is famed for its displays of pre-Colombian statues. We cycled to a hostel and learned about the many Spanish Immersion Programs in this old colonial town. That night and the next morning we researched the different Spanish lessons available and chose Nicaragua Mia Spanish School. We also took advantage of their home stay accommodations and were assigned a Nicaraguan family to live with for five days during our lessons. The instruction is for twenty hours over five days. Yesterday we moved from the hostel to a Nicaraguan family home where no English is spoken. When not in class, we converse with them in Spanish. We each have our own teacher at $100 for the week, and the home stay is another $100 each. This includes three meals a day with the family. After our first lesson of four hours I was conversing with my teacher in Spanish. She asked me questions in Spanish and I answered fairly well.

We completed our weeklong Spanish class and were thirsty for more. It is surprising how many people travel here for several weeks at a time on their vacations to study Spanish. Some have been coming here for years and say that this is the best way to learn. We believe that too because after class you have ample opportunity to practice what you just learned on the street and in the marketplace. Most locals we encountered were friendly and willing to help us learn. We conversed with our homestay family and can tell the difference already. The course is fast-paced and difficult, but the one-on-one teacher ratio helped me learn at my pace. In-between classes we explored Granada, a low-key but popular tourist destination and well suited for our type of adventure. We found a traditional Thanksgiving Day meal at Margarita's Restaurant in downtown Granada. We enjoyed the meal while watching American football in English at this American owned restaurant. We also enjoyed Reilly's Irish Tavern in Granada as they have some of the best chicken wings we have ever had.

We left Granada after a delightful one-week stay at the home of Carla and Julio. The room and meals, while talking with our hosts and their friends, was an enlightening introduction to Spanish.

We cycled fifty miles to San Jorge and the ferry to Ometepe Island — the island of two volcanoes on Lake Nicaragua. After the one-hour ferry ride, we arrived in Moyogalpa right after sunset and found a homestay. We don't like riding after dark and this find was convenient and cheap. We left Moyogalpa early the next morning and cycled around Volcan Conception to the other side of Ometepe. Heading west, we had great views of the other volcano, Volcan Madera. Madera is more wooded than Conception and swampy at the top including a lake in the middle. Hostel Little Morgan, outside of Santa Cruz, Ometepe was our choice and we settled into a woodsy cabin for two nights.

We were up early at 5:30 A.M. and met another couple who would hike Volcan Conception with us. A taxi picked us up at 6:00 A.M., as on Sunday the chicken bus doesn't run. At 6:30 we met our guide at the base of the 5,010-foot Volcan Conception and began our climb. The first hour was a fairly easy hike before the jungle enclosed us and the climb became increasingly steep. The almost daily rain turned the surrounding jungle growth into a muddy path. Five hours later we were at the intersection of the descending path. Our guide had repeatedly told us that no matter where we were at 12:30 P.M. we must begin our descent so we don't get stuck on the volcano after dark. It was 11:30 A.M. and we were told that at our pace it would take another two hours to the summit. I soon dropped out, as the route required climbing larger boulders and steep mudslides. The guide and the other guy continued. I didn't want to fall and get hurt, so I met Jocelyn and the other girl back at the intersection. Our guide said we hiked 80% to the summit, and that was fine with us. We were told that about one-half of hikers reach the summit, as the top of the route is very steep. As it was, we made it back to the road shortly before dark. We sometimes stood and surfed down trails of volcanic sand. It was a satisfying ten-hour hike through jungle, old lava streams, large rocks, mud, beautiful jungle growth, lots of pretty butterflies, strange looking mountain rats, and, of course, many howler monkeys. The males did not like us walking under their families and let us know with their loud growling. Back at the hostel, we enjoyed dinner and a few beers with new friends before our long, deep sleep. Our 'break' days are sometimes more difficult than our riding days.

We left Santa Cruz and cycled around the non-paved northern side of Ometepe Island. The sometimes rough road took us three hours as we crossed a few recent lava flows. In the middle of nowhere we watched a cart heading our way noisily ringing a bell. It was an ice cream cart that was several miles from any town! We purchased popsicles and could not believe this guy was pushing a heavy cart over the rocky road. I gave him a nice tip. We arrived at the ferry, purchased tickets, and had a good time talking to a cycling tour group also headed back to the mainland. They were riding a three-week tour of Nicaragua, Costa Rica, and Panama. Once back at San Jorge, we decided to get a room near the beach and plan an early start to enter Costa Rica tomorrow.

Jocelyn's Instagram Post:

November 12, 2015

In case anyone was wondering, we're safe and now in our 30th country, Nicaragua, at the "boom" surf break. Our goal is to rest and find some waves!

Leon, man. In Leon I met some amazing people. I hung out far too late, like 4:00 A.M. late, and I drank lots of *Flor de Cana!* Got some surf on waves and a volcano! Pretty nuts.

November 20, 2015

We've decided to stay for a week in Granada as we found an awesome homestay and Spanish school to immerse ourselves in. Seems crazy that we will stay for 7 days, but I'm excited to learn more Spanish and hoping it will be helpful the farther south we ride!

November 30, 2015

The toughest hike ever, and we only made it 80% to the top of Volcan Concepcion on Ometepe Island on Lake Nicaragua. The trail had places that were so steep it was comparable to doing lunges up rocks and rock climbing with very little zigzag action. I took 6 liters of water, and that wasn't enough for the two of us as we ran out about 2 hours before we made it back to the main road. It took us a total of 10 hours to hike up and down about 5,289 feet.

Though the hike was ultimately hell, I can say I made it to just above the thick cloud line. Yesterday there were no clouds and it was the perfect day to hike up a volcano. This hike will be forever remembered even after tomorrow when my knees will still be hurting and my arms will be sore from hanging on to tree limbs for dear life while descending down this sucker. I do know now that there is more hiking to do in my life story.

Costa Rica

Mike:

We had been warned by many people that the road from San Jorge to the border is filled with robbers and not to stop. Naturally we were concerned about this and hoped for the best. Along this road we saw many men in camouflage with rifles standing near trees. We thought they were soldiers but were not sure. Of all places to get a flat, this was not the place, but it did happen and we rolled to a stop at a farm entrance off the road. I quickly jumped into action and changed the tube. While doing this, a truck turned into the 'farm' with several men inside. They slowly rode by us, and I looked up and saw them sternly shaking their heads. At this, Jocelyn said, "Dad, we need to go!" I quickly reinstalled the wheel without aligning the axle and engaging the brakes and left. Since I didn't spend the time to adjust the wheel, it was not rolling straight but I didn't care. We were soon at the border where I completed the wheel installation. Checking out of Nicaragua was confusing on where to go and how many taxes were required since there were several people with official-looking forms who wanted money. After several minutes of searching I found the correct line and paid the small official tax. We had heard that the Costa Rica border had been mostly closed the last several weeks because of an influx of Cuban refugees trying to work their way into Central America, Mexico, and the U.S. There were hundreds of refugees camping near the border. I went inside and noticed that people were entering the country, so I went back and told Jocelyn. We steadily walked our bikes inside the small area and worked ourselves into one of the lines. Several people, mostly truckers, were cutting in front of us, but Jocelyn spoke up and we used our bikes to keep line cutters away. The official seemed perturbed with us and our bikes and quickly stamped us in and said, "¡*Vamonos!*" In other words, "Go!"

Since we hadn't had lunch yet, we stopped at a small outside market. The prices were 'through the roof' so we each bought a soda and left.

We would find these high prices everywhere as Costa Rica is a popular destination for tourists, especially Americans. When we returned home it seemed like everyone talked about Costa Rica for a vacation. We still recommend that for the money, activities available, and friendliness of the locals, Nicaragua can't be beat. With so many tourists in Costa Rica, the people don't seem as friendly as other Central American countries.

We rode through several towns looking for a place to stay, but everywhere was filled with Cubans . . . the Cubans with money. Those without money were camping. We thought of camping, but with so many refugees camping we were a bit concerned. We finally found a hostel with an empty room in the town of La Cruz. At $50, it was way more than what we had been spending through Mexico and Central America. In Nicaragua this would have been an $8 room. We washed our clothes and hung them outside on a fence. After that, we moved inside the main house living room. Later, I went out to the bar for a beer and noticed that our clothes were gone! I slapped myself for even putting them outside with all the refugees around — of course someone would want our clothes. I asked the bar and restaurant workers, who directed me to the manager. She then led me to their laundry room and said that she saw someone taking them off the fence and knew that the clothes weren't theirs, so she hung them in the laundry room. I was so relieved and noticed a dryer and asked if we could use it. She smiled and said, "*Si*."

We continued south to Liberia on a rolling, quiet road with many roadside crossing animal signs including anteaters. We looked all over for anteaters but never did find one. Liberia is at the crossroads for turning to Playa de Coco, and since we live near Cocoa Beach, Florida, we wanted to visit this Coco Beach. Before the turn, we saw a *finca*, an estate in a rural/agricultural area that offers rooms. We decided to stay in this inexpensive option and then head to Playa de Coco tomorrow. Across the street was a large outdoor mall that we wandered through before finding a dinner spot. If we didn't know any better, we were in "Anytown, U.S.A." In fact, most of the cars and shops had the same name as in the U.S., while most people looked American, and all we heard was English. Why would anyone want to live or visit here? You are physically leaving the U.S., but once here, it's just like home. I guess people are comfortable here.

We left Liberia, and twenty miles later were in Playa de Coco where we scored a room right across the street from the beach. This Coco Beach is on a bay unlike our Cocoa Beach on the Atlantic Ocean. Walking through town, we enjoyed good food and found an advertisement for a sunset sailboat ride. We inquired about several boats and found out that the 47-foot Kuna Vela sails unlike most other boats that just motor and feed the passengers drinks. The next afternoon we rode on a beached dinghy out to the anchored Kuna Vela. We sailed south to the next bay, Hermosa Beach, and picked up Sandie and Mike. This is typically a sixteen-passenger boat, and it was comfortable that there were only four of us. Captain Israel and crew Marvin were friendly and knowledgeable. We sailed to a quiet and calm cove and spent a few hours snorkeling with the many colorful tropical fish before swimming to shore and exploring a few wet caves on the deserted beach. We next swam back to the boat and were presented with two large snack trays along with drinks. The sunset was one of the best we have ever seen as the sky was lit with many amazing shades of red through the numerous clouds. The wind picked up and the spray flew as we returned to Hermosa Beach and then Coco Beach. Israel and Marvin expertly handled the boat in these gale conditions. On the way into Coco Beach, we assisted a stranded fishing boat with a tow. At this point it was dark, choppy, and wet. Marvin dropped us off on the beach. We met a few new friends in town before returning to the M&M Hostel.

 We left Coco Beach on Sunday and cycled south through the Congo Trail (formerly known as the Monkey Trail) to the small town of Potrero. Back at the hostel, a new Swiss friend had told us about this off-road trail, an alternative to the main road. He had traveled it with his motorcycle and said that it was difficult, so he wished us luck with our bicycles. It took us several hours but we made it through this mostly steep, loose dirt, and rocky road. Yesterday, Jocelyn told me that she had talked with our Cape Canaveral neighbor Janice's brother, Arnold, who lives in Potrero. Before we left, Janice had told me that she has a brother living in Costa Rica, but I had completely forgotten that until Jocelyn told me she talked with him after messaging Janice on Facebook. He invited us for the night and we found his house. There are no addresses here except for 100 meters from this and 50 meters from that. We had a good time with Arnold watching Sunday NFL in English before enjoying a seafood meal at a nearby restaurant. Monday morning we said goodbye to Arnold and rode south to Tamarindo Beach where we found Hotel Villa Amarilla. Manager Cinde welcomed us as family with a tequila shot in this small hostel-like hotel directly on the beach. We immediately rented two longboards and hit the surf.

The surfing has been fun, but we decided to move on. Two months ago we made reservations to fly home for Christmas. You might say we are taking 'a vacation from our vacation.' We cycled to the town of Nicoya and a warmshowers host who offered to store our bikes for a month. At Armando, Patience and Lucas' (fourteen months) country home, we packed a pannier each for our flight and rode a bus to San Jose Airport. The family was kind to store our bikes and gear until January 13th.

We returned to Costa Rica's Nicoya Peninsula after a Christmas vacation at home in Cape Canaveral, Florida. It felt so good to be a family once again, and we enjoyed every minute of our time. Armando manages a bicycle shop in Nicoya, and while we were gone he inspected our bikes and recommended a few items to be replaced. We were able to bring the parts with us — new bearings for Jocelyn's continuing headset problems, and another rear hub replacement on my bike because of bearing failure. This hub that was installed in San Diego had become increasingly noisy to ride. The previous hub had cracked in half on the drive-side flange back in Northern California. But who knows, as I could be at fault. Through Washington, Oregon, and California, I would stand out of the saddle and crank it up the hills. The hub gave way on a hill in California. I don't ride like that anymore. We returned to Costa Rica on January 14th and took a taxi to the new downtown San Jose bus station for a five-hour bus back to Nicoya. We spent two days working on our bikes, sorting all our gear with the new stuff we returned with, and playing with Armando and Patience's son, Lucas. Every once in a while you meet someone with an immense knowledge of bicycle theory and repair. Armando is one of those few we have met around the world that knows their stuff. It is people like Armando that help us get back on the road in better shape. Whenever we meet people, they assume we are bike experts. We are far from that but manage to stay on the road sometimes with the help of others.

We left Nicoya on a typical winter Costa Rican day — 90°F in the shade and 105°F in the sun. Our plan was to leave the Nicoya Peninsula by ferry to Punta Arenas to avoid a busy section of the Pan American Highway.

Three days later, we were cycling through the port town of Punta Arenas on our way to a long climb toward Jaco Beach. The ride was fast and furious with increasing traffic and heat. In Jaco, we found a hostel to take a break from the heat. Two days later after riding through the Costa Rican jungle we arrived at the Panama border. On the way to the border we crossed many bridges where we stopped and observed many large crocodiles in the rivers below.

The border crossing was interesting as once again it was a 'game' to figure out where to go and the proper procedures. In this case we had an early start and stopped at a border restaurant for breakfast. As we waited for our food I took our passports across the street to immigration to inquire about exiting. I learned that once again we had to pay an exit tax. When we flew home for Christmas the airport exit tax was $29 each. Costa Rica is full of taxes. In fact, at a restaurant there is an added 13% tax to the bill along with a 10% service fee (called the *propina* or tip) shared among the workers. I asked four people where I pay this exit tax and received four different answers by mostly pointing. I even walked into the border police station and was told, "No tax." Back at customs, I obtained two exit forms after standing in line. Exit forms are never stacked on a table for easy access. This is true for most of the countries we have visited. I took our forms back to the restaurant and completed our exit papers. I returned to immigration and asked several more people in Spanish, "Where do I pay the tax?" Finally, a kind girl led me to a van where another girl inside this van was collecting the fee. Armed with my receipts of $7 each I was able to get an exit stamp on our passports. Checking into Panama and exchanging our *colones* for U.S. dollars was a breeze. This is the second Central American country (the first El Salvador) that uses U.S. currency. Panama does, however, have *balboa* coins, which are the equivalent of U.S. coins.

Jocelyn:

December 3, 2015

Kind of hard to believe we have made it this far and are still together in our 31st country, Costa Rica. We will wander around here for a bit until our flight home as we need to take a break from this bike tour and ourselves. We will return in January to continue our world tour into South America!

December 8, 2015

Dad and I went surfing today for 6 hours. It was so fun but tough and I asked to change boards with thanks to the awesome rental place. I started out with a 9 footer as I'm a "longboarder" at heart, but after two hours I was reading the lines better and knew I needed a faster and lighter board. I got this 7-foot fish, and we were carving, giving some spray. Oh, man, it was fun! I paddled across this estuary four times to get to better waves with less people. I prefer lefts, so I found those with no one around except monkeys and crocodiles.

December 11, 2015

I'm home!!!!!! Started traveling at 6:00 A.M. yesterday and arrived home at noon today. On our first plane flight out of Costa Rica I had a severe allergic reaction on the plane, leading to my throat closing up and a rash down my entire body. It was a bit scary, but I'm semi-okay now and home with my Momster, bro Cary, and Yaki dog. She missed me and still loves me.

We flew home for a few weeks to spend Christmas 2015 with our family in Florida.

January 16, 2016

We returned to Costa Rica to prepare our bikes for the next journey south, tuning them up and repacking all of our stuff! In the meantime, we've become good friends with our warmshowers hosts Armando, Patience, and Lukas. He is my little buddy! Tomorrow we will be back on our bikes, a bit heavier, but we're so eager to explore new things and live in the constantly changing day to day bike touring.

Panama

Mike:

We cycled to the first major Panamanian city of David and boarded a bus to take us further south past a one hundred mile major road construction project. The road was down to one lane each way with several areas of gravel. We also have two friends we want to visit in Panama City who will be leaving soon.

We are happy to be out of expensive Costa Rica, but unfortunately the only road to Panama City is along the busy Pan American Highway. Along the way we camped at a few surf camps on the beach. At one on Palmar Beach there was also a hotel at $70 while the beach camping is $10. I'm glad we have a tent. There is something about hearing the surf lap the shore all night that makes sleep come easy. There were no rivers nearby so we did not fear the crocs!

The road widened to three lanes each way with clean shoulders about twenty miles from Panama City. Sunday morning found us cycling over the Bridge of the Americas after being stopped by the police. He told us it was illegal for cyclists to ride over this bridge as there are no shoulders. The alternative was crossing a bridge several miles inland. As we were discussing this, several roadies rode by on the way to the bridge so we talked him into letting us go. It was indeed a banner moment as we cycled over the bridge and around the historical part of the city to our hotel for the next three nights. I was last here July 5, 1998 when I was working for the Sea Launch Program. I worked on the Assembly and Command Ship in St. Petersburg Russia to help it prepare for launching satellites from Ukrainian Zenit rockets on a launch platform in the Pacific Ocean at the equator. On this day we transited the Panama Canal from the Atlantic to the Pacific and up to the new homeport of Long Beach, California. We arrived in old town Panama City and checked into a hotel that Jocelyn had made reservations for as rooms are hard to find. It was an easy ride after the bridge because on Sundays most major roads close one side to vehicles allowing cyclists on the other.

After checking in at the hotel we met our neighborhood friend Ginny and our new friend Jess that we had met in Guatemala. We shared lunch at a bayside seafood restaurant. Scenes like this are rare for us so we get excited when we meet friends on the road. After this we wandered through town and met two more friends of Jocelyn's for dinner. The next day Ginny flew home to Washington D.C. while we and Jess took a bus tour of Panama City that also included a stop at the famous Miraflores locks of the Panama Canal.

We were at a quandary on how to proceed to Colombia, South America. Because of the Darien Gap between Panama and Colombia there isn't a road. The Darien Gap is a jungle full of dangerous wild animals and insects, drug trafficking, indigenous Indians that don't take too kindly to people, and kidnappings. It is the only interruption in the 19,000 mile Pan-American Highway from Prudhoe Bay, Alaska to Ushuaia, Argentina. At only ninety miles it is a whole different world.

There used to be a ferry from Colon, Panama on the Atlantic side of the Panama Canal to Cartagena, Columbia. But this doesn't exist anymore although many sailboats sail the eastern coast south along the San Blas Islands to Colombia. We tried to get on one of these sailboats for a five day adventure down the coast, but the boat captain cancelled due to weather as this time of year it is windy on the Atlantic Coast of Panama. We switched to another boat where at first the captain said he would take the bikes but then changed his mind. Since the next boat trips were not available for another week, we decided to fly to Bogota. Our first choice was Medellin, Colombia, but that plane on Viva Colombia Airlines didn't leave until late afternoon, meaning we would not get out of the airport until after dark. The Bogota flight is a little further south but arrives during the afternoon. Yesterday Jess left for Argentina; we boxed our bikes and bagged all our panniers. The Panama City Airport was stringent on checking everything, unlike other parts of the world. We had to jump through a few hoops and it took over two hours to finally get through security after checking in our bikes and bags. The total coast was about $500. The sailboat trips are about that for one person.

Jocelyn:

January 21, 2016

The father daughter cycling adventures team has made it to Panama and are currently just one bridge from South America — my sixth continent! We will ride along the Pacific most of the way to Santiago and cut across to Buenos Aires if we make it before it's too cold!

January 24, 2016

We have cycled across the Bridge of Americas! The police stopped us just before going up this bridge and were telling us we couldn't ride on a bicycle and that we needed to go by car. Well, I straight up asked the officer if he was going to arrest us, and he simply said, "*Bicicleta es peligroso* (dangerous)," so I took that as an okay to keep going. He eventually figured out this is what we do and that we know it's dangerous, but we're going to keep doing it. So, he let us pass with many warnings and we had an amazing ride up and down this beautiful bridge!

We met up with my neighbor and high school friend Pepper for dinner and drinks. How neat is it to see friends in other countries; it's awesome! I also timed our arrival with our cycling friend Jesse that we met in Tikal. We ended up hanging out with him for a bit and even watched the Super Bowl, and Jesse and I partied all night till the sunrise. Even though we explored all the Flor de Cana rums, I remember that crazy night and the adventures we fell into.

Colombia, South America

"When I see an adult on a bicycle, I do not despair for the future of the human race."

–H.G. Wells

Mike:

We arrived in Colombia with hotel and airport transportation reservations. We loaded our bike boxes and gear on two luggage carts. The outside doors were not wide enough for the boxes, so we wrestled the boxes off the carts and sideways through the door and then ran back inside the same door for our bags even though the doors had "Do Not Enter" on them. At this, the alarms sounded and soon we were surrounded by gun-toting Colombian guards as part of our 'welcoming committee.' We explained that we could not exit the doors with everything at the same time. After a few minutes of them chatting amongst themselves, they left us alone. Our driver was there and shaking his head as we put our boxes and bags back on the carts. It was a long drive to the district of Candelaria or old town Bogotá and our hotel. My bike box was open and my cable lock fell out somewhere, probably on the plane. Fortunately, we had zip-tied most everything onto the bikes. We had boxed our bikes outside our Panama City hotel in the sun and heat and the tape did not stick well.

After a welcoming beer of Budweiser from the hotel, we reassembled our bikes and left on a walking tour. There are some countries that are proud to serve American beers even though their own country produces much better beers. We didn't get far when we saw the Bogotá Beer Company on a corner. It was close to dinner so we shared a pizza and pitcher. The next few days were spent touring this beautiful city at over 8,000 feet in the Andes Mountains. Our walking tours explored all the cathedrals/churches and the talented artistic graffiti that this vast city is famous for. The architecture of the old houses, churches, and buildings has Spanish colonial, baroque, and art deco styles. It houses several universities, libraries, and museums. The people are friendly and the food delicious. We are enjoying a traditional Colombian diet minus the meat.

I also worked a few repairs to the electrical wiring on our dyno hubs. Finding parts is always a challenge. Since my fairly new rear tire failed, due to sharp rocks cutting into the sidewall, I bought a replacement. It was difficult explaining to the sales girl that I wanted a thick tire. So I drew a picture and she understood and brought out an excellent spare for only $5. On our last afternoon we boarded a mountainside tram that rose to 12,828 feet for a magnificent view of Bogotá.

Speaking of dollars, it is satisfying to have our expenses drop considerably. Costa Rica was expensive and Panama wasn't much lower. Colombia is back to much lower prices thanks to the *peso*.

After three days of discovering Bogota, it was time to continue south. We timed it right because it was Sunday and traffic seemed lighter, at least for a while. Before we knew it we were in the thick of traffic trying to negotiate partly on the road and partly on many bike paths of which there are over 200 miles. The afternoon was tedious until we were outside the city. We felt lucky that neither of us was hit by a car, truck, or bus, as many drivers seemed to try. But we managed to outmaneuver several close calls. Outside of town, we soon began climbing and the weather turned cold at around 9,000 feet, so we stopped and donned our cold weather gear. The road soon dropped to 6,000 feet and warm again as we rode through the wavering Andes Mountains. The Andes are the longest continental mountain range in the world. They are a continual range of highlands along the western coast of South America. This range is about 4,300 miles long, about 120 to 430 miles wide, and of an average height of about 13,000 feet. The Andes extend from north to south through seven South American countries: Venezuela, Colombia, Ecuador, Peru, Bolivia, Chile, and Argentina. Near dark, we arrived in the small town of Silvania where we found a fairly new hotel that cost less than $12. We ate in town and then settled into our room for the night. It was a good start on our route south toward Ecuador.

During the next several days we rode through the Andes, which sometimes dropped quickly into wild downhills and oven-like valleys to less than 1,000 feet. With the temperature at 120°F we did struggle after the cold at elevation. The heat is intense, and since we are at 4° north latitude it will get worse. After riding through the hot valleys it was back up over 8,000 feet. Some days it would be cloudy and rainy and the miles came easier, but soon the hills began again with increasing steepness and frequency. We cycled through the town of Campoalegre where we found a hostel owned by an older couple. When we were in our room with the senora, a bell rang at the front gate. The senor answered and it was the national *policia* asking if there were foreigners in this hostel. At that, the senora put her finger to her lips to silence us. The senor told the *policia*, "No," and he left. Apparently in this country as in China, foreigners are only allowed to stay in government approved hotels. I remember in China entering some hotels and being told, "No," for a room. Also in some villages, people shunned us. We were forced to camp 'illegally' at times because of this. The hostel owners asked us when we would leave in the morning. When we told them 7:00 A.M., they were pleased as the *policia* start making their rounds at 8:00 A.M. A neighbor must have called the *policia* when we entered the hostel.

Last night thunderstorms brought lots of rain. Since Colombia is in a serious drought, this is welcome. We like it too because we cycled in the overcast and much cooler weather. We were out of the hostel by 7:00 A.M. and soon started climbing through the mountains. By 4:00 P.M. we were entering the town of Garzon where we found a *hospedaje*, which is low-cost lodging and basically a step above camping. At $6 each, we rented two rooms. These lodgings are basic, with a toilet, sink, shower, bed, and the all-important fan. It is open around the roof, so critters like large lizards do get in. But they eat the mosquitoes so they are welcome.

We once again started early into the foothills of the Andes. The foothills are 3,000 feet and sometimes drop to sea level before rising again. Sometimes there are shoulders — but mostly not. We stopped in the town of Atamira to share a liter of coke along with a few cookies. While there, another touring cyclist, Chris from England, rode by, saw us, and stopped. He is cycling from Alaska to Argentina for a charity. Together we complained about the ups and downs and laughed about it. That's all one can do as it can be arduous.

We continued toward our goal of San Agustin by Sunday as we want to watch the Super Bowl. The day started cool and the rain continued during the long and sometimes steep climb to the town. It was a real struggle to climb about 3,000 feet in three miles and took us almost two hours. Since San Agustin sits at 9,300 feet, there was some huffing and puffing. I walked the first half mile but Jocelyn excels at this type of climbing. I soon enjoyed the climb as it was a continuous up instead of the last few days of up, down, up, down. Once in San Agustin we struggled through the busy Sunday afternoon streets before finding a *hospedaje* off the main road. After cleaning up we went in search of the Super Bowl but ended up finding a pizza parlor. When we returned we found the game on our room TV complete with English commercials and the game commentary in Spanish.

We decided to take a day off and investigate the World Heritage city of San Agustin, a site of pre-Colombian ruins, founded in 1752. The site contains the largest collection of religious monuments and megalithic sculptures in Latin America and is considered the world's largest necropolis. Entire families were entombed together with one site having 49 people. The tombs were covered by huge slabs of rock and carved statues to protect the tombs or as headstones. The remains of the many ancient cultural groups up to 6,000 years ago are scattered over an area of over thirty square miles.

We toured the surrounding tomb areas around San Agustin by horse, spending six hours riding to three sites of tombs with statues before ending up at the National Architectural Park at San Agustin. The area contains 508 statues collected from many countries and is the largest collection of pre-Columbian art in South America.

Most of the statues are not from their original placement, as throughout the years tombs were unearthed and robbed of any valuables. In fact, many of the statues were destroyed as some people thought there was gold hidden inside the pieces. A variety of the burial sites are original. The statues are real, not replica's, and are dated about 2,000 years ago. We say this because we have been places where the relics are replicas.

One interesting aspect of the statues is that it is believed that people from Asia, New Zealand, Africa, Egypt, and Mesopotamia traveled and settled in Colombia. Our park guide carried a notebook that compared the statues to those from different countries. On examination, one can see similar facial features and styles when comparing these statues to those found in Egypt, Africa, etc. It appears there is a definite connection. There are slant eyes, round eyes, large African adornments, different types of ears, and similar tools shown in hands.

Descending from San Agustin took less than ten minutes, a huge difference from the two-hour climb. We backtracked about fifteen miles before making a turn toward Macoa. Soon, we were climbing again in the rain. Around 4:30 P.M. we started looking for a place to camp just to get out of the heavy rain and cold. The road was quiet and we soon found a restaurant and talked about our options as we slowly stopped our shivering. We decided to hitch a ride to Macoa. A truck stopped at the restaurant and we asked the driver about a ride. He agreed since he was headed there too, so after a hot bowl of fish soup we were laying in the back of his truck filled with jackfruit and descending on a winding road. We both lay literally on a huge pile of large jackfruit. After one stop, the driver saw how much we were shivering and gave us each a blanket. The only thirty more miles to Macoa took almost two hours over the rocky road. At one point the driver motioned to us to hide through a Colombian military checkpoint. I kept wondering if the guards would see our bikes, but we got through. My head was filled with thoughts about our driver detouring to a guerilla camp for them to kidnap us; after all, it was dark and the jungle road bumpy and winding. We have been in many situations where our imaginations ran wild. I was ready with my Delorme SE two-way iridium satellite communicator as it has an SOS button to activate when in trouble anywhere in the world. Fortunately we didn't need that. We arrived at a produce market in Macoa after 9:00 P.M. and immediately saw a large well-lit hotel sign off in the distance. To find the hotel was an adventure in itself as we negotiated the streets and traffic in the dark. This day the riding was cold and wet and the truck ride was quite the adventure — for our minds. I don't think we will do that again and we broke our number one rule which is to not be out at night with our bikes. We finally retired to bed quite late after gorging ourselves from the hotel's limited snack selection, including cold beer. Adventure isn't just about the cycling but also what happens off the bikes too.

Leaving Macoa was quite the challenge during rush hour, hills, and one-way traffic on most streets. Jocelyn's excellent navigational skills did get us out and into one of our favorite jungle rides as we descended the Andes Mountains. We had a pleasing ride through the jungle, rivers, waterfalls, and particularly tropical plants and trees. We haven't seen the full sun for over a week, so that was a bonus. We are slowly making our way to Ecuador. We have heard that the crossing we are headed to, not the typical Pan-American Highway crossing, is not always open. This is another road less traveled .

The next day we were up for an early start, but the heavy rain changed our minds. There was little water drainage on the heavily-flooded road, so we decided to do a wait and see. After a few hours the road was clear enough to cycle on, but after an hour the road stopped and became rocks, gravel, and mud. Every once in a while there was a small paved section, but the road was mostly unpaved. It was almost as though a company was given a certain amount to pave this road and did pave a mile here and a mile there but pocketed the rest. We deflated our tires to 40psi to help us cycle over the sometimes large rocks. Whenever we stopped, drivers would stop and ask if we were okay. We got a few offers for rides but politely declined. We continued riding and walking until the next town. This town did not have power like most as we headed into 'No man's land' commonly known as 'The frontier'. We found a room for $5 and settled down for a long night of reading.

Jocelyn:

January 28, 2016

We are here in Colombia! Our 33rd country on this around the world bike tour starting in South America. I certainly picked the best possible hotel in La Candelaria, the historic downtown of Bogota, Colombia. It happens to be right down the street from this brewery, Bogota Beer Company, so excuse me while I drink an IPA. This part of the city has artwork the style of graffiti all over the city. Beautiful. From its endless display of artistic freedom, to the old colonial mansions and bustling industrial sections, Bogota has quickly become one of my favorite cities! Did I mention over 300km of bike paths cross the city?! Oh yeah, and local brew pubs line the streets as well!

February 5, 2016

We've been riding strong since we left Bogota! Colombia is this ultra-unique country. The people are super friendly and the drivers are absolutely the kindest we've ever encountered, and the food is so *"tipico"* (too much meat for us.) It's rained the last two nights, which has cooled us down during the day and is helping reverse their major drought situation. The Andes Mountains are always in sight and they make me anxious! But we finally got to do some road climbing today and I am super stoked! Oh, and we've changed our route again, hehe, as we will try to drop straight into Ecuador after visiting historic San Agustín!

February 9, 2016

On our break day in San Agustin, we thought a five hour horseback ride throughout the mountainside would be fun! And it so was! Even though it rained the entire time, my horse was strong and would gallop away with my giggles! We rode to three sites with statues/carvings dating back 2,000 or more years. This park is an archeological site that is a massive place that was well thought out. Our guide seemed to think that back when Atlantis was in the middle between America and Africa people from all over the world traveled here to bury their loved ones. I quickly became interested in this concept, simply because the style of statues ranged between an Egyptian to an Asian tomb. There were over 500 statues that have been found in this region along the mountainside with more tombs. The number of tombs that have been excavated is unclear, because, unfortunately, many were raided for the wealth buried with the people.

Ecuador

"Life is like riding a bicycle. To keep your balance, you must keep moving."

–Albert Einstein

Mike:

After two more days over rocky unpaved roads we found a paved road a few miles from the border. The border was a delight as both Colombia and Ecuador Immigration was 1½ miles past the border in the same office. We checked out of Colombia and into Ecuador at the next line. It was a quiet border crossing and we were the only ones in the office.

Cycling the frontier area of Ecuador was a stark contrast to that frontier area of Colombia as the road was paved and the homes more modern. We stopped in the city of Lago Agrio, found a hotel, and were surprised that once again the American dollar is the currency of Ecuador. That makes three countries now that uses the dollar: El Salvador, Panama, and Ecuador. Now that we have been in the two most popular American tourist countries of Costa Rica and Panama, we believe that those countries north and south, Nicaragua and Colombia, have so much more to offer. The prices are way cheaper, the countries beautiful, along with friendly people.

We took the day off to rest and perform more bike repairs from the last week of mostly off-road cycling. Several components were loose and a few needed mending with our abundant supply of zip-ties. My brother-in-law Jim suggested Teflon pipe tape for the continuing loose headset nuts on Jocelyn's bike, so we walked through town and actually found a roll in a small hardware store. Back in Colombia we had purchased a large heavy crescent wrench, as we could not find a single wrench at the exact size that we used to tighten the headset's two nuts every few days. I wrapped the threads in this Teflon tape and tightened the nuts. This ended up doing the trick, and we never had to tighten again. Great idea — thanks Jim!

We headed west toward Quito but decided not to visit the enormous city and instead turned south through the Andes. Our climbing in the Ecuadorian Andes was slow and would take us all day to get 24 miles. We crossed the equator from the northern to the southern hemisphere. The official name of Ecuador — The Republic of Ecuador — literally translates to 'Republic of The Equator'. Its capital city of Quito lies smack in the middle of the imaginary line. The equator was discovered and mapped by a French geodesic expedition team in 1736.

Riding the Andes Mountains in Ecuador.

With frequent recurring hard rain it was a tough day. We were looking for a dry place to camp when around one corner appeared a small mountain village. For some reason there were three hotels in the one-street town. On further inspection two were closed, but we acquired a $10 room in the other. Jocelyn also cooked another delicious dinner.

Even though we were wearing our so-called waterproof jackets, they were soaked through and not from sweat. We wonder if there are any totally rainproof jackets besides the heavy yellow ones. I'm glad to say that our Outdoor Research waterproof pants worked great. I believe what we have are soft-shell jackets, although both were advertised as totally waterproof and breathable. A hard-shell jacket would shed the water better but not be as breathable. We have noticed that the Spanish we used in Mexico and Central America is not always understood here in Colombia. We are adapting to the new lingo.

It rained all night. Jocelyn read that it is now the rainy season in the Andes. On a trip like this you just go with the flow and can't always cycle a country in their best season, so we once again donned our rain gear and cycled off. Soon, a giant cloud descended on us and it rained hard, dropping the visibility to around twenty feet. It was difficult because the water was flooding down the road. We descended for many miles and my brakes gave out. I was looking for an uphill place to ride on just to stop. One of my nightmares is a fast downhill on a water-filled road — and this was it. My guide and mechanic, Jocelyn, tightened the cables and we continued. It was scary though. Near the bottom there was a roadside cafe where we gobbled down a few bowls of hot chicken soup after removing the chicken heads and feet. We met a bicycle racer from Quito who introduced himself and spoke good English. Since we were going the same way he offered us a ride in his truck to get us off the dangerous wet road. He enjoyed practicing his English and we learned much about Ecuador. An hour later he dropped us off at the intersection to our next town of Baeza. He had invited us to his family home in Quito, but we declined as we try to avoid large cities and are more interested in the old Spanish southern colonial city of Cuenca. We spend our days cycling soaked to the bone and evenings trying to dry everything for the next day. Just a week ago we were riding in 120°F heat and now 50°F wet. The golden rule is: Always have one dry set of clothes for night and don the wet ones during the day.

We had an early start from Baeza as it was not raining. After a few hours of climbing to 8,500 feet the rain started hard and we continued in the low visibility. Our goal for the day was Tena, about 48 miles away. We didn't think we could make it until we had a long, fast descent of almost 5,000 feet. Once that was done, the sun kind of came out and we were once again in the ups and downs but able to solar dry with good visibility. We pushed on until late and settled into a hostel just north of Tena. It was a good, hard, and wet day of cycling.

We crossed a river where Jocelyn decided she would like to fly fish. So we hung out by the river and had fun doing something different. By 11:00 A.M. we hadn't had breakfast yet and cycled into the tourist adventure town of Tena, which boasts all kinds of activities and 37 hostels. While looking for a breakfast/lunch spot we spotted a hostel and decided to take a break. As exhausted and sore as we were it was an easy decision. We walked through town, ate lunch at a Mexican place, and then shopped in the super *mercado* (supermarket).

Back at the hostel, we stripped our bikes, cleaned our rims of dirt and brake residue, and adjusted our brakes. I ended up replacing my rear brake pads again. We also enjoyed the pool. Our trip is a real beating on the bikes and us. It's not the climbing but the fast downhills in heavy rain and almost no visibility.

The morning brought a rare clear sky as we cycled out of Tena. We were cruising along at 2,000 feet with lots of ups and downs, but the scenery and wild sounds of the jungle were enticing. We are tired of being chased by dogs, in fact, dozens each day. Many times we have to stop and threaten them with a water bottle to stop the chase. So far that approach is still working. After 18,000 miles, I have only been bitten once in Azerbaijan as we cycled to Iran. I would say that we have been chased by over a thousand dogs. But it is heartening to observe some dogs just standing and watching us as we pedal by. Why most dogs get so agitated is lost on us.

Riding through a small town, we saw a sign for a *hospedaje* advertising camping. We turned off-road for about a mile. When we arrived, we were swarmed by mosquitoes so we decided to rent a cabin instead of camping. We are now in the area known as Amazonia. While the Amazon River is far to the east of us over the Andes, this area is called Amazonia as it is the beginning of the Amazon influence. We watched in fascination at the assortment of birds and heard so many different animal sounds. There were insects we have never seen before. The jungle is alive, and we feel fortunate to be a part of it. This was our first day in two weeks without rain!

Our goal of the Spanish colonial town of Cuenca would take several more days of climbing. Before that, we cycled over eight hours to make it to the adventure town of Baños, known as the 'Gateway to the Amazon' as it is the last big city still located in the mountains before reaching the jungle and other towns that are located in the Amazon River basin.

Baños, at an elevation of 6,000 feet, is one of the most popular tourist attractions in Ecuador due to its amazing natural beauty and its plethora of available adventure sports.

After a pancake breakfast at our hostel we once again started the morning in rain. It was a long day of climbing from 6,000 feet to over 9,000 feet over a steady forty miles. None of it was steep but instead was a gradual ascent. The rain continued all day, and once again we were soaked and cold. While riding through the town of Riobamba we found another hostel, and next door was an excellent Chinese restaurant where we each indulged in a large hot bowl of vegetable soup. Across the street was an excellent bakery where we purchased fresh croissants for breakfast along with chocolate cake and a cookie for dessert. We rode around the backside of Volcan Tungurahua hoping to see the always snow covered peak. But due to heavy clouds and rain we only had an occasional glimpse of the side with recent lava flows.

Our objective for the day was to meet up with the Pan-American Highway. We have cycled little on this highway, but it is the only road that heads south over the top of the Andes to Cuenca. We spent most of the day winding through canyons to find it. The best part of the day was that the sun was out for a few hours and it felt great.

This part of Ecuador is traditional in the way people dress and live. The women wear brimmed bowler hats colored to mark their ethnicity. Farming is king here and we were surprised how organized it is. After another eight hours on the bikes and 44 miles we made it to the town of Guamote where it was market day. We had a crazy time trying to navigate through the crowds while walking our bikes. We found Chuza Longa Home, moved our bikes inside, and explored this colorful town. Market day here reminds us of the market days in Asia. Everything imaginable is on the street for sale. We were fascinated by the trading of live and dead animals. Chicken feet were popular as people ate them and then dropped the remains on the ground. As we walked, there was a definite crunch. Jocelyn bought a cool colorful belt. Our pleasant and friendly homestay owner cooked vegetable soup for dinner and this morning a good breakfast was included.

We left Guamote on a beautiful sunny morning and pushed on through the Andes at 10,000 feet. We did climb to over 12,000 feet before descending to 8,000 and climbing back up. The afternoon rain caught us for many hours, but this area of the Pan-American Highway is a good road with wide shoulders, ample drainage, and surprisingly little traffic. We surprised ourselves and made it to the city of Canar, which is only 42 miles from our next goal of the Spanish colonial city of Cuenca. We stopped for lunch at a roadside stand where there were pigs cooking on a spit. We each had a delicious pork plate along with maize bread. While there, we struck up a conversation with Luis who lives here two months of the year and owns a masonry business on Long Island, New York the rest of the year. Luis is from Ecuador but moved to the U.S. many years ago to start his business. He was eating lunch with two friends and invited us for a local tour and a night at his home, a few miles up the road. We loaded our bikes in his truck and were given a tour of all the local historical spots in Azogues and Biblian before being driven to his beautiful home in the hills overlooking a valley. We had a good time with him and his friends and a good sleep in his huge comfortable house. He did invite us to his home on Long Island, N.Y., but we never heard from him again.

We left Luis' home, returned to the Pan-American Highway, and were soon in Cuenca where we found an enjoyable hostel about a ten minute walk from old town Cuenca. The highway became busy with two lanes each way and lots of bikers out for a Sunday ride. I immediately missed the simple Ecuadorian villages in the high Andes we have traveled through as there is a charm to this old style of living. But it is also fun to be back in civilization and enjoy a somewhat 'easier' life — whatever easier means.

After checking in and locking our bikes in a storage area, we spent the afternoon walking around old town Cuenca. There are cathedrals/churches everywhere you look. We tried to enter these churches but only found one open, and it is Sunday! On our walk back to the hostel we stopped in a *mercado* and bought lots of food as the hostel has a kitchen and we intend to spend three nights here. We spent two days exploring Cuenca. The city of Cuenca, at 8,000 feet, is a World Heritage Trust site due to its many historical buildings, stunning architecture, and the origins in the local caves of the first inhabitants that goes back to the year 8060 BC. They were hunters and nomads, following the animals and seasons. The Spanish settlement of Cuenca was founded in 1557 and named Cuenca after a similar town in Spain. Cuenca's population and importance grew steadily during the colonial era. Thanks to Andee for suggesting we stop here. A few weeks ago she saw an article about Cuenca in the newspaper.

While in Cuenca we needed to decide to enter Peru on the coast or in the Andes. We have talked with many people concerning this and also read many biking blogs about the safest way. The coastal area is isolated and conducive to robberies. Peru is an extremely poor country, so crime on tourists is high. After reading about so many touring cyclists taking the coastal route and having a bad experience we decided on the inland route over the Andes Mountains. Crime is also high there but it does seem safer. We have mixed emotions about bicycling through Peru. Obviously we need to be aware of others in the isolated areas. We have not had any negative incidents in Latin America. I was concerned about Mexico and the poor countries of Guatemala, Honduras, and El Salvador, but we were fine through it all. It's all a matter of being aware of your surroundings. So far on our world trip we have not let the media or others determine our route. But at this point we decided to stay away from the coast. I remember when we were on our way to Iran people thought we were nuts. Iran turned out to be one of our favorite countries, and we still email message with our Iranian friends.

We cycled to the town of Vilcabamba located in the "Valley of Longevity". We had no idea what kind of town it was and were surprised to see and talk with many Americans and Europeans who have lived here for decades because of the excellent soil and atmosphere for farming. We found another hostel, and after our usual cleanup we explored this pretty town full of all different types of people. This area has been referred to as the 'Playground of the Inca' which refers to its historic use as a retreat for Inca royalty. Located in a historical and scenic valley, it is a common destination for tourists, in part because it is widely believed that its inhabitants grow to an old age.

The Andes Mountains are beautiful to cycle through, but the rain does make it more challenging. It seems like it rains all morning or afternoon and all in-between. It also rains starting about 11:00 P.M. and then stops at sunrise and pauses for a few hours. Many sections of this road, Ecuador 682, are unpaved and quite muddy, but once again the vistas are incredible and well worth the effort. Many people who follow Jocelyn on Facebook ask why we are here now since it is the rainy season. We are here now because we are on a continuous trip south. "It is what it is," as the old saying goes. Raining or not, the Andes are amazing and we thrive on being off the beaten path. While at the South Pole I have read many books about the early exploration of South America along with the history of the Incas. My latest read, *Lost City of the Incas* by Hiram Bingham is about how Bingham in 1911 walked and rode by horse the Andes Mountains while searching for the lost ancient capital of the Incas, Machu Picchu. In the book he writes, *"It was the month of February. Unfortunately we knew nothing of the usual weather in the Central Andes during the so-called summer months. As a matter of fact, February is the very worst month in which to explore the highlands where the Incas flourished. The rain starts in November and continues well into April."* This is the same time we cycled through the Andes, and we were also unaware of this rainy season.

The next several days were difficult. The paved road disappeared and was replaced by a single lane with flowing mud. We were actually faster than most vehicles! The rain continued heavy and we cycled/walked by many mudslides. We found a hotel after dark in Zumba, Ecuador about eighteen miles from the Peru border. After this, it was another hard day to the border.

Jocelyn:

February 16, 2016

We have cycled to the equator in Ecuador! The past week or so has been tough with rain on and off the entire day. There have been large road climbs with a lot of the time on rocks, but we are freaking doing it, y'all! We're in the most gorgeous mountains traveling through indigenous villages. The lush greenery wraps our stinky, wrinkly, wet bodies, while the unique birds call to us as we inch up the hill, and little, black, furry monkeys jump from tree to tree with their dark curious eyes. My view consists of a powerful waterfall and the ability to trace the road along the mountainside in the Andes. I hope this road takes us closer to this "bad boy" waterfall tomorrow!

February 25, 2016

This was a solid, leisurely 11,000 foot climb out of Riobamba with sunshine and smiles and a donkey. The small farming villages lie around like puzzles on the sides of the Andes Mountains. We arrived around lunchtime in Guamote and it was rather busy, so we decided to wander inside the cobblestone town. To our surprise, the streets were lined with vendors selling everything you can possibly imagine. Hundreds of native villagers with their colorful traditional clothing wandered the busy, dirty streets. We walked our bikes around stunned. Though we've visited many markets, this one was by far one of the most alive, interesting, and hectic madness we've ever walked through.

February 28, 2016

Yesterday I found out about the police corruption first hand when during lunch a group of guys sat down near us and one starts telling us he lives in New York. We hit it off, so he invites us to his home in the hills. But first they take us around their town, all the while drinking beer. The driver is on the police force and we stopped at the station. He gave them $20 so that he could take off work and hang with the Americans. I got to wear the *policia* vest all day. We got stopped by some police as a joke, the officer driving our truck gives them beers and all is good. We arrive at Luis' beautiful house. We swap stories, but the police officer's stories were the most intense and frightening of them all . . . the end.

Peru

"Adopt the pace of Nature. Her secret is patience."
–Ralph Waldo Emerson

Mike:

We finally made it to the Ecuador/Peru border after several exhausting days. Ecuador was easy to exit, and checking into Peru was easy too at this river crossing called La Balsa. In fact, this crossing is known as 'the quiet crossing' as it is off the beaten path. The only people present were the border guards, a few people working in a small restaurant, and two taxis. After lunch we decided to take a taxi the thirty miles to San Ignacio, the first town. Since the taxis were small, we hired two. We found a questionable hostel with tiny rooms and saw Patrick from England who we had met several days ago in Vilcabamba. We met Patrick and his friend at a restaurant that evening along with breakfast the next day. The hostel was tiny and noisy, so we found another *hospedaje* that was much more open and comfortable as we were still tired and needed a break. Unfortunately the location of this one proved distressing. At midnight the local discos lit up with loud music followed by the 'chicken killing' at 2:00 A.M. We had noticed earlier that the building across the street from our window was full of chickens, but it was no big thing until 2:00 A.M. when two women arrived to slaughter them. At that time I heard what appeared to be a small child crying, but it was chicken after chicken being killed by what sounded like a dunking in scalding water. The chickens actually cried, and I have never heard that noise before. Each one lasted about 3 seconds before succumbing, and all the others cried with them. It seemed like an inhumane way of killing chickens. I know we all eat them, but it kept me awake all night and I don't know if I can eat another chicken. The crying kept me awake the rest of the night. Soon, the awful smell of dead chickens wafted to our window. Fortunately it started raining hard around 3:00 A.M. and that took most of the smell away.

Peru Achieved!

We left San Ignacio in the rain. We waited for it to stop but it never did. Our goal for the day was Jaen, and we accomplished that because the trip was along a somewhat flat river valley. We haven't had such a flat route for months. We arrived in Jaen near dark, found a hotel, and ate vegetarian Chinese across the street.

The Andes Mountains have been challenging in the rainy season as we have cycled from Colombia, Ecuador, and now the Peruvian Andes. But enough was enough and we are exhausted from the rain, so we will bus to the coast of Peru and see what adventure awaits us there. The last two months being soaked in the rain every day was hard and we crave to be dry. So far, in Peru, we have found friendly people, but the country is lacking in services of all kinds. There does not appear to be any kind of traffic laws as the drivers are everywhere and anywhere on the roads, passing on shoulders sometimes three at a time. There is absolutely no respect for pedestrians, and you take your life in your hands when attempting to cross the street. So far, in our trip, the Croatian drivers have been the worst. The Peruvians are right up there with Azerbaijan not far behind.

We walked to a bus station in Jaen to inquire about a bus ride to Chiclayo on the Peruvian coast. All four of the bus lines were not operating on that route due to the heavy rain and rock slides over the Andes. We were told, "No pass Chiclayo." They told us that another station may have a bus driving that route. We jumped into a moto taxi to the other station where there were eight bus companies. We went to one after another hearing, "No pass," until the eighth one said, "*Si.*" That bus was scheduled to leave at 10:00 A.M. — in forty minutes, so we rushed back to the hotel, loaded the bikes, and returned to the station. At 10:15 when the bus had not yet arrived, we were told 10:30. At that time we were told 11:00 and then 11:30. Well, at noon it did arrive and we loaded our bikes and gear, which was an adventure of jumping through hoops to get it done without damaging the bikes. Fortunately we have only done this a few times. We settled into our seats for the long 180-mile, seven-hour ride to the coast. None of the other bus companies were taking a chance on this trip except for the one we were on. But if you look at the bus company name, 'Towes Angel Divine' then it all makes sense. We were on a 'Jesus' bus — so of course we will get though safely! As it was, we had short stops while waiting to pass one lane areas that were covered in landslides. The rain was grueling through the pass and the driver stopped several times, but we made it safely. We arrived after dark, and through Jocelyn's excellent navigating she routed us to an area of many hostels where we settled in for the night.

The following day we rode through a coastal desert in the fabulous blue sky and heat for most of the day before finding another hostel in the late afternoon. We had lots of clothes to sink wash, and the rooftop had clotheslines for drying. This area has been notorious for touring cyclists robberies. We keep to the main road, meaning we are back on the Pan-American Highway and find a place well before dark. We decided that we would not camp unless there was no other choice.

We started early as we knew we were in for a long desert crossing. It turned out to be about 45 miles in 100°F heat, and we almost ran out of water even though we were well stocked before leaving the last town. We were also short on food and munched on walnuts through the ride. Once we were across, we stopped at the first market for a warm PowerAde and beer. It is difficult to find cold drinks even though there are large unpowered coolers everywhere. Peru is a poor country and power in rural areas is at a minimum. Continuing down the road we passed a fruit stand and scarfed down a watermelon and then continued to the first restaurant for a delicious broccoli tortilla. We finally left there at 6:00 P.M. and cycled to a hostel in the next town. Last night I went out to search for two cold beers, which turned out to be quite the challenge. I did find two, returned to our hostel, and relaxed with two beers after a challenging day in the desert. After that, Jocelyn and I decided to search for ice cream. The beer bottles were returnable, so I returned them to the bar where I purchased them. Upon my return, the huge Samoan-looking bartender asked where I was from. When I replied Estados Unidos (United States), he closed his eyes and concentrated for several moments while his three little kids hung on to him. He finally opened his eyes and blurted out in English, "Why are you here?" It took so much concentration to say those four words in English. His kids looked up at him and wondered what he'd said. I answered in Spanish and he was so relieved. Sometimes it is so hard and painful to communicate.

We cycled all day along a rocky and sandy road to reach the popular tourist beach of Huanchaco. At one point we split up, with Jocelyn forging ahead on the sandy road while I 'went on strike' thinking to myself, *Enough is enough!* I sat on the road feeling depressed and beaten. I kept watching Jocelyn until she was out of sight. It took a lot of soul searching to stand up and continue. We have come this far together and we must not separate. It took all I had to push my bike several more miles through the sand until the beach town where Jocelyn was patiently waiting. We spent an extra day in Huanchaco to surf and spend an afternoon resting on the beach.

After a long day on the Pan-American Highway we ate at a truck stop, and by 11:00 P.M. that night I was either throwing up or sitting on the toilet. We were both feeling rather poorly after a brief breakfast as I could only eat a few small pieces of bread. After two hours of lying in bed, we knew we could not make the sixty miles to the next town. Camping in the blowing desert sands did not seem appealing. The headwinds have been strong and the number and steepness of the hills increasing as we get closer to Lima, still about 180 miles away. We left the hostel and cycled to another one on the other side of town. That's as far as we made it. To our surprise this one had air conditioning, our first in months. After a visit to a pharmacy for an electrolytic drink, we ate soup and spent the afternoon in bed.

After a good rest we started early and spent ten hours on the bike just barely getting to the next town right after dark. It was a typical Peruvian desert day . . . hot, with headwinds and lots of hills. We are well prepared with ten liters of water per day, and sometimes it seems like such a hard battle against the wind. But you never know what is around the next sand dune. Today we were surprised with many small, pretty, deserted ocean coves.

The first thing we immediately noticed in coastal Peru is the revolting amount of roadside trash. It is everywhere — in the towns and deserts. The refuse piles begin the closer you get to a town, somewhat diminishes in town, and reappears after. The deserts are Peruvian dumping grounds. We did not see this in the Andes.

This morning I was feeling poorly again, but we pressed on with a relatively flat day. We were chased by a dog with no hind legs! Yes, this dog powered itself with his front legs with its rump dragging in the sand barking all the way. He probably lost his rear legs chasing a car.

After more desert riding we arrived in Ventanilla where we had a decision to continue on the Pan-American and head straight into the middle of Lima or take the coastal route beside the port and airport. There was a lot of traffic on the Pan-American, more than usual, so we rode the coastal route. At that, it was still another four hours to the old-town district of Lima where we settled in a *hospedaje*. We had heard that there were family friends staying at a hotel near us. We walked to this hotel and saw them through the window talking on the phone. We walked in to see Trish and her son Colin. What's funny is that Trish was talking with my wife Andee on the phone! They treated us to an excellent meal in a nearby restaurant, and they flew the next day to Cuzco and Machu Picchu. We spent two days in Lima and explored the old historical district including the Cathedral of Lima where the remains of Francisco Pizarro are interred. Pizarro was a Spanish conquistador who led an expedition that caused the fall of the Inca Empire. The cathedral is filled with beautiful art, and next door are museums that we also toured. Jocelyn had been following a touring cyclist, Antii, from Finland for a few years now. In fact, in 2014 we were in Kyrgyzstan at the same time he was. Through messaging, we found out that he was at another hostel down the street. We met him for breakfast the next day before he continued north. He eventually made it to the U.S. when we were still in South America, and he stayed at our house in Florida.

We left Lima and had two sixty-mile days thanks to the wind. The rude Peruvian drivers continue to bother me as they just don't care about pedestrians, bicycles, or anyone in their way. They would just as soon run you over. Lima is crazy just trying to cross a street even within a crosswalk and with a green light. It doesn't matter, as young and old often run across a street. It is sad and disgusting to see an elderly person run across the street with a green walk sign. The shoulder is used as a passing lane for both ways! We are always observant, because at any time a car may ride up to our rear honking and have one coming head on also honking. It is so senseless and frustrating.

Machu Picchu was built in 1450 and then abandoned in 1540 when the Spanish Conquistadors were thought to be looking for it.

Machu Picchu, the ancient Incan citadel set high in the Andes Mountains of Peru.

Jocelyn with a small wild llama.

A banner moment for the father and daughter duo.

We continued riding south in the heavily increasing traffic with a shoulder of potholes and dirt. While riding the white line I was almost hit twice. This part of Peru is nerve whacking during Easter week with much more traffic than usual with families on holiday and traveling. After a second close call I told Jocelyn, "At the next town let's find the bus station." After another fifteen miles we rode into the town of Pisco, and I was almost hit head-on by a car passing onto my shoulder. We found the bus station and Jocelyn purchased tickets to the next city. While unloading our bikes, someone ran up and stole my Arkle 'purse' bag off my bike. It happened so fast and we were never more than two feet from our bags. Security saw a man jump onto the Lima-bound bus. We immediately called for the police who arrived fifteen minutes later. We thought they could call ahead and catch the guy on the bus, but that's not how things work here. I immediately offered a large reward of many months typical Peruvian salary. Jocelyn left with two policemen and we thought they were going to chase the Lima bus down to get our bag, but she ended up going to the police station where they wrote down her passport number on a piece of paper. After that, we talked with the police for another hour. Finally, after nothing was done, we checked into a *hospedaje* next door and let the bus attendant who spoke a little English and the police know where we were in case the bag was recovered. We figured it was a long shot for the recovery, and once we leave here it will be gone forever.

Both of my cameras (still and video) were in this bag, along with my IPod, Kindle, and lots of other stuff. All of the videos I took in Colombia, Ecuador, and Peru are gone as they were not backed up on my laptop. I had the videos backed up on a USB drive, but that was in the bag too, which was pretty stupid on my part. Unfortunately we have no Andes Mountains videos. I lost my camera along with a camera SD card that stored all my pictures. But these files were on my laptop. Fortunately I carry my passport on my person or it would have turned into a big mess. No cash was stored in that bag either as we have kept two thousand dollars hidden in bags and inside the bikes. Each locked seat post contained five $100 bills rolled up inside the tube. The moral of the story, "Don't put all your eggs in one basket." This is an old but true saying. We were warned about cyclists' robberies on the Peruvian coast, and we are now an added statistic. I still kick myself for this blunder on my part, but we did learn.

It's odd how in the last several days I had been thinking about how much I don't like Peru or the people due to the trash and thoughtless drivers. I'm sure I am in the minority of touring cyclists on this subject. Peru is one of my least favorite countries. Bulgaria is another one. Jocelyn summed it up quite well after the incident when she said, "We still have our health, and maybe the thief has a family that will benefit from this."

It is only stuff, along with a few mementos from my late mom and dad that I have been carrying. These items from my parents will be greatly missed. There wasn't a day that went by, until the end of our ride, where I didn't look down at my handlebar and think about my parents' memories that were no longer attached. I had always removed those and my bike computer for safe keeping the few times we took a bus or train ride.

We bused the 112 miles from Pisco to Nazca to avoid the Easter traffic and lick our wounds from the robbery. We were so relieved to get out of Pisco. I guess that in the last almost 20,000 miles we were lucky there were only two bad things that happened to us. Bicycling around the world sounds glamorous, but crap does happen. It's a tough part of life but still a rewarding journey that we will not quit.

Jocelyn had read about the town of Nazca and the Nazca Indians and their ancient 2,000 year old geoglyphs. These 'lines' are in various animal forms and must be viewed by aircraft from above 1,200 feet. Yesterday afternoon we made the awesome flight to view this ancient culture and history.

Jocelyn:

The following is Jocelyn's excellent description:

In the desert of Southern Peru lies one of mankind's historical mysteries. The Nazca Lines, geoglyphs etched into desert sand, were constructed for religious ceremonies to pray for water and life/fertility. The Nazca Lines are possibly open air temples. The more famous lines portray familiar creatures, but there are thousands of geometric lines that can be seen throughout the valley. The Nazca people were a civilization dating roughly from 100 B.C. to 700 A.D. For eight hundred years they survived by constructing underground aqueducts that are still in use today. They lived in the harshest and driest of conditions, which their bodies adapted to. They were small people who rarely ate meat and didn't need much water. The people collapsed and faded from history possibly from an Inca takeover. They believed in human sacrifices, and many of the sacrifices were babies that had no sin, ultimately "pure". We flew over the most famous of the Nazca Lines yesterday. It was magnificent to see how large these images are and how precise the geometric shapes are. They were skilled and focused people. We both were air sick from the flight because of the abrupt left and right turning movements. After that, we visited the

Cementerios de Chauchilla, where a specific bird that buries its home into the sand helped archeologists find this enormous cemetery in the 1920s. Many grave raiders stole buried relics and moved the bodies, but it was finally protected by Peruvian law in 1997. The mummies are so well preserved because of the dry desert and the process the Nazca used before burial. The bodies were clothed in cotton and painted with resin. Most of the bodies found were identified as shamans who acted as a medium between the visible world and an invisible spirit world and practiced magic for healing purposes. They are jaw dropping to see, cross legged, facing the sunrise, and most were sacrifices. One interesting point is they have a red-toned hair color and wore their hair in dreadlocks. It was a bit creepy to walk around and see all these mummies within arm distance. But I highly recommend making the visit if you are traveling in Peru!

Mike:

Two riding days later we were back at the beach to once again find the strong headwinds that have entertained us for 21 days now. Along the way we have been sandblasted in the heat while being physically and mentally challenged. Peru has miles of unspoiled scenic beaches with no condos as in our home state of Florida. We look in awe of all the unridden lefts and rights (surf talk for waves). The towns are spaced far apart, so it is either camping behind a dune or wall or a small occasional *hospedaje*.

Yesterday we were barely making headway in the afternoon when a car carrier truck stopped ahead of us. He said that the upcoming 24 miles is a dangerous climbing coastal road for bicyclists as there is no shoulder along the narrow road. He offered to load our bikes on his truck for this section. We said okay as we were tired of the strong wind. I was in shock as we drove the high shoulderless road. In fact, there was only an occasional guard rail when the road was wide enough. Riding south on this road is dangerous as one strong gust of wind or from a passing truck would easily put you over the side to fall several hundred feet to the ocean. It was frightening just watching this from the cab as he maneuvered when oncoming trucks were sometimes just inches from us and we just inches from the side. When this section was over, he stopped and dropped us off.

Despite the wind, we made good time through the terrain of small hills while spending the entire day riding. Several days later we completed our ride to Arequipa, Peru after two weeks and 720 miles from Lima. Founded in 1540, Arequipa is the colonial-era capital of Peru's Arequipa Region. Framed by three volcanoes, it's filled with baroque buildings constructed from sillar, a white volcanic stone. Its historic center is anchored by the Plaza de Armas, a stately main square flanked on its north by the 17th-century neoclassical Basilica Cathedral, which houses a museum displaying religious objects and artwork. At 7,700 feet it was one of our easier climbs since it was over a three-day period. We dropped down into many canyons, sometimes several thousand feet deep, rode across the canyon, and then climbed out on the other side.

Our bikes had a well-deserved two week rest while we traveled to explore Machu Picchu and then to Hawaii for my niece Mariah and her fiancé Andy's wedding. Jocelyn had found a warmshowers host in Arequipa, Peru where we cycled to and stored our bikes. We boarded a sleeper bus for the ten-hour winding road up the Andes Mountains to the city of Cuzco. We arrived at 7:00 A.M. and were met by a van driver for a two hour ride to Ollantaytambo. From there we boarded the Inca Train for an almost two-hour ride through the stunning Andes to the small town of Aguas Calientes, which is about two miles from Machu Picchu Park. Jocelyn had booked us a room at Hostel Inka Wonder. We made reservations for the early morning bus ride to Machu Picchu.

We arrived at Machu Picchu Park at 6:15 A.M. It had rained all night and was still raining. The Andes rainy season is November through March and is almost over. A few months ago we bicycled into the Andes while in Colombia, entered Ecuador in Amazonia, cycled up to the Andes through the rest of Ecuador, and then entered Peru in the Andes. After two months of constant rain we went to the desert coast of Peru to dry out. Now we are back in the Andes by bus and it is still raining every day.

The clouds would sometimes lift and give us a good view of the ancient city for a few minutes. At 9:00 A.M. we began our three-hour round-trip hike to the summit of Mountain Machu Picchu. Machu Picchu translates to 'Old Mountain' from the Inca language. It was a difficult hike from 5,600 feet to just over 10,000 feet in the rain and cold. We were hoping it would clear at some point, but it never did. Back at the bottom it was still raining hard and we considered leaving but held back for another hour in the hope that the clouds would lift. They did about fifty minutes later. Seeing Machu Picchu as we did was breathtaking, spiritual, and difficult to put into words. Those who have seen it know what I mean. On this cycle tour we have discovered the Aztecs in Mexico, the Mayans in Central America, and now the Incas in Peru. The ruins of all these ancient civilizations have been humbling to experience.

Machu Picchu was founded in 1450 and abandoned in 1540 when the Incas heard that the Spanish had invaded Cuzco. They descended from Macho Picchu to the Urubamba River far below and followed it to Amazonia where they disappeared. Machu Picchu is a long process to visit with transportation and permits. It was a grand day to experience one of the most awesome historical and architectural sites in the world.

We bused back to Cuzco and spent a few days exploring this striking colonial city before our flight to Hawaii. The city sits in a large valley in the Andes at over 11,000 feet. Inside the valley are many hills on which the city was developed. We found a hostel a block from the central plaza and many wonderful old Spanish colonial streets and alleys to explore. Cuzco was the historic capital of the Inca Empire from the 13th into the 16th century until the Spanish conquest in 1533. Every day we traveled a different walking route to see where we ended up. We are living history in the many churches, cathedrals, museums, and small passageways — some with Arab influence. The many varieties of food makes the day delicious.

Jocelyn set off on a fifteen-hour trip to explore Vinicunca, also known as the Rainbow Mountains. This area is multi-mineral rich terrain and thus provides for extreme soil colors. The trek entailed a three-hour van ride, four hours of hiking to over 17,000 feet, breakfast and lunch, and a long trip back to Cuzco. She called it her favorite hike of all times. I spent the day walking the streets, exploring more churches and museums, and a little bit of shopping.

The next day we flew from Cuzco to Lima, to Los Angeles, and then to Hawaii for a total of 29 hours of air and layover time. It was a family reunion as my son Cary, sister Tish, brother-in-law Jim, niece Makani and her fiancé Jamie, and cousin Mary Jane gathered for the wedding of my niece, Mariah, and Andy, along with their two sons Sam and Shiloh. It was a whirlwind five days enjoying family and the beautiful island of Hawaii, and before we knew it we were back in Arequipa and our bikes.

Jocelyn's Instagram Posts:

March 7, 2016

Climbed and climbed out of Ecuador into Peru two days ago. After a long, grueling, painful, but breathtaking bike ride, we opted to take a taxi from the border into the nearest large town with accommodations. While in San Ignacio we moved to a nearby hostel from a hotel in less than two hours of arriving because they had no water. We stayed overnight and had the worst of nights. The bed was shaped like a "U" and loud noise continued till 5:00 A.M.! We decided to take a break day, found a quieter *hospedaje,* and have decided to change our route. Due to the rain, poor road conditions, and my father tiring earlier, we are hoping to hop on a bus to the coast tomorrow. I've been drinking way less because of health and personal reasons. But today a little celebration was in order because we are in our 35th country and I found Flor de Cana cheap beer in Peru!

March 10, 2016

"Do not, my friends, become addicted to water. It will take hold of you, and you will resent its absence!"

– Immortan Joe (from Mad Max)

I've been tripping on Shpongle (musical group) and the mass amount of sand that leathers my skin. Shocked at the amount of trash, frustrated with disgusting drivers, but despite the negatives, all of the Peruvian people we have met are so nice and kind! Totally opposite of what others have said about the northern coast and all the robbing that has occurred, but today we ran out of water. Nothing like some Shpongle, no water and some cookies to get me grinning from ear to ear!

March 14, 2016

Our first glimpse of the Pacific Ocean after over a month or so in the mountains was just north of Playa Huanchaco. We rode a beach rock road into this small, popping surf town just before dusk. The vibes were nice and the waves were rolling in, so we took a day off to go surfing, chill out on the beach, and eat international foods. The design of the local surf boats, *Caballitos de totora* (little reed horses), date back to 3,000 years ago (Obviously the name wasn't this 3,000 years ago.) and are possibly the first ever surfboard as fishermen surf the waves back to shore after casting their nets and collecting fish in the cavities of the boat. There is an ongoing debate in the surfing world as to whether or not this constitutes the first form of surfing. We left here a few days ago and I thought they were cool!

March 16, 2016

Today is my father's 63rd birthday! He hasn't had a good day, with a rough morning and a long day of riding. He also hasn't been feeling well and has been riding very slowly, but we still are averaging 80 km a day. I wasn't a great daughter today because I couldn't make it special. I did however tell the owner at lunch, and he brought us a pancake with chocolate!

March 19, 2016

A letter to my phone camera: When you see my face or anyone's face, what gives you the right to automatically select the "beauty" editor? Are you saying that I am not enough and that a baby-butt smooth-looking face is beautiful? Please enlighten me on your definition of beautiful. I didn't ask you to edit my face in such a drastic way. It's like you want to erase my past. I'm so glad I found the way to turn off your darn photo beautifier. I understand that those who like to wear makeup might look like this sometimes, or they at least try to, but I don't want to look like a babydoll. I want to look like the explorer and adventurer that I am. I'm sun-kissed, chapped lips, and freckled. So never will you see me post a photo as fake as this one where you even trimmed my eyebrows! I promise to never lie to anyone about who I am.

March 21, 2016

Met up with my friend Antti from Holland that I have been following on Instagram for two years now! Our bike tours finally crossed paths in Mira Flores, Lima, Peru. It was so fun to chat and hang out with him for breakfast! Wishing you all the best, Antti! Post note: My mom and brother hosted him in Florida when he was traveling north later this year!

Another very coincidental event happened today. Colin, a former student of my mom's from my elementary school and his mother, Trish, had a flight delay in Lima on their way to Cuzco. My mom read about their spring break trip, sent a message to Trish, and gave them my phone number to try to connect us while we were all in the same town. As the two were chatting, Dad and I found them in a restaurant very close to where we were staying! We shared a nonstop conversation full of laughs and a delicious dinner. Thanks to Trish, we were filled with good food and family time! They left to explore Machu Picchu and more.

March 26, 2016

If I listened to every single person that warned me about the dangers of cycling around the world, I wouldn't have ever left my house and might be dead from my own dangerous destructive self. Though we were robbed yesterday of some of our possessions, it was just stuff, mostly technology things. We weren't robbed of our memories and our past, present, and future adventures. The broken person who decided to steal our bag needed it, and maybe we helped them get back on their feet. We are hurt that some of the items were family mementos that are not replaceable. We are feeling pretty numb, upset about the police lack of concern or integrity, and mostly sad. But we got on a bus this morning and went 100 miles south from the scene. We let it go. Tomorrow is a new day, a new challenge, and a new adventure.

March 31, 2016

Sometimes the wind blows so hard that you have to turn around, put your head down, and dig deep into your being to find the want to continue. Even if the sand is stinging your skin, you can't stand up straight, and you literally have been covered with sand for two days. (Am I crazy to admit I've been daydreaming about walking across a desert?!)

What I see on the road is like sandy waves of goodness. We have had 21 days of solid 30+ side and headwinds. Today's sandy thought: I sure am getting a nice pedicure for the upcoming wedding!

April 2, 2016

The Nazca Lines, geoglyphs etched into desert sand, were clearly seen as we flew over the desert while visiting Nazca a few days ago. They were constructed for religious ceremonies to pray for water and life/fertility. The Nazca Lines are possibly open air temples, and the most famous lines portray familiar creatures such as Hummingbird, Astronaut, Whale, and Monkey! There are thousands of geometric lines that can be seen throughout the valley. The Nazca people were a civilization dating roughly from 100 B.C to 700 A.D. This was magnificent to see how large these images are and how precise the geometric shapes are all through the valley. Even though we both got very sick from the flight, I recommend taking the time to visit here. Oh yeah, I was so moved by this experience and being robbed that when I just happened to stumble into a tattoo shop that was open on Easter I agreed to a hummingbird tattoo!

April 4, 2016

We have made it to Arequipa! It took us awhile to find our warmshowers host house, but we did! Our bikes are safely stored for the next two weeks or so. Tonight we're taking an overnight bus to Cusco, and then tomorrow we're taking the train to Aguas Calientes, and Wednesday we will trek up to Machu Picchu! We have seen the most beautiful Plaza de Armas in Peru!

April 7, 2016

This was a tough hike today. The path was entirely made up of rock stairs for 1600 meters. It took us just an hour and fifteen minutes to reach the top and roundtrip three hours. I could only imagine the views of Machu Picchu from this *montana*. It rained for the majority of our visit causing hundreds of tourists to leave. We decided to wait around, and two hours later the sun came out and the entire place glowed with the light. Seeing Machu Picchu in person brought tears to my eyes.

April 10, 2016

Today I met the Rainbow Mountains in Cerro Colorado, Peru. This magical place was just found about two years ago, and tour companies started designing treks to visit the area. I signed up for a single day and was picked up at 3:00 A.M. to ride in a van for three hours to the start of the hike. When we arrived at the point, we ate a breakfast and began at 4,000 meters to climb to 5,300 meters. This took us over three hours, and despite the unreal elevation, the colors that wrapped our every movement were heavenly! Once we made it to the top, we were surrounded by snowcapped mountains, but you can't tell how cold it was by my outfit of choice and huge smile! I'm really digging treks these days, and my pictures will share this epic climb!

April 14, 2016

Just a day after this trek we took three flights and are now in Hilo, Hawaii for my cousin Mariah's wedding! We will be spending time with family and exploring the island till the 19th, and then we will be back in Cusco, Peru on the 21st!

April 23, 2016

We are back with our bikes!! Today we reorganized our panniers and feel 5 lbs. heavier — gear and persons . . . haha! Later, we took a stroll along the Plaza and found this crazy-looking man who is cycling around the world from Venezuela. We are pretty sure he won't make it very far with all that he has loaded on his basic bike! Haha! He has his broom, 6 spare tires, 3 spare wheels, and other stuff he carries, and now we both feel much better about the extra weight we carry. We got this! Our route has changed and we will slow down, feel less pressure to get somewhere on a specific date, and have over a month to explore Chile. No Bolivia visa mess, and possibly no Argentina.

April 25, 2016

I keep looking back to when we started this tour at the border of Canada last June. I guess you could say I'm amazed that my father and I have survived this leg of our world tour. We have had our ups and downs, but we both understand each other. Though he barely talks or speaks his mind, I know he is very proud of me for getting him here. We're forever grateful for each other.

Chile

"We confirmed that Chile lay in the shape of a long, slim sword. It is composed of a string of valleys lying between mountains and volcanoes and crossed by plentiful rivers. Its coast is abrupt, with fearsome waves and frigid water, its forests are dense and aromatic, its hills unending."

(*Ines of My Soul*: A Novel by Isabel Allende)

Mike:

A few desert days later we cycled into our last Peruvian town of Tacna where we spent the night and then cycled to the border to exit Peru and enter Chile.

Four days into Chile we noticed a huge difference between here and Peru in that the drivers are courteous and drive per traffic regulations. Plus, there is no honking at each other all the time as in Peru. Chilean drivers actually respect pedestrians in crosswalks. Cars stop and wait for a person to cross, unlike Peru where they appear to try and run you over. Even bus drivers are respectful and slow down or move over when we are cycling. We haven't had so many good honks in months.

So far we have not seen the roadside dumps as in Peru. I told Jocelyn that it is like riding in a whole new country! At first we just stopped and stared as the drivers patiently waited for us. But Chile is also more expensive and seems to have a better national infrastructure. Also, the Spanish that we learned in Nicaragua has slowly been changing the further south we go. The last few days when talking with the locals they don't seem to understand what we are saying, so we must improvise somewhat. We are also back in the land of the *peso*.

Southern Peru is full of canyons where you ride down one side, cross the canyon floor, and then ride up the other side. Northern Chile is the same way. The last two days we have cycled down and up numerous canyons with the deepest so far at 4,000 feet. We rode ten miles to climb out of that one. Now that we are out of the canyons, the riding in the high desert is fairly flat and the winds have actually been to our advantage for the first time in two months. Canyon riding is really fun and the scenery spectacular.

Yesterday we rode all day to a little past sunset, pulled off the road, and pitched the tent. Up to this point we have been getting up at 6:00 A.M., but now it is 8:00 A.M. with the sun. This is quite a change for us, and we both feel much more comfortable camping here than in Peru. The southern sky is alive with stars. I haven't had this astronomical view since my two winters in Antarctica. In fact, the Southern Cross was brilliant and staring at us. It is times like this that we would prefer a better camera, but we don't want the extra weight or size.

Today we stopped near the town of Pozo Almonte, famous for the World Heritage Site of Santiago Humberstone Saltpeter Mine. The mine was in operation from 1872-1960. It opened due to the demand of saltpeter in explosives, which also found a use in agriculture. After the Germans perfected the production of saltpeter without the mining process, the traditional way was abandoned. Since both Jocelyn and I enjoy history and 'old stuff', we spent a few hours touring this mine and ghost town.

We left Pozo Almonte late the next day since we were short on *pesos*. The ATM wasn't working, and the bank hours were 9-2. Once again we were cheated by a bank since they always charge more for a money exchange than the guy on the street. We did change dollars in Arica when we entered Chile with a street guy and received 670 *pesos* to the dollar. The bank only paid 630. The official rate was 675, so the street guy was once again the best way. We have found that banks around the world pay the lowest. We didn't have much of a choice, so we took it.

We continued south through the lava-rock desert. At one point we heard a 'popping' sound like a shooting gun. When we stopped to make a tuna sandwich at a shaded bus stop, we heard the loud popping clearer and it was coming from the lava. I walked on part of the flow while eating and discovered it was air pressure escaping from lava vents and popping as it escaped. The scenery is fascinating as we ride through this varied landscape. The miles come easy as the terrain is mostly flat and the wind still favorable.

We have not had this many good honks, waves, and thumbs up from car drivers, truckers, and even bus drivers since crossing Iran in 2014.

By far, this has been the friendliest country in South America. Today as we were nearing a rest stop we saw a pickup truck with all the doors open and Barry White blaring from the speakers. In front was an older guy who was dancing. As we passed, he called us over and handed us a plastic bag full of granola bars. I reached in to pick out two, and he said, "Total," so I took the entire bag. What a fun guy, and it was so random with Barry White playing! We talked for a few minutes, and he said in Spanish, "Please don't litter." That is another pleasing experience — no roadside trash dumping here.

The next day we stopped near sunset at a lone desert restaurant for dinner. No one else was here, and we thought it a good place to possibly camp. The senorita showed us a small, clean *cabana*, and at $10 we were sold, moved the bikes inside, and then spent a few hours in the restaurant. After drinking the four Coors beers on premises (After all, it was Saturday night.) the senorita showed us a bottle of red wine that was cheaper than the four beers. The bottle of wine had probably been sitting there for years. We bought that and settled in for the night.

The last few days in the desert have been long with camping and an occasional room. The days are hot and the nights cold. Last night Jocelyn found desert ruins to camp in and also started a fire from wood that she had carried for several days. Along with that, I had carried two beers that we enjoyed with the fire. I was up with the sun at 8:00 A.M. and attempted to warm up with a brisk walk through the desert. Thirty minutes later, I gave up and crawled back into my sleeping bag to get warm. From there I read my Kindle until 9:30 A.M. when it did warm a little. Once the land warms, the winds switch and come from the west. Jocelyn made tortillas with peanut butter, bananas, and apple for breakfast. We finally found a truck stop restaurant after a few days without anything on the road and had a delicious lunch, restocked our water, and continued south.

Heading south toward Santiago, we rode into the major port city of Antofagasta. After walking around the historical city center, I found a city hotel after nine tries. Most hotels that I checked with were 'anti-bike' which is a first for us. Many of the reception people were unfriendly, but then this is a big city and their attitude is quite different than in smaller towns. The hotel we finally registered in had a friendly staff and was happy to accommodate our bikes. After eleven days of riding we decided to take a day off for rest and to explore this interesting city. We met an

English-speaking gentleman who drove us around the surrounding area to visit the highlights.

We left Antofagasta and entered the Chilean Atacama Desert. The Atacama Desert is a plateau in South America covering a 600 mile strip of land on the Pacific coast west of the Andes. It is the driest non-polar desert in the world. Fortunately, the notorious Chilean winds continued to be kind to us. We had talked with several cyclists heading north through Chile who'd had a tough time because the onshore winds are fierce and can blow a bike off the road or can "head you" this time of year. Most people either wait it out or walk through the gusty parts.

Jocelyn preparing lunch in the Atacama Desert, Chile.

We enjoyed the varied scenery and camping as we worked our way through the famous Atacama Desert and back to the coast. The weather is getting colder as we head south through winter. We are in the tent early and don't get out until the sun warms up a bit around 8:30 A.M. That puts us twelve hours in the tent and gives us plenty of reading time on our Kindles. There is nothing like crawling into the sleeping bag early and reading with the quiet desert winds ruffling the tent. The last two mornings have been cloudy and cold, so we do have to stay bundled up until riding time. Jocelyn is not only the navigator but also the cook. The extra food and water weight can be difficult as we climb out of valleys, but it is a necessity. About every sixty miles or so there is a *posada* or inn that serves food and has bottled water.

Riding the beautiful Atacama Desert in Chile.

Once again we cycled to the coast near Chanaral and along the rocky coastline for a scenery change. We cycled by many small beach towns that are empty because of the off-season. Summer starts in December and runs until March, so it was pretty much deserted. The following two nights we spent camping on beaches. We enjoy falling asleep while listening to the waves break on the beach. With the high nearby mountains, we don't see the sun until after 8:30 A.M., so it is hard to get an early start. But it doesn't matter as long as we can pull over somewhere before dark to set up camp.

Yesterday we rode into the small town of Bahia Inglesa (Church Bay) with a beautiful beach. Since our route was taking us inland again we decided to spend the night in a bungalow complete with two rooms and a kitchen. We went to the local super *mercado* and bought lots of fruit and other stuff. Most of the other accommodations were closed for the winter, so this was ours at a cheap price. There were a few restaurants open and we had delicious local seafood. I opted for the abalone, which I haven't had in over 25 years. While growing up in Oxnard, California, I used to dive and pry abalone off the coastal rocks and islands, and my mom would cook delicious abalone meals. Abalone is all but gone in California now but plentiful here. What a treat it was to experience this again and reminisce about old times at home.

We worked our way inland again due to the lack of a coastal road. About halfway to our destination of Copiapo, I heard a faint "*Hola, Hola,*" and turned to see a cyclist headed the other way. We immediately stopped and met Sean Kane from Ireland. The funny thing is that he has been following us on crazyguyonabike.com and was sure he would run into us as he heads north — and he did! After a few minutes of swapping 'Tales from the road' we continued south and Sean north.

We departed Copiapo and climbed several miles out of the valley before settling down in a series of ups and downs. The riding was easy and we stopped at a highway rest stop to make tuna and avocado tortillas for lunch. There were even restrooms complete with potable water, so we refilled our containers before continuing south. Around 6:00 P.M., we started looking for a campsite in this mainly fenced area with one gate that had a 'Rancho Private Property' sign on it. We soon arrived at a *posada* (inn) and asked if we could camp there. The owner immediately invited us into his courtyard and said to put our tent there. We set up camp and then enjoyed a fine restaurant meal and another beautiful Chilean sunset before crawling into the tent. This *posada* has been in operation serving truckers and cars since 1903. Their history was hung on the walls. Throughout the night there was a heavy mist, almost rain, so we packed everything wet. We had an early start and made it to the next town of Vallenar by 3:00 P.M. We found a cheap hostel with a sunny courtyard and hung out our tent to dry. We also washed all our clothes and hung them out to dry on our portable clothes line. Today was such a treat, as by 4:00 P.M. we were strolling through the town in the daylight with leisure time and enjoying the local beer. It seems that since we entered Chile we always arrive somewhere late, near or after dark.

We are now in the southern Atacama Desert Mountains where there is more climbing. The surrounding mountains look as if they are painted on a canvas with various pastel colors. We spent the last two nights camping in the desert. At sunset the world around us is tinted orange, red, purple, blue, and finally, as the night moves in, black, as we seem to be covered by a dark blanket. Yesterday the fog rolled in from the coast. We were trying to reach the coast, but the sun set and the fog thickened so we decided to pull off the road and find a place to camp. We set up camp off the main road and behind piles of rocks. On a hill overlooking us we saw several people watching us from their homes, but since we are used to this we didn't think anything of this. The next part is scary though. After I took a picture of our camp we saw three highway workers approach us. They immediately told us that we should leave this area. We acted like we didn't know what they were talking about as we did not want to leave due to the heavy winds, fog, and dark. Eventually we figured out they were trying to warn us to leave. "The families up the hill are dangerous and will rob you," they said as they slashed a finger across their throats and motioned a gun with their hand. At this we were shocked and didn't know what to say. They also said, "The police will not come here." At this point we knew that we had to leave. It was dark and foggy and they said we could load our bikes and tent onto their truck and they would take us to a safe beach. Our original goal was the beach at another five miles through another mountain pass, so we took them up on their offer and loaded all our stuff. They took us to a beautiful secluded beach and we set up camp for the second time this evening. It was a mellow spot where once again we were lulled to sleep with the waves crashing on the shore. The three guys that brought us here were 'road angels' that possibly saved us from harm.

For the past few weeks we have been riding long days in the Atacama Desert while recording many miles. One day we saw what appeared to be a small fishing village and decided to drop down to the water and investigate the town of Guanaqueros. We love to explore small old fishing villages, so when we came upon another *cabana* we stopped and decided to spend the night after a short day. It is the off-season in Chile, as it was in Spain, so the prices are cheap and we are usually the only guests on the premises. We enjoy visiting the local markets and cooking our dinner.

When we crossed the U.S. we wrote in our first book about crossing the country 'one taco at a time.' We are now riding through Chile 'one fish at a time.' The fish is excellent and the wine unmatched. A large bottle of local wine is less than $3. The wine is not just cheap; it is excellent. After a tasty fish lunch, we spent a few hours strolling through the fish markets, watching the daily catch being cleaned, boats readied for night fishing, and the repairing of nets. This is the kind of place where I could spend a summer, eating in the many seafood restaurants daily, enjoying the local wine, and swimming in the bay.

The coastal riding is more demanding as the steep, long hills and valleys continue. We arrived at the junction to Santiago and split off to the right to follow the coastal route to Patagonia and Puerto Montt. The landscape has changed dramatically with the addition of large pine and flowering trees. Tonight, while looking for a place to camp, the fog started rolling in and the weather turned wet and cold, so we decided on a *cabana* in the small town of Papudo. We stopped at the local market and purchased pasta for dinner and eggs for breakfast.

We left Papudo and had an early morning steep climb to the Pacific side of the coast. Even though it was foggy, cloudy, and cold, most of the day it turned out to be a fun as we rode through an area that reminded us of Malibu, California as the coastline was beautiful and there were many large modern homes built on the coastal rocks. We washed our clothes last night but they remained wet, so we aired out our laundry in the hopes of drying. At the end of the day they were still wet. For several days now we have been working our way out of the Atacama Desert. We are always surprised when a local walks up to us and asks in perfect English, "Where are you from?" It happened again today when we were leaving a restaurant. This time there was a kind gentleman who told us he was the city manager and asked if we needed help with anything or a place to stay. We were just passing through and thanked him for his offer. After answering several questions about our trip, we spent the rest of the day riding until sunset. The kindness of people all around the world makes this trip special.

After another cold night with both sets of our clothes wet, we were on our way and rode past Concon, Chile filled with endless condos and continued toward Valpariso on a scenic beach bike path. While riding through Vina del Mar we spotted a hostel and checked the price as we wanted to launder our clothes and take a few hours off this afternoon. The hostel had two small single rooms on the first floor, so we took them at about $15 apiece, not bad in a city of $200 a night hotel rooms. We moved our bikes inside, found a laundry, and had a relaxing Mexican lunch.

The following day we rode inland away from the coast. After a few hours we entered wine country with rolling, charming vineyards. We passed three wineries that did not advertise tours or tastings, but the fourth one was a charm and we enjoyed fine wine and lunch at Matetic Vineyards. There was a hotel on premises and Jocelyn checked the price. At $300 per night we easily continued south in the increasing cold and rain as winter is setting in. The days are starting in the high 30s F and end in the mid to high 40s. We haven't had rain since in the Peruvian Andes, but that is now increasing as this is winter in Central Chile. A few days ago we were on a fast, long downhill. Jocelyn was ahead of me and I saw her almost fall as she wobbled to a fast stop. She had a major puncture that could have been a major accident, but she managed to stay upright. One large nail made four punctures in her rear tube. That is a record for us.

Along that line, two days later we were in another fast downhill when I noticed an oncoming truck parked on my side of the road. Too late, I noticed a large, black oil slick and swerved to avoid it. My rear tire went into a slide as I fought the handlebar to stay upright and was able to stop without falling, but this tweaked my knee painfully. Today an almost disaster happened when a full water bottle fell off my bike into Jocelyn's path. She hit that and fell hard onto the ground injuring her wrists and one knee. All of the above just shows how dangerous riding a bike can be and a trip like this can be over in an instant. We take for granted that we can just ride our bikes for miles and miles on any type of roads. These incidents keep us thinking how fragile we are on our bicycles.

This morning Jocelyn's wrists and one knee were swollen, plus there was a large contusion on her right leg. We decided to take a break day as cycling all day with swollen wrists would exacerbate the situation. Fortunately there didn't appear to be any breaks. When she fell, two cars stopped and several people offered assistance. I helped Jocelyn to her feet and thanked them as they left. We found a hotel in the next village of Malloa. I say village because that is how small it is. The hotel is on the Plaza de Armas with the church across the street and a restaurant and market on the other side. All towns and cities have a *"Plaza de Armas"*, the main square.

The *Plaza de Armas* (literally Weapons Square) is the name for the main square in many Latin American cities. Most cities constructed by the Spanish conquistadores were designed in a standard military fashion, of which one block would be left vacant to form the *Plaza de Armas*. It is often surrounded by governmental buildings, churches, and other structures of cultural or political significance. The name derives from the fact that this would be a refuge in case of an attack upon the city from which arms would be supplied to the defenders. We have visited and stayed in or near many *Plazas de Armas* and Malloa has the smallest one yet.

As usual, we are the only ones staying here. In fact, there is only a caretaker and no staff present. The hotel appears to be an old mission or church building — large and beautiful with high ceilings. It is cold, but there are two radiator heaters in our room and lots of hot water. Today we rested, napped, and cooked a delicious veggie lunch and dinner. We also enjoyed playing with the two resident doggies. It was a hoot watching them chase the local geese across the property.

Jocelyn's swelling had lessened and we were back on the road. We entered Chile a little over a month ago and have been riding up and down large canyons and gorges along with small to large hills with many long, slow climbs. But now we are in a much flatter region — at least we were for one day, and as a result we were able to add seventy miles on our odometer.

Once again we exited the main road to explore Saltas Del Laja and the enormous Laja Falls. Laja Falls consist of four horseshoe-shaped falls — one on each arm of the Laja River. The tallest at one hundred feet is the easternmost fall, but the western falls are sixty feet tall. Total width of all four falls — 1,365 feet.

We found a hotel overlooking this wide waterfall. I consider myself the king of finding cheap rooms. And since it is off-season, another cheap room was available with a little bit of negotiation since there was only one other room occupied. We could have camped but it is wet and cold. We explored Laja Falls with a long hike around the top and bottom. Jocelyn got soaked walking around the lower splash zones. The different views of the falls were incredible. We enjoyed lunch in the small village before returning to the hotel for a long nap. Jocelyn is recuperating from a cold and sore wrists and knee, while I am recovering from my twisted sore right knee from an almost fall. As touring cyclists, we take advantage of our rest days . . . and sometimes rest.

Sunday morning found us back on the road and into hills. The scenery change was awesome as the large forests, rivers, and bridges began. If fact, at around 2:00 P.M. the sun was shining bright as the fog and mist rose. It was the first time in over a week we had a clear sun and warmth. We were attacking the hills one after another when all of a sudden the sun was down and we had to find a place to camp. Hills can get you into a charging mood and make you forget the time. So we ducked into an open gate and rode until we found a space among the many trees. We quickly set up the tent, and since it was so cold we just crawled inside and decided to forget dinner.

As we lay down at 6:00 p.m., my mind was hoping the gate would still be open in the morning. We don't have our Sierra Design minus 39°F bags we used on our last trip, as we didn't want to carry them and their extra five pounds on this trip. This is the first time we could have used them.

We awoke and 'forced' ourselves out of the tent at 8:30 a.m. with a crunching ice noise under our shoes. That is a long time in a tent, but at times you just don't want to leave the bag. The temperature was under 30°F. Even though it was this cold, it did rain overnight which gave our gear another good soaking. Inside the tent was also wet from condensation. I remember on our tour through the Pamir Mountains in Tajikistan waking up in our tent with icicles inside along with frozen water bottles. It was below zero with a clear sky at over 14,200 feet. We rode uphill into the next town and consumed a large breakfast with several cups of hot tea since we had missed dinner the night before. About three soaking hours later we passed a hostel and I thought of my frozen hands and toes. I stopped and asked Jocelyn how she was doing. Her hands and feet were in the same condition so we decided to call it a day. After the usual after biking work of washing clothes and drying the wet tent and camping gear, we took a taxi to a market in the nearby town. We bought enough food for lunch and dinner, along with the mandatory Chilean wine. We returned to the hostel, cooked lunch, and later dinner before resting. Sometimes the end of the day's work is much harder than cycling sixty miles.

We headed south into the Land of Lakes through mostly rainy days. We asked a restaurant owner at lunch today where Patagonia begins, and he told us we were now entering the region with the Land of the Lakes, Volcanoes, and Fire. This district is an area of lush, green valleys, towering cone-shaped volcanoes, and emerald lakes — all at the base of the snowcapped Andes Mountains. We read that much of the district looks like the German and Swiss Alps.

Northern Patagonia is a delight to cycle through with many lakes fronting snow covered volcanos. We rode by Lake Llanquihue, the second largest lake in Chile. We talked with several people who said it was snowing here last week and to expect lots more in the near future. This region of Chile is the top outdoors destination with shimmering lakes, lush forests, and rolling farmland, punctuated by the snowcapped volcanoes.

We enjoyed a steady climb, followed by a fast downhill to Lago Ranco in search of a campground, but it was closed. The *senora* caretaker said we were welcome to stay, led us to a lakeside campsite, and switched the bathroom and hot water power on. We pitched our tent directly in front of the lakeshore with a stunning backdrop of the snow-topped Andes in Argentina.

The next morning was cloudy, but we enjoyed riding along the lakeshore with the magnificent view of the Andes. We rode through a small village and bought bread for a tuna sandwich. At that point it was close to sunset, and since most of this land is private and fenced we rode back a bit to a *hospedaje* sign we had noticed. It looked old but it was open and we were guided inside to a room. The *senoras* were pleasant and accommodating and excited that there were Americans in their home. In fact, several people came to greet us as they served an excellent fresh salmon dinner. As I have always said, this journey is all about the people you meet, and Chile is one of the best.

This morning we had a filling breakfast from the *senoras* and said "*Nos vemos.*" These two words mean "See you later." Throughout Latin America these words are preferred to "Goodbye." We had an invigorating Sunday ride, which eventually led to a dirt road when we cycled to Lago Puyehue for another magnificent view of the Andes and Argentina. While looking for a place to pitch our tent it started to snow so we settled into a lakeside *cabana*. A quick trip up the street to the *mercado* found us the ingredients for a hearty soup. The *cabana* also had a wood burning heater, so we bought extra wood and quickly heated the *cabana.*

After talking with many people about winter in Southern Chile, our goal of Ushuaia, another 1,000 miles, appears bleak, so we will stop our South American adventure in Puerto Montt. All of the borders with Argentina south of Santiago are now closing. Traveling south of Puerto Montt requires traversing many fjords by ferries that are also closing.

We had a grand last day riding to Puerto Montt on June 17, 2016 as the weather cleared and the beautiful and majestic Andes dazzled brightly in the blue sky. In Puerto Montt we found a hotel before a walk to the bus station for Santiago tickets.

On June 8, 2015 we had left Blaine, Washington at the Canadian border and started cycling south. We entered Mexico at Tijuana on August 4th and now here we are about one thousand miles short of our original goal of Ushuaia, Argentina, the southern tip of South America. From this start we have ridden 10,459 miles. Chile has been the longest country yet, and we have zigzagged 2,405 miles through this stunning country that is 2,670 miles long with an average width of less than 112 miles. The next part of our world adventure will start in Calgary, Canada as we ride across Canada to Nova Scotia. After that, we will head south along the East Coast of the U.S. and home to Florida.

We spent the rest of the day and the next morning exploring Puerto Montt by foot. The next day we boarded the bus at 4:00 P.M. and arrived in Santiago twelve hours later at 6:00 A.M. We cycled through downtown Santiago in the dark morning looking for a hotel. The prices were high, and after walking out of one the doorman gave me a card advertising an apartment. I walked to the apartment building while Jocelyn watched the bikes. I found the proprietor and rented a room for four nights for a total of $100. It was centrally located near the Santiago *Plaza de Armas* built in 1541. Surrounding the square are several historic buildings to explore.

Jocelyn's childhood friend, Danielle, resides in Santiago with her husband Maximo and son Max. We met with them several times as they guided us around Santiago. We also met them a few times at their apartment. They recommended a bicycle shop, Taller Chicle, and owner, Carlos, where we had our bikes boxed. Carlos told us that two years ago he met a cyclist heading south at this same time. South of Puerto Montt this cyclist was stopped by the snow and fjords and ended up walking his bike across a southern border and then east and not south to Ushuaia. Thanks to Danielle and Maximo for also arranging our transportation to the airport. We soon boarded our flight to Calgary reminiscing our last year in Latin America and thinking of our upcoming Canadian ride.

Jocelyn:

April 28, 2016

Chile — the valleys are insane. Hate climbing when I can see the top and it takes an hour or so to get there. Gets you all weird in the head, man! We're out of shape, lol. I'm so giggly inside and out that this is unreal. There is nothing like camping out in the desert. Literally, or quite possibly, my favorite camping landscape! I don't even care about the sand that accumulates inside my sleeping bag. There are random buildings in the middle of nowhere that provided shade, places to warm up soup, and to take cold showers.

April 29, 2016

We are cycling through a *salar* (a salt flat in the Chilean desert) where the Earth cracks and breathes equal to each breath of my own. I am equipped with six liters of water because the Atacama Desert lifts me to Mars, hah ha! I am collecting firewood when I see it because it is cold at night and there aren't any trees. We went on a tour of a ghost town called Humberstone, a World Heritage Site, that had saltpeter mines. Dad and I took turns while one guarded the bikes, and it was definitely off the beaten track! We had fun exploring the sodium nitrate mines and looking up some information later that related to this era of production. Very interesting stuff!

May 1, 2016

Reflection: When we first met, I was sitting outside a shack, in the middle of nowhere, drinking a Coors. You lay down in front of me and took a nap. I was graced to watch the powerful wind travel through your mane of hair. All at once I felt at peace. That's when I realized there is something so soothing about watching a dog's hair blowing in the wind.

May 4, 2016

We have a proper camping place in the lonesome Atacama Desert. I've been collecting firewood for two days now and am ready for this exact time. There's always a heavy west wind, and today was not any different. We found this old broken-down dwelling, and that surprise led us half a mile off the road. It looked like a pile of sand or rocks, but as we walked up to it we found an old house of sorts with shelter to start a fire! This was a great find and camp spot for a great fire and a good night! And it was here when the sun shouted to the night sky that it just wasn't ready to rest yet! I danced with it till my legs couldn't move anymore.

May 8, 2016

Hello, world, said Mr. Hand, a stone sand creation or formation in the desert. It is called *La Mano del Desierto*. We took a great picture of our bikes leaned against the palm of the hand. We have ridden 213 miles in three days, and I just had to jump for joy. "Just starfish it!" Tonight, we are in this stretch of the Atacama Desert where there is no place to hide. While we were setting up camp we heard a few hollers and honks from the friendliest of truck drivers. Two have stopped to ask if we need water and some bread, or if we need a ride! These are the best of times, camping life, bike friends, and it is freezing! I've had to wear two layers of clothing today at just below 60°F! This means I have two more layers of clothing to last me through the winter here in Chile. Brrrr — in Northern Chile, it's been a nice 80°F during the day, but at night it drops to below 30°F! Every day it seems to get colder. But I haven't dug out my shoes yet!

"*Posadas*" or in my terms, desert restaurants, can be found every 100 km or so. We never pass one up. It's a typical truck stop or cafeteria-like meeting place with a set two course menu and "extras". We get the menu choice, always. We chow down, feed the local dogs, and in return we leave even happier with smiles that could turn someone silly!

Mano del Desierto, a 36-foot-tall hand protruding out of the Atacama Desert sand.

May 17, 2016

I'm pretty sure we have made it to the end of the Atacama Desert full of downhills, uphills, and around the bends. I rode into the largest tumbleweed I've ever seen and balanced one on top of my head for a cool memory. This made such a silly picture that I have giggled for days.

May 21, 2016

We are just bicycle touring in Chile, and I tend to get a bit excited and take us on some dirt roads. We don't stay long either way, and I'm happy for days because of it. I guess I don't care. I give thanks to my legs though they aren't muscular. They look like hot dogs or legs filled with beer. They have supported me for over 20,000 miles on a bicycle around the world, and we are currently in Chile.

May 25, 2016

For the past two days we've been riding along the hilly coastline of Chile along some parts that I have renamed "Royal Boutique Way" because the houses are massive and all have infinity pools dropping into the rocky cliffside. It's richer than Malibu, California, and we were impressed riding in Concon and farther south to Vina del Mar.

May 27, 2016

I had a lunch date with my father along the Ruta del Vino, where they make the best Chilean wines in lush vineyards. Vina Matetic was the first one open! It doesn't get above 50°F now, but I'm still wearing shorts, and of course I'm still being called a *loca* (crazy in Spanish)!

May 29, 2016

It's been an interesting and fun two days on small roads in thick, cold fog. While on a major highway going downhill at about 40 mph I ran over a large nail puncturing my tube in four places and causing me to swerve to a sharp halt on the wheel. I only have my front brakes working, so the sketchy stop worked and I was safe. Two days later, today, my dad's spare two-liter plastic water bottle goes flying out of the bungee hold landing right before my front tire. I go flying and skid across the bike path, while hands and wrists took the force of the crash. Guys in a car behind us came running as I was pinned under the bike. I was hurt pretty bad but got up and swore at the water bottle like it was at fault. But I was projecting my distrust of falls and it was my entire fault. The flat tire was a warning. The universe talks to us and I'm trying to listen.

June 3, 2016

Riding beside the sunset is one of the most peaceful moments in my daily rides, especially because this was the time when we got a glimpse of the Andes Mountains with pink sparkles that danced upon the snowcapped range. Today we are just north of Los Angeles, Chile. We've been racing the cars and trying to keep warm, and that means we put our pants and shoes on! I don't know why, but my feet were still frozen the entire day.

Interesting post: I've sure drank around the world and I didn't just go to Epcot! If only I had written down all the different beers, wines, and other alcoholic beverages I've tasted. These two have jumped to my favorites in the Chile beer group, which happens to be very grand! *Salto del Laja* and *Puffe*.

June 6, 2016

Gone are the days that it barely reached 60°F. Now it doesn't rise above 38°F. Last night we stealth camped amongst a large forest of pines and the temp dropped into the 20s. We are enjoying these last winter weeks together, savoring the solitude. I'm actually not looking forward to being back in the English-speaking part of the world.

June 9, 2016

Total around the world combined miles 22,234 (35,782 km). We are just five days away from finishing our south tour segment. Right now, we have around 2,300 miles in Chile, and that is more than our original goal to bike tour at least 1,500 miles. Los Lagos, Chile.

June 12, 2016

I've been off the grid for two days and I've just found out about the shooting at Pulse nightclub. I'm literally in tears thinking of all the beautiful people I've met there, of the bartenders I know who work there, and flashbacks of all our amazing, fun, and safe times my friends and I have had there. My prayers go out to everyone. Where can we find out about who has been killed in this tragedy? Pray for Orlando!

I could stay here for the rest of my life and be content, yet I don't want to be content. Since finding out about the Pulse shooting, I feel even more encouraged to get home, but I will remember the excitement of watching the sunset dance upon the Andes Mountains and how we stayed in this tent for 14 hours because it was below freezing! I finished reading a book, too, and thanked Marcia, the owner of this closed for the season campground, as she stoked the hearth just for us.

When I looked upon this river, I thought, *I think it's time I give it up. You've heard it all. Now let it be.* My mind tends to hurricane inside my skull. I can't keep it off and it sure wrecks a lot. I'm caught in a stroke of my pedal and the world. All in all, I'm still lost, unsure, and loved. I want you to be free, to feel safe, to love, to smile, and to laugh, and I just want you to hug. Hug those you know and those you don't. In order for all of us to be okay, we should spread our wings and love each other.

June 13, 2016

Today we are in Puerto Octay, Chile. We had lunch here (a terrible pizza) and are currently staying in Frutillar. We arrived here after sunset with a thick fog, so we haven't seen it fully, but friends have told me about this special town and it looks awesome. Tomorrow is our last day of cycling on this part of our world tour. We will bike tour through the famous Puerto Varas into our destination city of Puerto Montt. Though it isn't Ushuaia, Argentina, we have cycled this far south and together as a fatherdaughtercyclingadventure team. This is all so unreal.

June 14, 2016

Los Lagos is filled with little hills that will get you in a sweat and with fast descents that will freeze your ass. Ha ha! Sometimes there are challenging little curves that are right up against the lake and are somewhat flat! Our last day of riding south was filled with sunshine, volcanos, birds singing songs to us, and one stupidly steep hill! We are in a winter wonderland, bike wandering, touring, taking videos, and preparing for our journey north.

June 16-21, 2016

We are in Santiago, Chile! Cerro San Cristobal. Went up on the *funicular* (cliff railway) to the top of San Cristobal Hill and could see the huge city below though the smog was thick. We toured the Santiago Metropolitan Cathedral in the *Plaza de Armas*. Construction of the Santiago Metropolitan Cathedral began 1748 and was completed in 1800. All the other cathedrals before this have been destroyed by earthquakes. *Muchas gracias* to my new friend Carlos at Taller Chicle Bike Shop for helping us box our bicycles for our long flight home tonight.

The most important post during our days in Santiago includes my childhood friend, Danielle. She and I played in their pool in Cocoa Beach, watched movies, acted kooky crazy, had a breakfast club, and were giggly girls ten years ago. We found each other again in Santiago and spent time in her home with her husband Max and young son Maxi! They escorted us to many places and took care of our traveling needs. Our time together was over too soon, but I know we will meet again!

Enjoying a roadside lunch

Jocelyn found a tumbleweed!

Canada

"Oh the places you'll go."
–Dr. Seuss

Mike:

We landed in Calgary, Canada minus my bike. At our intermediate stop in Houston we gathered our bikes and bags and proceeded through customs before re-checking it all to Calgary. My bike and many other bags didn't make the flight because the flight load needed to be lightened. Thom from Calgary's Prime Ski, Board, and Bike Tune Shop met us at the Calgary airport and drove us to the shop as we had scheduled for our bikes to be reassembled and tuned. Thom next drove us to our Airbnb house where we enjoyed a basement studio for a few nights. My bike arrived the next day and was delivered to the house. I reassembled my bike and then rode it to Prime Bike Shop while Jocelyn rode her free rental bike. The afternoon was spent cycling around Calgary and shopping for a few days of food at the Safeway grocery store. We were in culture shock as we walked down the aisle and saw all of our favorite brands of food. Our rental bikes had racks, and we filled up one of our panniers and a backpack full of food.

The craziest difference is how our day has changed; in Chile the sun rose at 8:30 A.M. and set at 5:00 P.M. Here, in Calgary, the sunrise is 5:20 A.M. and the sunset at 10:00 P.M.

We joined our next Airbnb hosts, Linda and Ralph, in a Banff National Park hike with a fellow touring cyclist's family that they met in Cuba late last year. Linda and Ralph have cycle toured and hiked in many countries, and they met the family of Derek and Kathleen along with their two children Anna (12) and Jasper (10) from Ottawa who have been bicycle touring Western Europe, Colombia, Cuba, Western United States, and Canada for a year. Anna and Jaspar received quite an education during their year off school as they toured on their bicycles. The eight of us drove to Banff National Park near Lake Louise and hiked twelve miles in Paradise Valley past Lake Annette, up Sentinel Pass at 8,600 feet, and down Larch Valley to Lake Moraine. The Rocky Mountains are incredible and the views stunning. What a great day sharing "Tales from the road" with three cycling groups!

We flew to California to attend my niece Makani and her fiancé Jamie's wedding. Andee and my son Cary met us at Los Angeles Airport. My family was together again and on a road trip as we drove north to Arroyo Grande where we met my sister Tish, brother-in-law Jim, and my niece Mariah. At the wedding I walked Makani down the aisle and Jocelyn changed hats from her bicycle helmet to a minister's hat and married Makani and Jamie. She did a great job, and it was a superb day. We soon headed south to visit Andee's brothers — brother Jeff and his son Perry, and brother Chip along with Chip's wife Kerry and their daughter Meg. We drove to San Diego for a 4th of July celebration at Tish and Jim's house. We had cycled to their home last August on our way to Mexico. A week later we returned to the airport and dropped Cary off for his flight home to Florida, while Andee, Jocelyn, and I flew to Calgary. Once again, Andee was to drive our support vehicle for a few weeks as we cycled to Winnipeg, Canada. This trip just got better!

My wife Andrea joined us with a rental car in Calgary and set up camps each day for a few weeks until Winnipeg as we rode east across Canada.

In Calgary we rented a car and drove to our next Airbnb host's home. We had already met Linda and Ralph and were going to stay with them a few nights and explore the Calgary area. We retrieved our bikes with thanks to the guys at Prime Bike Shop for their excellent service. Our timing was excellent as we arrived in time for the world famous Calgary Stampede Rodeo. We attended the opening parade and ceremonies of the rodeo and enjoyed the entire day with the rodeo events and many categories of exhibitions. We have never seen rodeo Chuck Wagon Races, and it doesn't get any more exciting than that! The following day we drove to Banff National Park to explore that beautiful part of the Rockies.

Jocelyn:

June 25, 2016

The best hikes are when you have no plan or idea of what hike you want to do and you arrive late in the day and set off for a short 11km loop in your Chacos sandals. Today, a group of three families of touring cyclists got together and ended up hiking to Lake Annette along Paradise Valley, up over Sentinel Pass, down into Larch Valley, and down to Lake Moraine. 7 ½ hours and 20 km later we got our adventure fix for the day.

We had heard that the pass was a bit rocky with a good bit of snow still, and in fact it was all rocks with much snow. Naturally we scrambled and rock climbed where it got rather scary, and I don't scare easily. At the end I wasn't a fan of walking in the snow in my Chacos, as slipping down the steep mountainside was heavy on my mind. With that being said, if I could, I'd go back there tomorrow in hiking boots.

I almost had a panic attack up here as the loose rock field was very heavy, but the views kept me gasping full of shock and excitement the entire time. It was during this moment that I remembered climbing Volcano Conception on Ometepe Island in Nicaragua when I swore then I wouldn't ever hike on rocks again because I hated it. Ha! I didn't hate it this time as it just challenged my body, my mind, and my willful strength to keep moving forward. The Canadian Rockies got it going on, and now we are heading to California for my cousin Makani's wedding!

June 26, 2016

First stop in Southern California always includes Mexican food! Mom, Uncle Jeff, and Cousin Perry met us for the food coma event. We had lots of errands to complete and some traveling north to drive and reach our destination in Arroyo Grande for Makani and Jamie's wedding.

July 2, 2016

The wedding went so well and I rocked the ceremony as the officiant, while Makani and Jamie took our breath away with their constant beautiful smiles and sparkling eyes. We were graced with lovely weather and a perfect setting at Peacock Farms!

July 4, 2016

What a fun day with my godparents, Aunti Tish and Uncle Jim, at their neighborhood 4th of July block party in Pacific Beach. Oh, I finally made it to the beach! So great to see you, Maddie and meet your awesome girlfriend Kim! I rocked the red, white, and blue with American love while meeting some Europeans at the local pub. I am sure they know I am a bit crazy!

July 6, 2016

Cary headed east to Florida to take care of the house and my princess dog Yaki, while Mom, Dad, and I are flying north to Calgary for the next leg of our world tour. Our Airbnb hosts were so kind and took us to the places we needed to buy supplies and then a perfect street spot to watch the 2016 Calgary Stampede Parade. We visited the Calgary Stampede Fair Grounds on July 8th and watched the rodeo including chuck wagon races. For most of the eight races, we were in the standing area on the ground where you could really feel the pounding hooves of the race beneath your feet. This is one of the largest rodeos in the world, and we were able to see most of the fair in one day. I highly recommend this if you are ever in Calgary during the July festivities.

Dad decided he wanted to take Mom to see Banff National Park that we had explored a few weeks ago. He splurged on a beautiful hotel that we rested in after a long day of hiking the glacier fields in Banff. For the record, we almost made it to British Columbia! Waterfowl Lakes in the Canadian Rockies should be on everyone's bucket list!

Mike:

We started riding again with Andee driving point as our support vehicle like she did from Washington to California. Jocelyn found a bike path to circumvent busy downtown Calgary, but we had to stop a few times to check the route on her phone as it was confusing. A cycling couple stopped and offered to guide us out of town on this path. They told us that a few years ago the bike path was flooded and now it was a bit convoluted to follow. After they guided us out of the city we continued along a canal path and were soon at Lake Chestermere. We found Andee waiting at a restaurant for a late lunch while watching the sky turn black with dark clouds and hearing distant thunder, so we opted to stay in a motel.

On our first full day we rode along the rolling grasslands of Canada on the Trans-Canada Highway. We spent the afternoon in the rain (We sure get rained on.) and gusty winds while entering the Badlands of Canada. We stopped and talked with Stan who is walking to Nova Scotia, the same place we are headed. He started 37 days ago from the West Coast in British Columbia. He is walking for a charity and said he left Calgary last Tuesday. When we said we left Calgary yesterday, he replied, "You guys are fast." Compared to walking, of course we are fast. Stan was pushing a jogging stroller loaded with 100 pounds of stuff. We made it to Crawling Valley Campground in Bassano where Andee had our camp ready. It is difficult falling asleep in Canada as the sun sets at 10:00 P.M. and it isn't dark until 11:00 P.M. Sunrise comes quickly at 5:30 A.M.

It was another good riding day without rain and thunderstorms. Today we rode seventy miles to the city of Medicine Hat. Our research of campgrounds didn't show any regular campsites east of Medicine Hat, so we settled for a campground in town where we enjoyed a fire and barbecue. We also spent time removing lots of gear for Andee to take home. We figure that if we have a bike problem now, parts should readily be available if need.

I have been thinking of how much I miss South America. It was more challenging to cycle that part of the world and mix with the locals than it is here. What's funny is that while in Latin America I thought of how much I missed Asia as it seemed so much more exotic to cycle through. That part of the world was more exciting and interesting than Latin America in some aspects. Cycling around the world opens one's eyes and is so full of new challenges every day. I think it was more interesting and also daunting trying to fit into the Asian culture, be it Turkey, the Stan countries, Iran, China, or Southeast Asia. I would desire returning to Southeast Asia for a few more months of cycling and to visit the countries that we didn't have time for. Out of all places, we have found the friendliest people in the world in Morocco, Iran, Southeast Asia, and Latin America.

It rained most of the night in Medicine Hat, but fortunately the thunderstorms stayed away. Andee cooked a filling breakfast of tortillas, eggs, and avocado in the campground kitchen. We packed our wet tent and rode east into the increasing hills and rain. In the late afternoon we arrived at Eagle Creek Campground, and since there were no other campgrounds for another forty miles we decided to call it a day.

The next day was long with hills and headwinds, so we splurged on a motel in the town of Swift Current. The scenery was filled with diversity as there were bison, coyotes, and deer. We watched a deer chasing a coyote as we rode along the highway.

Monetary wise Canada is a good place for Americans right now. $1 Canadian is .75 U.S. In other words, we have a 25% discount on everything, every day.

The riding days continued to be wet with the winds changing throughout the day. Andee rides ahead, finds a campground, and sets up our tent. It is such a pleasure having her accompany us. The ice cooler with fresh food is welcome as we can cook a varied menu compared to food stored on our bikes without Andee's support. That will go away soon though and it will be back to noodle soup, beans, and tuna. The Canadian campgrounds have minimal facilities unlike the camping we did from Blaine, Washington through California. Most of the sites on the Pacific Coast have electric and water. In Canada, the campsites are more rustic but beautiful, full of trees, and cheaper.

Jocelyn:

July 10, 2016

So thankful to have my mommy here and for the next thirteen days she will be our support like she has been for the last 5 years, but even closer right now! Our Canadian tour began with a rather late start, mechanical issues, with strangers/new friends guiding us all the way out of Calgary via bike trails, intense head winds, and my Momster being our cheerleader, like always.

July 12, 2016

The ever evolving, eroding badlands landscape is home to the magical, mysterious hoodoos, a tall thin spire of rock that protrudes from the bottom of an arid drainage basin or badland along with other geographic features that continue to change and are sculpted and carved by the forces of nature. Dinosaur Provincial Park is one of the few remaining pristine prairie habitats on the Northern Plains! And, oh yeah, the history that has been found here is out of this world!!! We took a half day to explore this very diverse landscape within the Canadian Badlands.

Did I mention that it is tornado season here and the weather is sporadic and runs through the prairies very fast? One minute it'll be as hot as Costa Rica and the next it's hailing. Of course, the winds are crazy, too. But yesterday we got hit hard in just a matter of minutes and we couldn't put our rain gear on fast enough. It's good fun but could become rather dangerous.

July 15, 2016

My Momster, the teacher, librarian, friend, and mother to all things, enjoys driving along on the trails, and one of her favorite things is finding and writing postcards to her schools, kids, and family. I'm going to miss her. We already get separation anxiety when we leave the campground each morning. I find myself wanting to pedal fast and far so that I can hang out with her more during the day. I love my mom, and it should be Mother's Day every day!

We rode to the Saamis Teepee in Medicine Hat, Alberta known as the world's tallest teepee! Momster took some amazing pictures with the blue skies and clouds, green grass, and our bikes positioned in the perfect spot. It is probably the most unique picture we will take in Canada!

July 18, 2016

We are in the "rough riders" territory and riding long days to make it to Winnipeg by Friday (a total of 357 miles). The long, straight roads and heat with mustard fields on both sides makes my mind wander and feel like I have gone a bit crazy. But don't you know already that I am crazy? Mom finds a good deal for our lunches and usually meets us on the road, which can be a truck stop in the middle of nowhere. Did I mention the road construction? We could use some encouragement about now trying to navigate all the detours and obstacles on the roads.

July 19-20, 2016

Mom was on her usual ride ahead of us exploring when she sensed that the weather was turning. She stopped in the small town of Indian Head and found a kind woman in the town's visitor center to chat with about the area, history, and always the weather! After checking out the local KOA, mom felt that without shade or shelter we might need to stay in another location. She returned to the visitor's center and met the husband of the kind woman, and they offered to let us camp in their backyard behind their 1895 historic home. We rode into town after only 51 miles and easily found John and Linda's home. They suggested that we visit the local lake, so we drove out there to have a very nice seafood dinner and stroll around the scenic area. We ended up being welcomed into their home later and staying in their living room as a huge hailstorm with loud thunder, massive lightning, and forceful winds came barreling through two times during the night.

We were all thankful that we were inside and to have met this couple, shared a hearty homemade breakfast, and walked around the neighborhood. One of their friends helped us with a bike issue in the morning. If you are traveling across Canada, this isn't a place to drive by without a stop at the Indian Head Farm, lunch at Sherry's on Grant Street (She's the mayor.), and a side trip to Katepwa Lake! Best part of nature exploring was being directed to the community farm where we picked three baskets of delicious Saskatoon berries. Thank you to the Korts for making us feel right at home in Indian Head. Post note: Get hail coverage for your rental car!

Mike:

Lunches have been fun as we explore old 'one horse' towns with interesting diners and old hotels. The food has been good along with the friendly people. Andee spends her days chatting up a storm with the locals and visiting museums. She can go anywhere and feel right at home. Jocelyn and I are doing the sweat work, but her research and ability to find interesting places to visit is so much more. Occasionally she will be at a fast food restaurant, will call Jocelyn so that we can 'place our order,' and then she will meet us to share our lunch.

We wanted to spend two nights in Regina and backtrack to the tourist town of Moose Jaw. Andee found an Airbnb host in Regina that was a much better deal than a hotel/motel. Sarah and Curt's home had lots of space for us and a large patio for our bikes. Plus we enjoyed their two dogs Oscar and Felix. We took a day off from riding to visit Moose Jaw which has the bootlegging tunnels made famous by Al Capone during prohibition in the 1920s. These tunnels provided a place for him to transport whisky to trains headed south to Chicago. Al Capone loved Moose Jaw and called it "Little Chicago". After exploring a few more tourist areas we bought two cans of waterproofing spray for our tent as it has leaked in heavy rains. Monday afternoon was spent applying this silicone spray and more maintenance on the bikes as there is always something that needs fixing.

Tuesday morning we cycled to Indian Head, Canada. We like exploring these small towns whether it is for lunch or the night. Andee met a lady in Indian Head at the welcoming center who invited us to camp in her backyard. Since the weather was looking stormy again, we were invited inside as hailstorms are bad during this time of year. We moved our gear inside and then drove north to explore the local lake country and enjoy a pleasant restaurant for dinner. Two strong hailstorms rushed by that night, as this is typical summer prairie weather. Our rental car sustained many hits and we would have to deal with this force of nature later.

Jocelyn's bike had side play in the rear wheel that caused a vibration. Linda rode with us to the local bicycle mechanic Bruce who works out of his garage. The rear hub cones were loose, so Bruce and his son fixed this and we were once again back on the road.

For the next several days we continued to Winnipeg while enjoying many good camping sites. Upon entering the outskirts of Winnipeg, Jocelyn heard a loud crack from her crank and had to jump off her bike as she could no longer peddle. She called Andee who went in search of a bike shop. Andee found two bike shops several miles ahead and suggested Portage Cycle and Sports for the repair. We walked our bikes several miles and found Dave who described the problem of stripped cranks caused from loose pinch bolts which connect the crank arm to the crank. He suggested changing the entire crank set including stem, bottom bracket, arms, and chain wheels as this assembly comes as a kit. We avoided the heat and went to lunch, and Dave had the work done an hour later.

It is amazing that in over 23,000 miles of cycling this has been only the third bike failure where we could not ride. The first was in Montenegro, on the Balkan Peninsula, where my rear wheel rim cracked from a large pothole in a fast downhill and was not rideable. The second was my rear hub cracking in half while riding up a hill on the coast in California.

The next day we took Andee to the airport in the morning rain. It was sad to see her leave again as she adds a loving and humorous touch to our ride. Jocelyn and I sometimes get into a routine where we are just focused on the riding and argue about simple things, sometimes forgetting why we are here. Andee has kept Jocelyn and me together on many occasions.

We returned to the hotel expecting to ride, but the stormy weather was causing flooding rains so we decided to stay put. In fact, tornadoes touched down here yesterday and Long Plains First People's Nation (an indigenous Indian community) evacuated to this hotel through the Red Cross. Our night was spent indoors watching movies and munching.

Jocelyn:

July 23, 2016

Mom found another awesome campsite on an island community park surrounded by Crescent Lake in Portage La Prairie. She really knows how to sniff out a good deal as well. This community park only charged a very small fee and allowed us the use of the bathrooms all night, and they scored us an invitation to eat at the "private" golf country club. After setting up camp, we wandered around and enjoyed the cool, clean park with only one other bike touring family of three that we met earlier that day on the road. The sunset was beautiful and we slept well in Manitoba. This was our last family camp night, and we gave our extra provisions to the elderly groundskeeper. He left with a big smile and a hearty wave!

Mom headed into Winnipeg, and after a few hours I called to let her know that my bike had a major problem and that I was walking it to wherever she was waiting. She found two bike shops, and after walking five miles we went to the first where the young man assured us that it could be fixed and that we would be able to pick it up later today. We stayed in a hotel, where a First Nations Tribe was evacuated to from their reservation due to the storm we experienced. What a night! Fortunately the bike was repaired. We had breakfast at an old, famous restaurant, and Mom flew home. I already miss her so much.

Mike:

Our first ride without Andee turned kind of depressing as we missed her positive and happy ways. It was so fun having her help to make us welcome everywhere we rode. The first day it took us over two hours to exit Winnipeg on this quiet Sunday. When we were back in the quiet countryside I was engulfed in a huge swarm of bees. Thousands of black dots buzzed through me, and I tried to maintain steerage and not move as the bees covered me and started stinging. I have never been through an attack like this before, and through the stinging I didn't flinch because if I did they would have attacked me further. I'm just glad I am not allergic to their stings. Fortunately my head buff covered my entire head including my mouth. Between this and dog chases, I don't know which is worse.

Manitoba Province is known for unpaved road shoulders. If fact, many countries have unpaved graded gravel shoulders. We spent our time between riding on the road and on the gravel shoulders depending on the traffic. Fortunately most drivers respected us, but at times we thought we were back in Peru with restless drivers.

After a long day it started raining and we raced to Pine Tree Campground. We have never been so engulfed by mosquitoes as here. In fact, when we checked in, the manager said there was no refund if the mosquitoes were biting. We had a difficult time setting up our tent, as the swarms of mosquitoes were there to torment us. It was raining and we had our rain gear on, but the mosquitoes worked their way inside our rain gear. About a mile or so back was a gas station/restaurant, so we walked there for dinner instead of trying to cook. What a miserable walk. After dinner at the gas station, we walked back and tried to sit in a screen-enclosed room. But even that was filled with mosquitoes. Sunset is now around 9:30 P.M. and we were in the tent before 9:00 P.M. After crawling in, Jocelyn swatted all the mosquitoes and we had a good and long sleep. As we lay in the tent, the mosquitoes buzzed between the rainfly and the tent. They knew we were in there. The next morning they were still there waiting for us and knew when we would exit. The next day we swatted away large attacking horse flies that enjoyed following our bikes. Flying bugs do love Canada.

Jocelyn:

July 25, 2016

We have made it to our 4th Province of Canada — Ontario, and there are now more hills, way more lakes, AND WAY MORE MOSQUITOES! I ride loaded and dirty along the TransCanada Highway because I cannot outrun those bugs!

We just keep riding. If you know me, I like those hops, and IPAs with double are better. This local Kenora, Ontario Blonde Ale is solid. It's refreshing, and it has a pilsner, pale ale, malted wheat flavor that's perfect for a starter beer for the evening. We shared two pounds of mussels tonight, and they were choice at the Lake of the Woods Brewing Company!

Mike:

We experienced one of our favorite Canadian rides so far as we rode a hilly 55 miles along many pretty, bright-blue lakes. It was an enjoyable ride with good shoulders and just enough hills to make it a bit challenging. At the end of the day we reached Crystal Lake Campground on Vermilion Bay, Ontario. At our campground two nights ago I had my first puncture since Nicaragua. I still can't believe I did not have any tire punctures in South America, even after all the rough roads we traveled.

We continued riding and putting in long, beautiful miles even though whenever we slowed the mosquitoes and blackflies swarmed us. We haven't seen blackflies since the west coast of New Zealand in 2011. Blackflies congregate around lake areas. Fortunately they don't follow moving targets, but they do bite fast. We are in long stretches of nothing and last night camped in a rest stop that had bear-proof trashcans where we stashed our food items. This picnic-only area had no camping signs, but since we didn't want to ride after dark, we were determined to stay even if we were asked to leave at some point. We've spent the night in many rest stops. When we awoke this morning there were two other cyclists camping near us. By the time we left they were still in their tents. After three hours, we entered the small town of Ignace, Ontario and after lunch decided to get a cheap motel room since there are no other campgrounds for another sixty miles. After several days of camping it sure is a pleasure to wash clothes, have a shower, and get away from the flying and biting things.

Jocelyn:

July 28, 2016

We ran out of water yesterday, and after 75 miles we decided to set up camp at a picnic rest area that simply states camping is illegal. But after talking to locals, they said most bikers camp there. So yes, I've stealth camped, and yes, I've done illegal things, but these days I never trespass. When there isn't a sign, I'll "free camp" while practicing Leave No Trace (LNT) principles of camping, and I never do anything illegal. I get anxiety if I do, but what solidified our choice for staying was the Revell River and the bear-proof trashcans. Plus, it was getting dark and we didn't want to continue riding. Unfortunately, our Sawyer filter broke after only filling two water bottles, which is quite ironic as I sent my Sawyer filter back home with my mom and the one we haven't ever used we kept and it broke after this one use. We had a quick dinner and never got out of the tent again. The mosquitoes are vicious here.

Mike:

We cycled another long day in the increasing hills and headwinds. The day seemed to last forever, but we spotted a Liquor Control Board of Ontario (LCBO) sign above the general store in Upsala and decided to have a beer. Off in the distance was a large lake and what appeared to be a campground. The proprietor said that it is a campground, so after purchasing a 6-pack we found a campsite on the lake and each of us had three beers while sitting on our picnic table in the shade.

For those not familiar with alcohol sales in Canada, it is somewhat confusing as it is controlled by the government with limited sale times and set prices. It was fine up until Ontario, which has very limited hours. Most days' sales stop at 6:00 P.M., but in larger cities sales are open until 8:00 P.M. or 9:00 P.M. on Fridays and Saturdays. We do enjoy beer after a long, hot day on the road. In the U.S., beer is available anywhere and anytime in small markets and grocery stores — but not so here. Some smaller towns may have only one LCBO store. We stopped at a small country store for a break of Twinkies and chocolate milk. The store did have an LCBO license and the guy ahead of me purchased two 24 packs of Busch beer. The cost of that was an astounding $87! The bottom line is that to enjoy a cold one it takes a little bit of luck and timing. We set up camp on Lake Upsala and then returned to the general store for dinner ingredients.

The next morning, Jocelyn cooked us a six-egg omelet with hot dogs and broccoli. There are increasing hills now, and we made it to Kakabeka Falls and inquired about camping at this provincial park. The price was $41 with no electric or water. After exploring the falls, we continued to the Happy Land Campground down the street and paid a still high $34.

This morning we had a short day so we 'slept in', whatever that means in a tent. It seems as though some days you just don't want to leave the tent. Earlier this year, while in the country of Panama, we met a fellow traveler, Gabrielle, whom Jocelyn became friends with. She is from Thunder Bay, Ontario and said to look her up if we ever pass through. Her parents, Elaine and Steve, offered to host us, and we were immediately welcomed into their home. That evening we enjoyed a delicious barbeque rib dinner with Elaine and Steve's neighbors, Rhonda and Kevin. We had such a good time and enjoyed all the company. Once again, we are reminded that this trip is all about the people we meet.

The next day we drove with our hosts to Fort William Historical Park for an informative tour. From 1803-1821 Fort William was the inland headquarters of the Northwest Company, a commercial empire that at its height stretched across North America into Europe and China. Fort William was the main transshipment point for goods coming in from the east and furs from the west. All goods came in and left Fort William by large canoes that traveled weeks and sometimes months to get here. The fort contained costumed staff who portrayed the individuals and groups who lived and worked in and around Fort William. The portrayed year was 1816, which marks the 200th anniversary of the occupation of Fort William by the forces of the Hudson's Bay Company. The Hudson's Bay Company and the Northwest Company were in competition for the control of the fur trade. These companies eventually settled their disputes and merged. It was a fascinating visit into history.

We had a good visit with Steve, Elaine, and Gabrielle. They were wonderful hosts with lots of food, drink, and conversation, but it was time to get back on the road. Elaine drove us out of town to avoid the poor Thunder Bay roads and busy morning traffic. In the late afternoon we stopped at a motel/licensed store for a cold beer. While there, we met Virginia from Canada getting back into tour cycling after her husband passed away. She is celebrating her 65th birthday with a tour of Canada. We were headed the same way and compared notes, but she continued riding while we decided to stay at the motel.

Jocelyn:

August 2, 2016

I met Gabrielle (Brie) in a magical hostel while cycling through Panama. She was backpacking her way up to Guatemala. We hit it off, and after hanging out for a few hours she invited us to stay with her parents in Thunder Bay, Ontario! A couple of times while cycling I have thought of her, the beers we drank, and how cool she was. When I started route planning across Canada I included a tour of Thunder Bay on that line! So happy to have met up with her again and her awesome parents and their coolest neighbors! They truly are "super" hosts, and we have appreciated spending time getting to know them! We will take one more rest day and tomorrow will head out of Thunder Bay and go on the northern Lake Superior route! It is at these times that I know I have made friends from around the world and we share memories that include family and exceptional dinners. Brie and her family are now friends that I'd welcome into my home forever, anytime, anyplace I am. That's how genuine and loving they were to me and my dad.

Mike:

The next morning a storm was brewing and we were immediately soaked as we climbed two large hills and negotiated through many road construction projects with blasting. We were passed by three touring cyclists who we waved to and said hi, but they never replied as they passed us going uphill. One of them wasn't peddling and all three bicycles were motorized. Later in the day we spotted another touring cyclist headed the other way who crossed the road to meet us. We talked with Chad from Boston who is headed west to British Columbia and then to San Diego. In fact, he said, "Are you the father and daughter who wrote a book a few years ago?" When we said yes, he was so surprised to meet us on the road. He said that before his trip he read many touring books and enjoyed ours because it was interesting and real. How random it was meeting someone on the road who has read our book.

It soon started raining again, sometimes with lightning and thunder. At this point we found another roadside motel and once again talked with Virginia who saw our bikes outside the motel. This motel was full, but there was another motel next door. We told Virginia that if there were no rooms there to come back and we would share our room with her. The motel sold food and we bought two steaks and rice, barbequed the steaks, and had a delicious meal washed down with our camping wine.

Our day's goal was to watch the opening ceremony of the Summer Olympics. We continued around Lake Superior in the periodic rain and achieved the town of Marathon after a long day. We quickly settled into a motel and found the only beer store, bought snacks at a grocery store, and settled into our room for the 2016 Summer Olympics opening ceremony. It was fun as we watched the Canadian version of the Olympics.

Before leaving Marathon we dropped down to Lake Superior and Pebble Beach. It was a cool morning to tour the beach of pebble rocks that have been polished over the years by water and ice along with a beach full of driftwood. Soon we climbed out of town and continued east. We continued into the drenching rain until we spotted lake cabins for rent along with an LCBO license sign. The camp store had a well-stocked store, so we enjoyed a feast that evening while watching more of the Olympic Games.

Jocelyn:
August 5, 2016

Today we met Chad from Boston! He is cycling in the opposite direction to Vancouver and then down to San Diego. I was so grateful to see another happy cyclist, and we both stopped to talk. Lately we have encountered many rude cyclists who ride past while not even saying "Hey" or "Hello." I love talking to fellow cyclist friends. Well, we got to talking for a bit and he happened to say, "You guys wouldn't happen to be the father/daughter team that wrote that book awhile back where the dad broke a rib taking a selfie?"

"YUP!"

Haha! He told us we are his inspiration.

WOW! I cried and said thank you for reading and sharing our love for riding. I love this bike life!

August 6, 2016

A new friend recommended we find Pebble Beach on Lake Superior in Ontario. One of my favorite sounds is of waves moving in and out upon rocks. This is so soothing, relaxing, and it gave me some free time to enjoy the Canadian seaside. I took a video of the weather we have ridden through, and it's not always sunshine, wildflowers, and lakes, or is it? If anyone is interested in riding the Lake Superior TransCanada route, I will highly recommend it as it has easily become one of my Top 5 routes from around the world. Someday I will return to ride all the way around the lake and will encourage friends to join me!

Mike:

The last few days have been a bit difficult for me with the increasing steep hills and headwinds. With few services on this road we have found three good camping spots along the lake that are part of the Ontario Parks Network. Although expensive at $41 Canadian, they are in scenic locations right on Lake Superior. Yesterday, at Agawa Bay Campground, we met Dale and his wife Cheryl, long time bikers who have bicycle toured and hiked in many places around the world. They are also sea kayakers and quite the adventurous couple and will be biking Southeast Asia later this year. After setting up camp we had a cooling swim/bath in the lake. That evening we enjoyed snacks, beer, and a fire at Dale and Cheryl's campsite.

After eight days from Thunder Bay we reached Sault Ste. Marie to complete a long ride with few services. We met and saw several people cycle touring, including three guys on cycle/scooters. It was unbelievable watching them go uphill powered like a skateboard with their feet as there were no pedals. This form of touring, and they carried panniers, seems a bit bewildering and taxing to us.

I finally had my front derailleur replaced in Sault Ste. Marie. While riding through Central Asia two years ago I fell onto rocks and bent the cage. I didn't know it at the time but it was also cracked. Shifting was getting more difficult in South America, and during the last several days of large hills north of Lake Superior I sometimes had to get off the bike and manually shift the chain. The derailleur cable was also frayed. The mechanic changed my cracked and bent Shimano Deore XT derailleur with another one that was two levels in quality below mine as we didn't want to wait for a like replacement. It worked well on the bench and on an unloaded test ride, but it took the next several days tweaking the cable tension to optimize the shifting under load and hills.

We left Sault Ste. Marie and spent several more days in the rain. I still don't understand why Ontario has such poor roads. In fact, we talked with many local cyclists about this and they all say they will cycle in the U.S. and other Canadian provinces, but they will not cycle across Ontario due to road conditions and traffic. The other provinces have more four-lane sections on Trans-Canadian Highway 17, while Ontario has only occasional four-lane sections and sometimes passing lanes. It can be frustrating in the rain, as most drivers, whether cars or trucks, will not slow down on the two lane roads. If the oncoming lane is clear they will move away from us when passing, but if not, they refuse to slow and they pass within inches. We have actually been flicked off by many drivers while we ride the white line or directly inside of it. It is that old mentality of "Why is a bicycle on the road?" We just cheerily wave back to them. Common sense dictates that when approaching a bicycle and you cannot move over, just slow down a bit. But that doesn't happen here. The government goes to the expense of grading the shoulder but only paving a few inches. We have ridden on the unpaved parts at times, but that can be dangerous also as it is sometimes deep and loose.

By late afternoon we were struggling and stopped at a country store for a cold drink and noticed many flavors of smoked rainbow trout, so we bought that and beer as the proprietor told us about a campground a few minutes down the road. We found that and quickly settled into a pleasant lakeside campground. After a swim in the lake we had a delicious dinner of rice and smoked rainbow trout.

The weather finally turned sunny after several wet days. A few hours later the rain started again. It was a struggle with the hard rain and increasing traffic. Several days later we arrived in North Bay and were immediately welcomed by another warmshowers host. Shannon has spent many years backpacking and working around the world. Our bikes went into her garage; we had a warm shower, put our wet clothes in the washer, and sat down with a delicious snack along with hot tea. That evening we enjoyed a tasty spaghetti dinner. The next morning Shannon cooked breakfast and we were back on the road.

The weather started clear, but within a few hours we donned our rain gear as we continued cycling in the hills toward Ottawa. After another long wet day we were hoping to camp but came upon a fishing and hunting lodge with cabins on Antler Lake, and we settled into one for the night. Shannon had packed us with the leftover spaghetti and we heated that for a second delicious night.

In Deep River we stayed with Michael and Danielle in their cordwood masonry house where the walls are made out of lengths of wood held together with a type of motor. The walls are unique and thick, which provides for excellent insulation during the winter while keeping the interior cool during the summer. They prepared a delicious meal along with quite an assortment of beer that we sampled. After dinner Michael briefed Jocelyn on the side roads to Ottawa paralleling the too busy Trans-Canadian Highway. They have cycle toured throughout Canada, the northern U.S., along with Ireland and England. Michael also explained the many bike paths to and around Ottawa.

After a night in their basement we were sent off after a delicious naan, spinach, and egg dish. We quickly were off to the 17 and rode to Ottawa on old farming roads where we surprisingly found the Whitewater Brewing Company out in the middle of nowhere. Michael and Danielle had told us about the brewery and restaurant, so we enjoyed a delicious pizza along with two pints of their fine craft beer. This fueled us another thirty miles to a KOA Campground that Jocelyn had set on her map. It was another long day on our bikes, and since sunset was soon we ordered wings and salad from a local pizza place that was delivered to our campsite after dark.

Jocelyn:

August 11, 2016

My mom is assisting me in transcribing these Instagram notes, so she wanted me to remember that today is my mom and dad's 37th wedding anniversary. Dad and she are often apart on these special days, so I will allow this one additional entry!

Did you know that "Winnie the Pooh" or adopted name "Winnipeg" was born around or in White River, Ontario, Canada? This black bear cub was adopted by Lieutenant Harry Colebourn in 1914. She was actually found by a trapper after a hunter had killed his mother. The bear was adopted for just $20 by Harry who was a horse veterinarian from World War I. Winnie quickly became the mascot for their group as they trained across the country. Lieutenant Harry took the bear to London, and upon finding out that he needed to go to France for the war, he found him a place in the London Zoo. Winnie stayed there till he died at 20 years old. During his time at the zoo, the friendly bear met Christopher Robin and his father A. A. Milnes who couldn't help but write about the special bond between the two. Christopher Robin nicknamed her "Winnie the Pooh", and he even shared birthdays with this actual bear. I've seen many black bears in this area and can't help but think how those bears could actually be connected to Winnie. My question is: Why did they color him golden brown like honey? Mom loves her history connections!

August 13, 2016

Today would have been my grandma Polly's 91st birthday! She knew me as the wild child, so often I think about how accepting she was of me.

August 15, 2016

I saw another baby black bear cub on the highway today. I kept looking for a momma bear but didn't see her and the cub didn't cross the busy highway when I was cycling through Sudbury, Ontario. Today is a Sunday and we met many Mennonites while riding in their horse and buggy rigs. They have such an interesting life, faithful in all things, and living in simplicity. They always wave hello, and we have tasted some of their darn good homemade sausage!

August 18, 2016

I have been pouting about the constant rain, but I'm also furthering my understanding that the now is accepting what is happening as it comes, feeling it with exceptional force, and propelling the energy to just keep on moving forward in a positive manner. I know that bike touring for the last six years has taught me so much, like how to be grateful, live in the now, and believe in the ride.

August 21, 2016

Three nights ago our warm showers host told us about his favorite brewing company, and it happened to be only thirty km off our route, but being who we are, we decided to make the trip and eat lunch there. Well, 100 km later, we made it to this glorious watering hole at 3:00 P.M. We each had two pints of Whitewater Brewing Co. "Farmer's Daughter" blonde ale with some pizza. 60 km later we found a campground and I walk in, and guess what? The front desk chick says to me, "Jesus, woman, you are hot!" I was so red, so tired, and so bloody wild looking at this time. But the day was marvelously full of farms and hills, all the while tracing the Ottawa River and melting in my seat over those two pints of beer. That was our welcome to Ottawa!

Mike:

This next day it was off into the rain again as we cycled to another host in Ottawa. Back in Banff National Park we had met a family that spent a year cycling in various parts of the world. After another long day, Kathleen greeted us into their Ottawa home. Husband Derick and kids Anna and Jasper were spending a week away at a family cottage. Kathleen welcomed us, and we were so excited to see her smiling face again. It turns out that it was her birthday and several friends came over to help celebrate. After a delicious meal we walked to a local park to watch a concert from the popular Canadian group, The Tragically Hip. This concert was being held in a stadium south of here, and the park was getting a live feed from there and projecting here on a giant screen. There were hundreds of people spending a Saturday night in the park. It was a fun evening.

Sunday morning, Kathleen guided us in the rain across the Ottawa River to Gatineau, Quebec where we met our cycling friends Nick and Virginia. We first met them in Dushanbe, Tajikistan in 2014 at a warmshowers host before tackling the Pamir Mountains on the way to Kyrgyzstan. We met them again in Kyrgyzstan where we were waiting for our China visas. In Vietnam they were in the southern and us in the northern mountains. We have met so many people all around the world, and it is special to reconnect with them in their homes.

We thoroughly enjoyed our visit with our cycling friends, Kathleen and Derick, along with their kids Anna and Jasper, in Ottawa and Nick and Virginia in Gatineau, Quebec. On Sunday Nick and Virginia cooked us an excellent barbeque lunch and dinner. We reminisced about our time together in Tajikistan and Kyrgyzstan. Monday was a windy and rainy day so we took the day off to relax, catch up with computer work, and watch a few adventure films on Netflix. Nick works evenings, so with Virginia we went back to Kathleen and Derick's home on Monday evening for a delicious dinner with their family.

Today is Tuesday and we toured Ottawa and Gatineau by bike. We met Nick at the Mill Street Brewpub for lunch. We visited many of the historical buildings, markets, and rode through Little Italy and Chinatown. On our way back to Gatineau we cycled through busy Ottawa and was surprised at the number of cyclists and how courteous the drivers are. Virginia cooked a tasty pasta dish to fuel us the next day.

After a big breakfast, Derick, Anna, and Jasper met us on their bikes and guided us out of Quebec. Thanks to Nick, Virginia, and Derick, Jocelyn had our ride to Montreal mapped out on bike paths. Although the path often zigzagged, we enjoyed getting off the regular road and had a pleasant three days of riding. In the late afternoon we found a campsite about twenty miles short of Montreal. The following day, Jocelyn once again was great with her navigating as we rode across islands with bridges and ferries, along the Ottawa River, Montreal canals, across major highways, and through to the east side of Montreal. Once there we were exhausted and found a cheap motel.

Jocelyn:

August 26, 2016

During our stay in Ottawa we saw an awesome light show over the Parliament House of the Canadian capital. This is a must-see show for anyone visiting! It's always so fun and great to reconnect with friends we've met on our travels. We met Kathleen and her family in Banff and hiked up Seminole Pass together. Her family took off a year to cycle around various countries around the world! Kathleen is one of the most inspiring women I've met, and she rode with us into Quebec today! Need I mention that it was pouring rain? But it's so fun to be able to wear shorts and sport our tan lines!

We met Virginia and Nick, our tour friends, while cycling in Dushanbe, Tajikistan. We decided to take a 4x4 ride to the start of the Pamir Highway together. After that almost disastrous adventure, we were bonded. We met each other twice in the Pamir Mountains as they took the Pamir Highway (high route) and we took the Wakhan Valley (low route) on our way to Kyrgyzstan. We then saw them one more time in Osh, Kyrgyzstan. They finished their tour in Singapore and flew back to Quebec. They invited us to their home if we were ever in Canada. Well, we cycled in and stayed with them for a few days. We cherish those moments we've had with them. Thank you, Nick and Virginia, for hosting us and for being awesome cooks. We love you!

Mike:

We have cycled around the earth! The circumference of the earth is 24,901 miles at the equator. We have reached that and more. In 2011 we cycled from Florida to California at 2,650 miles; in 2012 we cycled six weeks around the South Island of New Zealand at 1,099 miles. Those two journeys started our world ride total at 3,749 miles. When added to our third tour of Marrakech, Morocco to Bangkok, Thailand (2014) and Washington State to Puerto Montt, Chile, and Calgary, Canada to Quebec (2015-2016), we have over 25,000 miles (40,234 km). After 29 months, four tours of cycling in a period of almost five years, we are still going strong and together. There have been several difficult times between this father and daughter, but we have persevered thanks to patience and my wife Andrea's calming ways to keep us going. Physically and mentally, I have been up and down in some difficult situations from the sheer difficulty of a trip such as this. But we are still riding, as both of us are headstrong and will not give up on our pursuit of this incredible journey around the globe. People look at us and our bikes, and they seem to always be looking for a motor. We always point to our legs and say, "No motor." Often they walk away in disbelief.

We reached 25,000 miles in Canada!

Jocelyn:

August 28, 2016

We've cycled just over 3 ½ years in the last five years, and I've had four birthdays while on the road. This year I'll be celebrating my 26th birthday somewhere on the East Coast of the U.S.A. I sometimes feel burnt out and tired as we are 36 miles from 25,000 miles, that's technically around the world. I do think of my past, what I have quit before, but I've gained so much perseverance, a desire to go on, and a love for the unknown. I'm comfortable in my own skin. I love me! So, I'm on the losing side of 25, but I'm not afraid of age anymore.

Today we went island hopping, and I think we crossed over more than four bridges and took one ferry to find ourselves in Montreal, Quebec!

August 30, 2016

We have done it! The circumference of the world is 24,901 miles or 40,075 km. We decided to make this milestone our goal while it rained. We haven't done anything special to celebrate, and we don't feel a need. Our panniers represent how we are feeling, a bit sagging and dirty. I think once we hit Nova Scotia all we have to do is drop down to Florida and that'll be the end of our world tour.

We left Montreal and traveled along the St. Lawrence Seaway toward the historic Quebec City. The province of Quebec is much more bicycle friendly than the province of Ontario. Quebec has many bike paths and many signs alerting drivers to respect cyclists. As a bonus, so far all the shoulders are completely paved.

Mike:

We feel like we are back in France as the signs are in French and French is the language of Quebec. We always ask, *"Parlez-vous Anglais?"* (Do you speak English?), and most do. We enjoy the quaint villages, beautiful homes and churches, friendly people, thousands of acres of sweet corn, of which we buy and cook at camp, and delicious blueberries. Another bonus is that the people of Quebec have a choice of when and where they can purchase alcohol. We find beer at almost all stores and restaurants and about $5 cheaper a six pack than in Ontario.

Yesterday, when we checked into Motel Levis in Levis, Quebec, a bicycle touring couple from Delaware checked in after us. We quickly shared our stories. Chip and Nancy were here to start another one-week tour of this area. They have bicycle toured here several other times along with other parts of the world. Nancy invited us to share dinner with them, so they drove us to a microbrewery down on the waterfront of the St. Lawrence River.

The following morning, Chip drove us to the Québec ferry for our ride across the St. Lawrence River to Québec City. Québec City sits on the Saint Lawrence River in Canada's mostly French-speaking Québec Province. Dating to 1608, it has a fortified colonial core with stone buildings and narrow streets. The main district's cobblestone streets are lined with restaurants and boutiques. We had a good day exploring by foot all the history of this area. Thanks to all our friends that recommended we take a day off here to visit Québec City.

When we returned to our motel room we found a note from Motel Levis saying that we were their guests for the night and that they refunded tonight's fee. This motel is a 'Bienvenue Cyclistes' place where cyclists are welcomed and catered to. There is a shed in the back where bikes are locked and tools available for repairs. Thank you to Jean-Yves of Motel Levis for his generous contribution to our ride.

We continued riding all day until we found a campground with a grocery store right next door. At $21 Canadian, it was our cheapest camp yet and also had the most amenities, including a full kitchen at our disposal. At the store we bought lots of vegetables and had a grand dinner, along with ice cream for dessert. This downtown campground even had a pool and spa, but by the time we had eaten and cleaned up we were ready for the tent.

Yesterday we left Riviere du-Loup on the St. Lawrence River and started to New Brunswick on the Petit Temis Interprovincial Linear Park Rail Trail. This bicycle trail built on the bed of an old railway covers eighty miles with plenty of scenic lookouts, lakes, rest stops with toilettes, and rustic camping. Last night we found a campsite in the village of Cabano on Lake Temiscouata. We then crossed into our sixth Canadian Province of New Brunswick and cycled past the city of Edmundston where we found another campground. We hope to find more trails such as this.

The next several days Jocelyn found less traveled roads through the Canadian Appalachian Mountains. One day we met a kind lady who stopped on the road and told us about an apartment she rents to hikers and bikers on a daily basis. The village of Perth-Andover is on the International Appalachian Trail (IAT). We settled into the apartment and Eileen took us to a store, and once back at the apartment we cooked a filling dinner and breakfast the next morning.

Eileen directed us to a rail trail about one mile from the rental apartment. It was a great find and another day riding along an old railroad route. We spent all day on this trail, crossed the St. John River, and found a campground in Woodstock, New Brunswick. While preparing to cook our dinner, a plastic piece on our MSR Whisperlite International fuel pump that attaches to the fuel tank broke causing a gas leak. It has been a good stove as we have used unleaded gas around the world for fuel. We will not be able to cook until we can find a replacement.

Jocelyn:

September 2, 2016

Yesterday we got hit with a cold front, and today we are fighting the headwinds. I did find a concrete statue of a farmer holding hay in the middle of a field and stopped to snap a picture. That was a bit different!

September, 2016 — My brother Cary's 31st birthday

We are riding one boss-ass trail of 140 km into New Brunswick from Rivière-du-Loup, Québec! There are many outhouses, a few camping areas with wood, and lots of waterholes. This is a fine rail trail around the New Brunswick area.

September 6, 2016

Five years ago as of today, we started our bike tour across the lower eight states of the U.S. Some neighbors joined us for our send-off as we departed with the rising sun from the Atlantic Ocean in Cape Canaveral, Florida. Without our family and friends we wouldn't have been able to stick together this long. Thank you to those who have cheered us on, who have known me before this journey, and who will still stick around to see if we will make it legit and finish! We've cycled together for four tours, just over 30 months, and have crossed 37 countries.

Re-entered the U.S.

"Not all those who wander are lost."
–J.R.R. Tolkien

Mike:

On September 8, 2016, we re-entered the U.S. after exiting from San Diego, California into Tijuana, Mexico on August 4, 2015. We cycled into the town of Houlton, Maine near the border to visit our neighbor's mother. Jean spends her winters next door to us in Cape Canaveral, Florida with her daughter Andrea and son-in-law Tim. Jean has two lots with cottages on Lake Nickerson where we spent several nights. Andrea flew in the day after we arrived.

We had a terrific time visiting with Andrea and Jean, while enjoying home cooked meals and favorite restaurants in the small border town of Houlton. We also indulged in a different kind of transportation by exploring the entire lake one end to the other in kayaks and a canoe. This awesome peaceful setting has been in their family for generations. Jean's husband Pete, who passed the previous year, called this lot "Tranquility Point". The cottages are full of history and mementoes representing this large, jovial family. Our last evening was spent in front of a lakeside fire pit. Jean kept the fire going as we each enjoyed a large bowl of seafood chowder, easily the best we have ever had.

Jean and Andrea have been super hosts, but it was time to get back on the saddle. They fed us breakfast and drove us back to Jean's in-town large historical home where the bikes had been stored in the garage. The neighborhood is old Americana in a 200-year-old town full of white houses and big yards. We said our goodbyes and said, "See you in Florida!"

Jocelyn:

September 7-9, 2016

We have spent two nights with our friends in Houlton, Maine, and tomorrow we leave and go back into New Brunswick from Calais. We won't officially reenter the United States till around Sept. 23rdish. I have fond memories from just a few days ago when I was kayaking all over Lake Nickerson, sleeping in the lakeside cabin loft, watching bonfires, and sharing wine with the best seafood chowder. This special place is called "Tranquility Point" in honor of Pete, a former Air Force commander. Thank you, Andrea and Jean, for sharing this lovely place.

Mike:

We found U.S. 1 and headed southeast to Calais. U.S. 1 runs all the way to and through Florida. The Maine scenery was breathtaking, and at the end of the day we found Greenland Cove Campground on East Grand Lake. We were immediately welcomed by our next-door camping neighbors, Colin and Jill. After we set up camp, another neighbor, Ron, brought us fresh-cut tomatoes and four cooked ears of corn on the cob. Since our stove is non-functional, this was welcomed. After dinner we were invited next door to Colin and Jill's fire where we talked into the night. They are from Woodstock, New Brunswick and filled us in on some history of that area. A few days ago we had stayed in Perth-Andover. They told us how the town received its name. There is a downtown area, Perth, and a bridge over the St. John River to another downtown area. Hence, the town got the name Perth-Andover for the people on the other side — that part over the bridge.

This morning it started raining around 5:00 A.M. When we exited the tent it was still raining, and Ron invited us into his trailer for breakfast. We packed everything wet and cycled the three miles back to U.S. 1. In many cases campgrounds are situated on lakes, sometimes several miles down from the main road. In this case it was a three-mile climb up the muddy road back to US 1. Jocelyn and I decided to stealth camp next time before riding down to another campground. Many hours later, in the increasing rain and wind, we finally found a place to take a break at the Waite General Store. This was the only store open since we left the campground. The owner, Wayne, told us that a strong cold front was moving north. He showed us the weather radar on his phone and asked if we had shelter. We didn't but decided to try and hitch a ride the thirty miles to Calais. That didn't work in the very light Sunday traffic, so I asked the store clerk if she knew of anyone with a truck that could drive us. At this point the lightning and heavy rain had set in, so we thought about hanging out at the store until it passed. The clerk kindly called Wayne who had already left, and he returned and drove us to Calais. Wayne was a real 'road angel' who delivered us out of the storm to a motel in Calais. We strung up our clothesline in the motel room and draped our wet tent and clothes.

We left Calais, Maine, crossed over the St. Croix River, and re-entered New Brunswick in the town of St. Stephen. Our day was spent on a sightseeing route around the Bay of Fundy. The Bay of Fundy is a bay on the Atlantic Coast of North America, on the northeast end of the Gulf of Maine between the Canadian provinces of New Brunswick and Nova Scotia, with a small portion touching the U.S. state of Maine. It is home to the highest tidal range in the world with extremes to 53 feet. After a delicious fish lunch we continued to New River Beach Campground and settled in at a Bay of Fundy campground.

The next morning we rode on New Brunswick 1 to the city of St. John and proceeded to the Nova Star Cruises Digby ferry to check on departure times. We were going to spend a night in St. John, but we boarded since the ferry was leaving within the hour. The forty-mile ride took a little over two hours. On arrival at Digby, it was a two-mile ride to the Digby Campground where there were several others campers. It was a ten-minute walk into town and a delicious but expensive seafood dinner. Digby is supposedly the scallop capital of the world, so we indulged in this tasty treat. After stopping at an ice cream shop we walked back to camp and settled into the tent for the night.

In the morning we decided to take a break and explore this quaint and interesting fishing village. It's hard to believe that we have biked over 3,100 miles through Canada since July 10th as we have taken many days off to explore. Sometimes we will bicycle tour a town and in others we will walk. Most campgrounds will be closing at the end of this month. The seasonal people will winterize their trailers and leave them in place, hoping they will be okay after the long upcoming winter. The season starts in late May. We have enjoyed all the campgrounds throughout Canada whether they are private or provincial. Our original plan was to cycle more north to Prince Edward Island, north of Nova Scotia. We had even talked about cycling Newfoundland and Labrador. But we have run out of time. I will be leaving for a business trip to Denver at the end of this month and will fly out of Boston September 26th. In the meantime, we will cycle out of Digby tomorrow morning and head northeast across Nova Scotia to Liverpool and south to Yarmouth. From Yarmouth we will ferry to Portland, Maine and continue south to Boston.

Yesterday we left Digby riding north before heading east across the Nova Scotia Peninsula. Last night another cold front came through and the morning temperature was around 32°F. After an all-day ride we entered Kejimkujik National Park and found a scenic campground among the tall tress bordering a bright-blue lake. The park consists of 230 sq. miles of rolling hills and waterways and closes in a week. We were expecting it to be expensive, but at $25 it is much cheaper than the $41 provincial parks. This morning we turned south at Liverpool and continued a few more miles to Hunts Point Beach where once again we saw the Atlantic Ocean after a long absence.

In the historical town of Shelburne, established 1783, we stopped at the Boxing Rock Brewery in town, but the tasting was strange as you are allowed a 'splash' of what is available and then one small 4 oz. sample of one you like for $2. As I have said many times, Canada has different and confusing alcohol rules. The local campground was closed, but after five days in campgrounds a motel was welcome.

We left Shelburne, Nova Scotia hoping to make it just halfway to our ferry departure port of Yarmouth. Jocelyn found another rail trail, but after six miles of a rocky trail and plant overgrowth we decided to head back to the main road. When we found a road to exit the trail, we saw a sign that read, "This rail trail is not maintained. Enter at your own risk." It was rough and we walked a few miles of it. The going was slow back on the hilly 103 West, but we persevered and entered the outskirts of Yarmouth in the rain and close to sunset found a campground. We quickly set up the tent, and after a hurried dinner we were inside before the hard rain hit. Nova Scotia is going through its worst drought in 134 years. Many campgrounds and homes are out of well water and have to buy their water. In fact, that is why many campgrounds are closed.

Jocelyn:

September 14, 2016

Yesterday we rode into Saint John, New Brunswick. We decided to cycle to the ferry, and with thirty minutes to departure we walked right on! Bye to New Brunswick as we motored across the Bay of Fundy! My dad managed to capture an epic picture of me walking into the ship. Props to him for always taking photos of my backside with cool scenery, haha! We have cycled seven out of the ten provinces in Canada, covering 3,100 miles so far. Tomorrow we will start a small bike tour around the western part of Nova Scotia.

September 16, 2016

We are cycling through the Kejimkujik National Park, and I appreciate the campsites and environmental awareness of the area. I took pictures of some old, weathered buildings that demonstrate the hardiness of the people. My mom would like to explore this place!

September 19, 2016

Yesterday started out a bit slow as I guided us onto the Shelburne County rail trail. There was a lot of ducking under tree limbs, walking through rough roadways, and massive rocks that literally made us jump out of our seats. About 10 km in we saw a sign on the trail, "Abandoned railway, rail not maintained, enter at your own risk!" It made sense now, so we left that and cycled another 100 km into Yarmouth, which was totally unexpected. The rain fell, the large headwind disappeared, and the massive hills sort of rolled away. Now our Canada tour is over! We will get on the ferry tomorrow and hit Portland, Maine around 2:00 P.M.! Way to go — eh!

Mike:

We left our camp in heavy rain and rode directly to the ferry port in Yarmouth. After purchasing our tickets, we found a motel ten minutes away where we dried all our clothes and camping gear. Cycling across Canada was a grand adventure. We will miss the many provinces and new and old friends that we stayed with along the way. The scenic vistas through the mountains, hills, and lakes were stunning. The varying lake colors were awesome. The wildlife was impressive, but the mosquitoes were notorious.

This morning we had an early wake up and were at the ferry at 7:00 A.M. The ferry left at 8:30 and arrived in Portland, Maine five hours later. It was a relaxing trip while sitting in large, reclining seats while reading and snoozing. There are several outside areas to walk, but they were all wet from heavy fog during the entire trip across the Gulf of Maine. After going through U.S. customs, we cycle-toured the downtown area, stopped for a beer at one of many breweries, cycled south onto U.S. 1, and found a motel.

We spent an extra day in Portland, Maine to walk around the waterfront and old downtown areas. Portland is one of those cities where you can get 'stuck' and spend several days, as it is that entertaining. The next morning we continued south along another rail trail before riding on the coast and zigzagging back to the rail trail and U.S. 1. We had an enjoyable ride before finding a motel near the historic town, Kennebunkport, Maine, as the rain was coming again, and the campgrounds we passed were closed for the season. Historically a shipbuilding and fishing village for well over a century, Kennebunkport has been a popular summer colony and seaside tourist destination. We rode through New Hampshire and camped for one night before entering Massachusetts on the beachside during a bright, sunny day.

We crossed the Merrimack River on U.S. 1 into the town of Newburyport, and to our complete surprise we found Andee and her sorority sister, our next host, Margaret! The circumstances and timing of us meeting them like this were incredible, as we had decided to have lunch in Newburyport after seeing a portside restaurant while riding over the bridge. They saw us on the bridge after which we turned off into the harbor area. We rode right by Andee when I heard, "Mike!" When we turned our heads, there she was!

We enjoyed a wonderful reunion and lunch, sharing many laughs and great food at Michael's. After lunch, Margaret and Andee drove off in Margaret's car to see the sights while Jocelyn and I rode through several more historic towns before arriving in Magnolia Village just south of Gloucester. Margaret has lived in this cool little beach town for many years. These pioneering towns were established during the early 1600s, and we thoroughly enjoy riding through history. Margaret was an excellent tour guide who also knew all the best seafood restaurants. We explored the famous town of Salem known for its 1692 witch trials, during which several locals were executed for allegedly practicing witchcraft. We then enjoyed a seafood dinner in Gloucester Harbor and saw two of the boats from the television show, *Wicked Tuna*.

Jocelyn's Instagram Posts:

September 21, 2016

We left Yarmouth in the rain and fog, no different than many days cycling, but today we were on a long ferry ride to Portland, Maine. This town is where history feels alive, or was it all the craft brews and delicious treats that we enjoyed? Portland is for the foodies and beer lovers who enjoy the harbor views. What a beautiful day to experience the big tide waters!

September 23, 2016

We tasted one of the best chowders in Portland, and I am pretty sure all around the world. I can truly say that Gilbert's Chowder House is the place for lobster shrimp chowda!

September 26, 2016

We have been riding and camping in the good-old USA! Today we are in Kennebunkport where the Bush family has their summer homes, and it was amazing. We cruised down to Hampton Beach in New Hampshire and are currently staying with the super hostess, Margaret, in the Gloucester, Massachusetts area. AND, my mother surprised us for the long weekend to bring us some things we wanted for this part of our journey south. It feels like a daydream with her here. WOW! Dad was shocked and we all enjoyed a delicious meal on the dock at Michael's Harborside in Newburyport. The next few days were busy with sightseeing in Salem and a seafood dinner where the boats for the *Wicked Tuna* television show are moored. Margaret knew exactly where my father and I wanted to go, and we both were all giddy at the sight of the fishing boat *Hard Merchandise* featured on *Wicked Tuna*. I can't explain what a joy it is to see my mom, with her (and my) Alpha Gamma Delta sorority sister laughing about good times. Friends and family have been the glue that has helped to keep us moving on this journey. I have really loved meeting Tucker and sharing a cuddle session with this sweet doodle dog!

Mike:

Two days later I flew to Denver for several days of medical and physiological testing for the upcoming South Pole 2017 winter season. I work as a satellite communications engineer for the United States Antarctic Program, and this would be my third winter there. I am writing this book from the South Pole, so obviously I passed all the required medical testing. When I was in Denver, Andee and Jocelyn explored Boston before Andee returned home to Florida. This was such a cool surprise for Andee to make this unexpected visit. She and my son Cary are a significant part of this world cycling team, and without them supporting us on the home front this trip would have ended a long time ago. Jocelyn and I will forever be grateful for their encouragement and assistance.

I returned from Denver early Sunday morning and we were back on the road two days later after ten days in Magnolia, Gloucester. Seaside Cycle in Manchester gave us an excellent tune-up and replaced our drive chain after 3,500 miles from Calgary. Margaret and her dog Tucker were entertaining hosts who made us feel like we were at home. It was time to move on, and we decided on a route suggested by Margaret that would enable us to explore more of this historical part of our country.

Our first day found us back in Salem at Winter Island Maritime Park Campground. This campground is built on land that was a key defensive area for the city of Salem. The first fort was built in the 1640s, and the latest is called Fort Pickering complete with the Fort Pickering Lighthouse. An old moat is all that remains of the fort. After setting up camp we explored more of Salem.

The Salem to Boston Ferry left at 7:00 A.M., so we woke early, broke camp in the dark, and were at the ferry at 6:30 A.M., right in time for sunrise. After a quick one-hour ferry ride to Boston, we walked down the wharf and boarded the Boston to Provincetown ferry. This was a rough and wild ferry ride with many people seasick, and this was the first day in the last four that the ferry was running because of high seas. When we arrived at Provincetown, Cape Cod, we found an almost closed for the season motel and settled in for a day of exploring. In 1620 Provincetown was the first stop of the pilgrims on board the Mayflower. We spent the day exploring historic Provincetown while also enjoying the excellent local seafood.

We departed Provincetown and cycled around the Cape Cod Peninsula mostly by bike paths and rail trails. Cape Cod has an excellent paved bike path system that winds and meanders up and down sand dunes giving way to many beautiful ocean views. We reached Brewster and a warmshowers host, Susan, who was excited to hear about our adventures as we were just the third cyclist group she had hosted. She had previously invited two couples to dinner, and we joined the dinner party with excellent company and barbecued steaks. It was an enjoyable evening and her two extra beds were comfortable. We left before the sun was up as Susan went to work.

We cycled to Hyannis and boarded the Martha's Vineyard ferry. It was a beautiful and calm day on the ocean, unlike two days ago when we ferried to Provincetown. An hour later we were riding down the ferry ramp to explore Martha's Vineyard, a longtime New England summer colony. A few hours later we arrived at Martha's Vineyard Campground where we settled in for the night.

The next morning we bike toured to Edgartown but didn't have enough time to take the three-minute ferry to Chappaquiddick Island, as we were scheduled to leave Vineyard Haven on the 12:45 ferry to New Bedford. We had wanted to spend two nights on Martha's Vineyard, but the effects of Hurricane Matthew were starting to appear and the ferries stop running during windy conditions. We arrived by ferry in New Bedford, Massachusetts.

Speaking of Hurricane Matthew, our Cape Canaveral home (about six hundred feet from the beach) only suffered tree damage, thanks to Andee and Cary making it a fortress with our storm panels and long water-blocking bladders against the doors to prevent water intrusion. I had a hard time sleeping as I thought about Andee and Cary. Cary and I were texting all night to let me know what was happening.

The effects of a cold front and Hurricane Matthew brought rain all night with considerable flooding, so we decided to spend an extra day here. We "ubered" to the New Bedford Whaling Museum and spent several fascinating hours learning about the colonizing of New England, whaling around the world, and the end of the whaling period. It was from New Bedford that 21-year-old Herman Melville set sail aboard the whaling ship *Acushnet* on one of the most important sea voyages in American literature. Out of Melville's adventure came the classic novel *Moby Dick*.

Whaling flourished in the 1850s as more whaling ships sailed from New Bedford than from all the world ports combined. After whaling peaked in 1857, a slow decline continued until 1925 when the last whaling ship, the *Wanderer*, sailed from the harbor. The New Bedford whaling industry employed people from around the world who settled in this area.

The next day was bright and sunny but cold as we set off for another warmshowers host in Westerly, Rhode Island. There are two major bridges to cross over the Narragansett Bay. We approached the first bridge from Newport, Rhode Island to Conanicut Island and did not see any 'No Bicycles Allowed' signs, so we proceeded into the traffic. There was no shoulder and lots of traffic, and we soon realized we were in a dangerous situation. Suddenly a police car appeared and stopped us. We were told that bicycles are not allowed on this bridge and that he would not allow us to continue and "be killed." At that point he called another officer who quickly appeared, and they offered to take us and our bikes over the bridge. They were both kind as they helped us load our bikes and unload on the other side. We approached the next bridge and did see a 'No Bicycle' sign, so we stopped on the side to hitchhike over the bridge. A kind man with a pickup stopped to drive us across. The strange thing about this bridge was that there was a rail enclosed walking area plus a wide shoulder. We could have easily ridden across this bridge although it was windy. Thanks to two of Rhode Island's finest and John from Conanicut Island for being three 'bridge angels' this day.

We cycled another thirty miles to Westerly, Connecticut and met another warmshowers host. Tom has traveled many areas of the world, works on a clam boat, and he also forages for wild mushrooms that he sells to restaurants. He spends his winters paddling and hiking throughout Florida. We talked late into the night about — what else? — traveling the world. In January 2017, Tom stayed in our Cape Canaveral home with two traveling friends, Judy and Linda. Cary and Jocelyn were able to join them for a paddling session in Cocoa Beach. That evening they cooked a delicious seafood dinner. The next day they continued south. It was such a pleasure to repay Tom's hospitality from Connecticut.

We left Westerly and cycled to Mystic Seaport, Connecticut and toured the old shipyard, a 19th century seafaring village, and many seafaring exhibits. On premises is a working shipyard that uses traditional as well as modern tools to preserve many historic vessels. At the Seaport are the

1882 full-rigged ship *Joseph Conrad* and the old whaling ship *Charles W. Morgan*. The *Charles W. Morgan* was built in 1841 in New Bedford, Massachusetts and is the last survivor of nearly 2,700 registered American whaling ships. During her whaling days, spanning eighty years, she made 37 voyages around the world. The *Charles W. Morgan* is the last wooden whaling ship in the world.

In 1981, Andee and I sailed down the Intracoastal Waterway from Swansea, Massachusetts to Port Canaveral, Florida on a 46-foot catamaran named *Banana Split*. The owners lived in one hull and we in the other. 35 years ago we tied to the Mystic Seaport dock and visited this attraction on a warm fall day.

Jocelyn:

October 5, 2016

We left Margaret's house and rode south back to Salem to camp. Today we packed up our tent and gear at 5:00 A.M. and boarded the ferry from Salem to Boston at 7:00 A.M. We had a fairly good ride (I puked a little.) on the ferry to Provincetown at 9:00 A.M. So now we are in this Cape Cod historical town wandering around and exploring the monuments. We walked to the top of a tall tower that was finished in 1910 to commemorate the first landfall by the Pilgrims in 1620. Cool fact: This structure is 252 feet tall and is the tallest granite structure in the USA.

October 6, 2016

I am very concerned for my home state of Florida as it is preparing for a category 4 hurricane named Matthew. Depending on the time, my hometown of Cape Canaveral could disappear due to water surge across this barrier island. I live eight houses from the beach, and my brother and dog are staying home. I'm a wreck. I feel numb that I can't do anything. The prep work takes so much time and in the heat is difficult for me, more so for my mom (shutters, water-bladders across doors, filing the tub with water, and the clean up after that can take weeks.) We haven't faced a hurricane for years, but in 2008 my house was flooded by Tropical Storm Fay. Our tour just might end here shortly. I love you so much. You are the most amazing brother and I'm so thankful you are who you are. Stay safe and keep me posted. My mom evacuated to the mainland to stay with our good friend Donna. I know she is going to be fine, but we are all anxious to see this storm pass quickly.

October 7, 2016

Meanwhile, we are on Cape Cod National Seashore cycling around Provincetown on a lovely day. Thank you all for the positive vibes, prayers, and love toward my family, friends, and community. My family is safe and our house is fine! Hurricane Matthew ended up sliding farther east and hitting the Cape at exactly low tide! The best part: There was no storm surge in our neighborhood.

October 8, 2016

Yesterday morning we decided to try to make the ferry to Martha's Vineyard. When we did, we had no plan, but it seemed like everyone else did! We ended up cycling toward the middle of the island and camping. This morning we cycled to Edgartown (watched the ferries going to and from Chappaquiddick) and rushed back to Vineyard Haven to catch a ferry to New Bedford. We have had a good discussion about the Kennedy family. Someday I need to read more about our famous families in New England! We arrived into New Bedford and strolled around the dock area.

October 10, 2016

"Welcome to Rhode Island" was different as I accidentally took us on a "toll bridge" and halfway to the top we got pulled over by the police. For a minute there I was trying to decide if I should stop or keep going. The police officers were super nice and escorted us across to the Island. From there we had to hitchhike across the next bridge. It took like an hour to get a ride. It's a bummer as it's so hard to hitchhike in the U.S.

October 12, 2016

Mystic Seaport, Connecticut is where we found the *Draken Harald Harfagre*, the largest clinker-built (a method of *boat* building where the edges of hull planks overlap) Viking longship built in modern times! It left Norway in April and just arrived here October 2nd. We met the coolest warmshowers host on Long Island Sound with a lighthouse on his property. We decided to cycle some of Long Island and then ferry back to Connecticut this weekend. This is my 30th state to cycle in, and I am feeling that life is good.

Mike:

A few days and warmshowers hosts later, we rode the Cross Sound Ferry from New London, Connecticut to Orient Point, Long Island, New York and cycled south while exploring the old towns on Long Island. It was fall harvest time, and we enjoyed many stops at fruit and vegetable farms to admire the pumpkins, flowers, apples, apple cider, and roasted corn.

Jocelyn's 26th birthday in New York City.

Several days later we ferried back across the sound to Bridgeport, Connecticut before continuing south to Stamford, Connecticut where we visited, Annie, a college friend of Jocelyn. For the second time, the first being in Gloucester, Massachusetts, we met Leroy who has spent the last 2 ½ years walking the perimeter of the U.S. There are people slower than us! We settled into a motel on this Saturday night and met Annie, her mother Mary Beth, her uncle Bruce, and her uncle's sister Vickie at a fine Italian restaurant in old downtown Stamford. We enjoyed an entertaining meal with a fun group.

Jocelyn:

October 15, 2016

Yesterday we took the ferry from Port Jefferson, Long Island to Bridgeport, Connecticut and found Leroy who has walked around the perimeter of the U.S. more than 12,000 miles in the past two years. We first saw him in Massachusetts. He is also homeward bound.

> *"Each friend represents a world in us, a world not born until they arrive, and it is only by this meeting that a new world is born."*
>
> –Anais Nin

This is a favorite quote of mine. I just met up again with the ever-inspiring Annie and her awesome family. I met Annie in college, and she's been super supportive of our ride and what we're doing. This has been a bit unbelievable to meet her along our trip and to just get to hang out. Reconnecting is always fun.

Mike:

On our way to New York City we stayed with another warmshowers host in Mount Vernon, N.Y. Raj and Denise have a house full of various road and tour bicycles. They were married a year ago as they cycled through Northern Europe. They cooked an excellent meal, and it was entertaining listening to their cycling adventures.

Monday morning, we cycled through the increasing traffic toward New York City for a 26th birthday Jocelyn will never forget. We entered Manhattan on a waterfront bike path, and Jocelyn navigated us to a cool ride right through Central Park. At this, we were inspired to be brave or foolish, and we cycled down 7th Avenue through Times Square during the lunchtime traffic! What an exhilarating and dazzling ride as we maneuvered through throngs of people, cars, and taxis! Our shoulders were brushed a few times by trucks, but we managed to keep the rubber on the ground. I can't begin to say how riveting this ride was as we stared at the massive building-attached video displays advertising everything from the latest Broadway plays, television shows, jewelry, clothing, etc. It was difficult for these two 'looky-loos' to keep our roaming eyes on the road. We found an outside café for Jocelyn's birthday lunch and then proceeded to the striking and iconic multi-cabled Brooklyn Bridge with a massive elevated wood bike path and walkway. Once again we maneuvered through masses of people and other bikes for an unforgettable view of the Brooklyn and Manhattan skylines.

After that memorable ride, Jocelyn found our way to the Belford, New Jersey ferry where we took a 45-minute ferry ride into our next state. Our next warmshowers hosts Dan and Toby served us an excellent pasta-shrimp dinner as we excitedly talked about our riding day through the city.

We had a pleasurable visit with our Middletown, N.J. hosts Toby and Dan. Toby is quite the cook, and we probably gained a few pounds from the breakfasts, lunches, and dinners. We spent all day Tuesday exploring N.Y.C., and we rested the next day in Middletown.

Jocelyn:
October 17, 2016

For my 26th birthday we decided to cycle down Times Square in New York City. What a wild ride for sure! Dad describes it well, and all I can add is that we managed to not get hit. We crossed the East River on the Brooklyn Bridge and took several pictures, like celebrities sharing our pride for this wonderful city. I'll be back! We played tourists for a few days and went to the 102nd floor of the Empire State Building. The bikes waited patiently at our warmshowers hosts in New Jersey!

October 19, 2016

We voted with our mail-in ballots. This time I am sure that my vote means something, and we have a few weeks to see what happens as this process has been very sad and both political parties have been rude to each other. The American process is corrupt and needs to be fixed.

Mike:

We continued working our way south through New Jersey in heavy rain. A cold front was coming through, which brought cold along with the wet. As we continued through New Jersey most campgrounds were closed. We thought about camping in a few anyway, but with the 'No Trespassing' signs we decided not to. In Cape May, New Jersey we met Jocelyn's high school friend Lauren, her husband James, and son Aiden. They treated us to a delicious lunch in a downtown Cape May restaurant. At this point

Jocelyn had just heard from a nearby warmshowers host. We biked two blocks and were immediately warmly welcomed by Carol, Mark, and son Christian. Carol and Mark's house is busy with warmshowers guests since they are near the Delaware Ferry. That evening we enjoyed a delicious dinner and conversation. The next morning the rain stopped, but a strong southwest wind was blowing and since we were invited to stay another night we decided to stay and explore Cape May.

Jocelyn:

October 22, 2016

The early morning ride to Cape May was cold with freezing temperatures and 40 mph gusts of wind. It is fall and our bike touring along the East Coast has taken a new turn as we move south. It was quite a thrill to have a high school friend, Lauren, drive two hours to have lunch with us. Oh, wait! That's never happened before! Then we connect chatting and remember that her husband, James, was a student in Mom's class at Cape View. It's a small world after all!

October 24, 2016

We've cycled a bit along the Jersey Shore down to Cape May. Today we took the ferry to Lewes, Delaware and now we're chilling in a ghost town, Ocean City, Maryland. But we've also had amazing hosts that have become new friends and family. Lately I've been meeting ultra-inspiring humans who I bond with, and it ultimately makes it way harder to leave, perhaps because we are getting so close to home or maybe I'm still looking for a home for myself and a partner. Perhaps we are shown beautiful souls to see that the world is there within us all. And perhaps I didn't need to ride my bike around the world to find that I am loved.

Mike:

I am still amazed at how some people welcome complete strangers into their home. Some warmshowers.org hosts seem a bit cold and offish, so much so that I don't know why they participate in this program, while others like Carol and Mark welcome you like family. The next morning Mark guided us to the ferry where we rode to Delaware and into Maryland. For several days now we have debated if we should continue south home to Florida or head west to Washington D.C. Yesterday we decided to go ahead and head west. It was complicated as there are only two ways to cross the Chesapeake Bay — north across the Bay Bridge (US 50/301) at 4.3 miles or south from Crisfield by small courier boat to Smith Island and maybe find another boat from Smith Island across the bay. Bicycles are strictly forbidden on the Bay Bridge, plus hitchhiking in Maryland is illegal. Jocelyn called the courier boat and was told it does run but only occasionally, so we decided to continue west and try to find a ride over the Bay Bridge. That ride turned out to be Greyhound Bus. The ride scheduled to Annapolis, Maryland west of the bridge was scheduled for 10:00 A.M., but due to a bus problem it didn't leave until 1:00 P.M. Thanks to a friendly and caring transportation official, we were able to get on that bus even though Greyhound bus drivers have strict rules on bicycles — boxed or wrapped in bubble wrap. There was no way we were going to box our bikes for a ride over the bridge from Salisbury, a total distance of sixty miles, but we were prepared with bubble wrap that I purchased from K-Mart. At first the driver said, "No bikes," because he didn't want to be liable for any damage. When we told him we would take full responsibility for any damage, he said okay. Greyhound does have a complicated bicycle policy, and it depends on the driver, but bikes are free.

On approaching the Bay Bridge, I counted eight 'No Bicycle' Signs. There were three lanes, one closed for maintenance, and there was no shoulder or walking path. This is definitely a no bike or walking bridge. On the other hand, at the south end of the Chesapeake Bay is the 23 mile long Chesapeake Bay Bridge-Tunnel. We heard that at this bridge there is a service to carry bicycles both ways.

We arrived at the Annapolis Greyhound bus stop around 2:00 P.M. and decided to get a motel and explore old town Annapolis. We enjoyed happy hour in the oldest tavern/bar in Maryland, Middleton Tavern built in 1750, where we sampled many small dishes of local seafood. After dinner we strolled through the United States Naval Academy and the waterfront district.

As I have said before, my wife and I sailed three months in 1981 on the *Banana Split*, a 46-foot catamaran, from Massachusetts to Port Canaveral. I have been reliving our 35th anniversary of this voyage as Jocelyn and I bicycle south. We had anchored for a few days in Annapolis, MD and also sailed up the Potomac River to spend five days in Washington, D.C. in

1981. Andee enjoyed the historical sights, but with the early frost on the decks we decided to stay in the south to raise our family.

We left Annapolis under cold and windy conditions. Jocelyn continued to find the smaller country roads until the outskirts of Washington D.C. Our capital city greeted us with rain, so we donned our rain gear and headed to the Capital Building and the Washington Mall. We met a new friend, Michael, who was cycling for the afternoon and offered to guide us on our bikes. We cycled with Michael as we circled the mall area from the Capital Building to the Lincoln Memorial. We even bicycled to the White House and had our picture taken posing in the front. Cycling this area of D.C. is easy and a fantastic way to tour though this museum and monument-filled city. After lunch in Georgetown we rode to Arlington, VA and another warmshowers host where we spent three nights so that we could explore our nation's capital.

After two full days of exploring the monuments, memorials, and the Smithsonian Museum of Washington D.C., we were ready to get back on our bikes and head south. We also met our neighbor Ginny again, who works in D.C. We had met her in Panama City, Panama back in January. That is only the second time we have met with friends twice.

As we rode south along the East Coast of the U.S., we made a detour to visit Washington D.C.

Jocelyn:

October 29, 2016

Going into D.C. from Annapolis got a bit tricky when we had to cross three road blocks. I ran ahead and checked out the situation, and there was a bridge, so if that bridge was out, then the road would be closed. But it wasn't, and we snuck in and over the creepy quiet area. It was actually enjoyable up until we rode by the Washington Redskins FedEx Football Stadium. We noticed a considerable difference in common courtesy and were honked at several times. I smiled because it made me miss Asia, Central America, and South America. I'm happy to hear a honk, as a honk means you see me! But I wasn't happy to see how local cyclists disobey the rules of the road. Sorry, but I'm not going to run a red light or even a stop sign.

A highlight for sure was to be able to cycle right up in front of our own USA National Capital Building and snap a few pictures. I've been to visit many capitals on this world tour, but I guess my own, by this bicycle, brought me to tears. My heart went racing and the chills feathered my arms for hours after. I'm still in awe of how beautiful Washington D.C. is and how we were able to represent our country as simple Americans around the world.

Upon arriving in D.C. we cycled down the National Mall and made our way around to the White House. I've never been here before and this was, in fact, very emotional and just real to me. Like, here I was, where history is constantly being made and within this next month change is drastically evident. I don't know how the election results will affect this change, but I know from what I have seen in this part of our country that it is going to be a close call.

We walked through the Vietnam Veteran's Memorial Wall at sunset. My dad was in this action on a navy ship in the Tonkin Gulf off the coast of Vietnam. We have cycled across Northern Vietnam and met many lovely and kind people. I prayed during this entire memorial walk for the world, as prayer is one action I feel confident in doing. Though I do not practice a religion anymore, I find peace in praying and quieting my mind to a superior movement, feeling, or desire.

I am so happy that we had time to visit with Pepper, a friend from home who we last shared time with in Panama! Last January, we went out to eat and I had the same shirt on then! We are friends for life from the same neighborhood.

Mike:

After three nights we were ready for the road once more and headed into the pretty Virginia hills with many trees in full fall color. Halloween night we spent in a somewhat creepy campground/trailer park with lots of trees and leaves. There was a party in the trailer park area that kept us up part of the night, followed by howling dogs the rest of the night. The following day we rode to Richmond, Va. where a school friend of Jocelyn's, Leslie, hosted us in the Richmond Hilton. At first we were a bit concerned about where we could park our bikes until the desk manager told us, "Just take the bikes to your room." Our bikes enjoyed an elevator ride to a comfortable seventh floor room. Leslie soon met us and we had a good evening eating dinner and visiting while Leslie drove us around Richmond.

Halloween 2016 in Virginia. We got lots of honks.

A fine campground but a spooky cook.

A few days ago the tension adjustment bolt on my B-17 Brooks saddle broke, leaving the saddle un-tensioned and uncomfortable. Jocelyn called a few bike shops in Richmond and found Shift Bicycles that carries the Brooks saddle. We rode to Shift Cycles and I selected a different type, the Brooks Cambium rubber saddle that does not need tensioning. Glen, the owner of Shift Bicycles, has an extensive shop for touring cyclists. He is also a warmshowers host. We then cycled on the Virginia Capital Trail toward Jamestown and found a county campground.

We spent the morning touring Jamestown, VA, which is the first permanent settlement by the Virginia Company in 1607. This settlement was recreated from original plans of the Virginia Company in London and opened in 1957. The actual location of Jamestown wasn't found until 1994 on Jamestown Island a mile or two east on Jamestown Island itself. After the Jamestown-Scotland Ferry, we had lunch at the Surry Seafood Company on the other side of the James River. We never tire of people approaching us and inquiring about our ride. We had talked with a gentleman and his wife from North Carolina while we were waiting for lunch. When we asked for our check, our waitress told us that he paid for his lunch with a $100 bill and told her to use the rest for our lunch! We never got his name. As I have said many times, this trip is all about the people you meet all around the world as in this generous gentleman and Leslie from Richmond.

Yesterday we rode in more traffic than we have ever ridden in the U.S. to travel from Smithfield to Virginia Beach. I still don't know how Jocelyn does it, but she did manage to find occasional roads through smaller neighborhoods to connect us to Virginia Beach. The riding was tedious as we rode on streets and sidewalks to our next host's apartment. Alphonso, and his four bikes, lives close to the bicycle shop where he works. He has been touring for many years throughout the U.S. and Mexico. With over 36,000 miles under his belt he is quite an accomplished touring cyclist. An extra day was spent in Virginia Beach as we explored the beach area.

Jocelyn:

October 30, 2016

Hanging out after a long 42 miles of steep hills, inpatient drivers, and actual sunshine! The weirdest part about today was that three people literally stuck their big-old heads out their windows and yelled unclear, mean things. So weird.

October 31, 2016

Happy Halloween, trick or treat, dreams do come true, bike girl, AND today I cycled with a wild, full mask of an old man with a long white beard and hair (from the movie *Wrong Turn*)!

We met up with an old friend Leslie, and she ended up hooking us up with a hotel room. We took her out to some delicious dinner and drinks. Leslie and I have known each other for over fifteen years, and she was my inspiration in basketball and track. So it's cool that we like to hang out with each other and party hard together a bit.

November 4, 2016

We cycled the Virginia Capital Trail from Richmond to Jamestown Settlement. Two sunshine-filled warm days of goodness. Took me a bit of time to realize I cycled this back in 2013! Ha ha! I enjoy Virginia, but only the back roads. Today we cycled into Virginia Beach, with ruthless terrible inconsiderate drivers. Ugh. I realized that I don't want to battle the traffic anymore. We're not just putting our lives on the line; we're also slowing down the lives of others. The traffic was so bad that I wanted to end the ride here. But I guess we'll keep going to Florida because in one month we are done. I'll take it day by day.

November 5, 2016

Virginia Beach — I hope to never, ever see you again! Rude people, smoking inside restaurants, and constant traffic. I only had some fun because I'm staying with a friend, but I am never coming back here. I will stick to the country side of the state; that's where the lovers are!

Mike:

We left Alphonso on quiet Sunday roads and headed southwest to visit one of Jocelyn's friends north of Raleigh. We have zigzagged all down the East Coast to visit certain areas and to play tourists. Yesterday we continued west to Lake Gaston where we were hosted by Rachel and her parents Peter and Julia. Three years ago Jocelyn and Rachel rode the Transamerica Bike Route from Virginia to Washington State. Once again we were treated like family with a comfortable room and excellent food.

A few months ago I had a toothache but the pain left after a few days. The pain started again several days ago but this time would not quit. Jocelyn and I spent Thursday trying to find a local dentist for an exam and possible extraction. Many dentists take Fridays off, and here was no exception. I finally found one back in Roanoke Rapids where we stayed two nights ago and was told that the dentist would work me into his schedule. Rachel drove us and our bikes back to Roanoke Rapids and dropped me off at the dentist. A few hours later I left the dentist minus one tooth. Rachel then drove us to a motel where I was exhausted with a sore and bleeding mouth. At first the clerk at the motel said, "No rooms till 4:00." It was 1:30 and I was hurting badly. We waited a bit and I approached the check-in desk, opened my mouth, and mumbled about needing a room now as blood trickled out. There was an additional clerk standing there who immediately gave me a key. After a long nap. Jocelyn and I walked to a nearby restaurant where I ate soft macaroni and cheese.

After another semi-restless night we were back on the road. I didn't think I could make it far, but with flatness and a good tail wind we were able to record 49 miles before I decided it was far enough.

Jocelyn:

November 7, 2016

I'm back! North Carolina, what up? It's been awhile! To those friends who live in NC, I might be cycling by! Still unsure of the route so please let me know where you're at! We are currently heading toward Raleigh.

November 11, 2016

We've had some great days of cycling out of Virginia into North Carolina. We are connecting with my friend Rachel, who I rode the Transamerica Bicycle Route from Virginia to Washington State in 2013 with, and I got to hang out with her amazing mother Julia, again! It was so nice of them to open their beautiful Lake Gaston home to us for two nights. We really got to relax, which made it tough to leave today! I think the ultimate blessing I realized was that this friend of mine who I hadn't seen in three years was still my friend. We still laughed, giggled from memories, and were weird together. It was fantastic. Thank you for being awesome, being a true friend for life, for literally helping us out, and for getting my dad to a dentist!

Mike:

We continued riding southeast toward the coast and Wilmington, NC through the cold and rain. Wilmington is a big city and the traffic was tedious. But Jocelyn did find a bike trail through the middle of the city that guided us to another host's house. She had contacted two college sorority friends of hers, Sarah and Lindsey. Lindsey's friend Mary invited us to stay in her house. We all met at a bar where it was Taco Monday night with $1 tacos and $2 Latin beers. Sarah had bought a copy of our first book and brought it to the bar for us to autograph. The next day we rode to Carolina Beach and headed south to the Fort Fisher/Southport Ferry. After a four mile ferry ride we continued south through North Carolina to enter South Carolina at sunset. It was interesting that highway 17 in NC has a small shoulder and immediately this shoulder disappears in SC. Another sorority sister of Jocelyn's, Mary, invited us to stay in her parents' vacation house in North Myrtle Beach. We arrived there at dark after a long day. Mary's friend Gina picked us up and drove us to visit Mary, a bartender at the Crab Catcher restaurant in North Myrtle Beach.

We had a fun evening while enjoying delicious seafood. When it was time to leave I asked Mary for the check but was told that the guy I was sitting next to had paid it! I had struck up a conversation with him and he was fascinated by our ride and ended up paying for our evening. I never did catch his name either. A few weeks ago another gentleman had bought us lunch. We decided to take a day off in Myrtle Beach before heading south to Savannah, Georgia.

Jocelyn:

November 15, 2016

In Wilmington, NC we met two friends, Sarah and Lindsey, from my days at Western Carolina University, along with Mary, Jeffrey, Jason, and my dad of course at a bar for Margarita Monday! I got to see my sorority pledge sister Sarah, too! It's literally been way too long.

November 16, 2016

Yesterday we cycled 64 miles and it was a long day with the fact that my dad had to get a tooth pulled a week ago and he has a new Brooks saddle. We were averaging 9 mph. So that made it long and I had to stop and wait on him a lot. Our bodies can go-go-go now. For me, I don't feel exhausted unless I cycle 80 miles or so. We are in North Myrtle Beach where we cycled into the sunset and for a little bit after sunset. Yup, we're moving homeward bound rather quickly!

It took some confidence to bike into Myrtle Beach at night, but we made it because my sister that I hadn't met yet had set us up with her parents' home. We met the most amazing Gina and then MayLay and had the coolest of nights in town for a few days! Thanks to them for hosting us, serving some good drinks, letting us borrow a golf cart, and a family home. Life is so fun and wild and loved. We are loved.

Mike:

After two nights in Myrtle Beach, with one day on the beach, we were back on the road and continuing south to Georgetown, SC. Most of today's riding was on the busy U.S. 17. There was no other road south so we endured it. Jocelyn did find occasional side roads, but they all eventually wound up on U.S. 17. Eventually we arrived in Mt. Pleasant,

SC, a bridge ride away from Charleston, and spent two nights so that we could tour the area.

In the morning we rode a boat to Fort Sumter and explored where the Civil War started. That afternoon I reminisced my old navy days by touring the aircraft carrier *USS Yorktown* (CV-10) and the destroyer *USS Laffey* (DD-724). I served aboard the *USS Hoel* (DDG-13) as an Electronics Technician Radar (ETR), and touring these ships with the same radar electronics equipment I worked on brought back so many memories.

We left Mt. Pleasant on a quiet Sunday morning and cycled over the bridge to Charleston. Jocelyn led us on many side roads out of Charleston toward Savannah where we will visit her friend Nicole. Nicole cycled with us from Blaine, WA to Oxnard, CA last June to August, while Andee and son Cary drove our truck and set up our campsites. Our ride to Savannah, GA turned out longer than expected, as we traveled on smaller country roads rather than the busy four-lane U.S. 17. These roads are quiet and peaceful and also a challenge for Jocelyn to navigate our way south. Many times these roads turned to dirt or sand, but we found our way. We are also staying in more motels than camping since either our timing is off on arriving near a campground too early or the campground does not allow tents. I never would have believed it, but there are many campgrounds in NC and SC that are for RVs only. In fact, Jocelyn talked on the phone with two campgrounds where we planned on staying, and both said, "No tents." I can't imagine why. Up North they do not allow tenting in the winter because water is cut off and one must be self-contained in an RV, but the campgrounds around here don't close.

A few days ago Jocelyn was bit by an aggressive dog. We have been chased by hundreds of dogs around the world and fortunately this is only the second dog bite. I was bit in the country of Azerbaijan about a mile from the Iran border. Fortunately Jocelyn's bite was a quick one with few punctures. At this point we both jumped off our bikes and used them as a defensive shield. The dog finally backed off. It was a scary event, and since then we become nervous when we hear barking dogs. The dog was in front of a trailer, but no one responded even with several loud air horn honks from Jocelyn's bike.

Jocelyn:

November 20, 2016

I got bit by a dog today. It all happened so fast and I was totally worried about the dog running out into the highway before he bit me and then after! He was vicious. I dismounted and had to use my bicycle as a shield. I also used my air horn on him to try to shake him out of the "attack game." After about five minutes of him trying to attack us, he gave up and went back to his house. We quickly rode away and about a mile down the road I stopped and told my dad I was bit. There was one puncture and some scratches, some bruising, and a bit of swelling. It did freak me out. We almost did all the right things when he came running out of his house. We stopped, we yelled, but I didn't dismount in time. So, I guess it's my fault. I'm just glad he didn't get run over. If you are a cyclist, please! Please! Please! Do the right things so that a dog won't die chasing you as it is a game to them. Dad and I are tied now in this competition as he was bitten in Azerbaijan. Ha ha. Not funny.

November 21, 2016

Georgia is on my mind, and I will see my BFF soon! Nicole, be ready for the Rice team action!

Mike:

We arrived at Nicole's apartment, and the next day Andee and Cary picked us up and we drove back to Myrtle Beach where Andee had reserved a few nights at a resort for a Thanksgiving celebration. It was fun to chill out for a few days as a family again. Soon, Andee and Cary dropped us back at Nicole's and they drove home to Florida.

Jocelyn's Instagram Posts:

November 22-26, 2016

Mom and Cary drove up to Myrtle Beach for Thanksgiving, and we are staying in our timeshare exchange place. It is nice, but a little cold by the beach here, and mom likes the comfy beds and big bathrooms! Dad and I can get by almost anywhere now. We ate a turkey dinner with a nice couple and then walked around to digest our food. Dad is ready to get home and sleep in his own bed. Mom and Cary headed south after an early breakfast and ride back to Savannah where Nicole stored our bikes. We will stay another night there, and then I think we are charging home!

Mackin and I giggled for hours on the floor like old times. It is so nice to spend some quality time with my best friend again. I've been around my dad for far too long.

We met our family for Thanksgiving in Myrtle Beach, South Carolina.

Mike:

We had a good start to our final week of riding by getting 72 miles in eight hours with the increasing south headwinds. We were pleasantly surprised by the bicycle-friendly state of Georgia. There are only two roads south: I95 and U.S. ROUTE 17. U.S. 17 in Georgia has a good shoulder and not much traffic. There was one distressing moment when I heard a car close behind me. As I turned to look, I glanced in my left mirror and saw a small black car coming up fast with the right wheels on the shoulder. With just a second or two to react I abruptly turned to the grass and watched as the car sped over the paved shoulder I had just left. The driver finally 'woke up' and saw Jocelyn as I yelled out to her. She didn't hear me but the car jerked around her. Touring cyclists have a love/hate relationship with rear view mirrors. I always ride with two. They sure saved me today.

Anyone who has bicycle toured knows that one has plenty of time to think while on the road. Today I reminisced all that we had done in the last five years. If you would have asked me five years ago if we would have cycled the world, I would have said, "No way." The bottom statistic line is:
- 5 continents
- 37 countries
- 33 months
- 28,000 miles

To sum up the adventure, I like the four words: blood, sweat, tears, and smiles, lots of smiles. We have been fortunate to travel and discover this wonderful world by bicycle.

All of a sudden we rolled into our home state of Florida. I say all of a sudden because it seems surreal to me that we are headed home to Cape Canaveral and that we are almost there after all these years and 28,000 miles!

We crossed the border in the late morning and found a motel in Mayport, Florida with the threat of extreme thunderstorms as a cold front moved in. Since Savannah, we have endured headwinds but hope that changes to a tailwind when the cold front passes through tonight.

Jocelyn:

November 30, 2016

We made it to the Florida line today! This is my home state, and I'm feeling ultra-bittersweet that our world tour is almost over. In three more days we will be riding down our home streets.

Cycling into our home state of Florida.

December 1, 2016

We are on the coast and are seeing the erosion of the beaches due to Hurricane Matthew. Vilano Beach coastal road was collapsed! We stopped for lunch at the Beachcomber Restaurant for a date with some mahi tacos, red beans, and rice! After lunch we saw our first armadillo that I saved from crossing the road at the Flagler County line. I saved a turtle the other day. I take roadkill off the road almost daily. The road is a dangerous place, and I feel like it's my job to do things like this. And it should be your job to watch out for all the things on the road! Make the world a better place.

Mike:

After another long but beautiful Florida coastal ride, we arrived in Ormond Beach, just north of Daytona Beach, after sunset. The next day we arrived in Titusville and cycled to our final warmshowers hosts. Chris and Beth build touring bicycles and have gone on many adventure cycling tours. Thanks to Chris who told us about a new and excellent bike trail through Titusville. It is part of the Maine to Florida bike trail still under construction. The non-profit organization, East Coast Greenway Alliance (ECGA), is in charge of the 3,000-mile bike path that will stretch from Calais, Maine to Key West, Florida. The project has been underway since

1991, building different segments of the trail that will eventually link together. We have ridden various sections on this Greenway in all states since Maine.

Jocelyn:

December 2, 2016

We spent the night in our own Brevard County with a bike-savvy couple in Titusville. Of course we could talk to Mom and get a ride home in the truck, but what would that prove???? Tomorrow we are going to ride home our way, in style, and celebrate!

Mike:

On our final ride we entered Kennedy Space Center and continued through Merritt Island to our barrier island home on the Atlantic Ocean. There was one most disturbing incident on Merritt Island when a driver tried to intentionally hit Jocelyn. We were riding along on a quiet side road when traffic was backed up a bit and the cars behind us waited until they could safely pass us. A few cars back a driver yelled out, "Get on the sidewalk, assholes!" As he passed he intentionally swerved toward Jocelyn, narrowly missing her. We have bicycled around the world, and this disturbing insightful incident occurred on our very last day.

We finally crossed over our last bridge, and as I wondered how many thousands of bridges we had traversed in this world I shouted to Jocelyn, "It's all downhill from here!" I remembered the pub bartender in New Zealand in 2012, saying, "It's all uphill from here," when we told him about our ride. We had one more stop to make. It was Andee's birthday, and we stopped at a florist shop where we bought her flowers. Jocelyn strapped this bouquet to her bike for our final ride home. With blood, sweat, tears, and smiles in our eyes and minds we rode that last riveting mile that we had dreamed of for so many years. It was an emotional moment when we arrived in Cape Canaveral where Andee was waiting on the roadside to take pictures and give us a huge 'Welcome Home' hug. Jocelyn gave her the flowers and we both exclaimed, "Happy birthday!" Andee burst into happy tears!

Welcome home in Cape Canaveral, Florida — 5 continents, 37 countries, over 28,000 miles in 33 months of cycling.

After a brief lunch at our neighborhood La Cantina restaurant, we rode home to a neighborhood welcoming committee before returning to a beachside park where we met more friends who rode with us to Florida Brewing Company. We appreciated a long-awaited but overwhelming reception with friends as Jocelyn and I were there, but not really there. A few hours later we rode that final one mile home in the dark, walked our bikes into the garage, dropped the kickstands, and walked into the house. Our ride was over. At that we were somewhat anxious and apprehensive, maybe even a little depressed, wondering what was next in our lives.

We will miss our daily routine, but more than that, all of our new friends from around the world.

Jocelyn:

December 3, 2016

Today is Momster's 61st birthday. She is grateful to have us ride home safely and have less to do with the finances and worrying about us on the roads. We kept in close contact during this final ride, and she was doing her last minute preps for our reunion. She stealthily caught us on Merritt Island and snapped pictures and then again in our Cocoa Beach area, and we stopped to meet her at Cape View Elementary across the street from

Cherie Down Beach Park. We had flowers for her, and we all cried. I'm not sure what Cary was doing, but it didn't take us long to meet him for lunch at La Cantina! There we sat and joked and talked with our neighbor friends over some cold Amber Bock beers. Finally we cruised down our Harbor Drive and rode into the driveway thrilled to see a map of the world on a shower curtain hung between our front two palms! Neighbors were there with balloons and cheers! I was so thrilled to be back with my Princess Yaki dog. She is my other world and we make cute pictures!

Later we rode back to Cherie Down Park and met some riders to join us on our way to Florida Brewing Company for a big celebration. Mom had a cake for us, and her friend Carrie brought a small one for Mom's birthday. We had delicious food from the Romano family's DiLorenzo's Restaurant in town with additions from the neighbors and our dear friends Susan and Richard. We shared a slideshow of our pictures from our many parts of the world tour, and people just asked us lots of questions. It was a long and loving day that I was grateful at the end to be able to crawl into my own bed with Yaki!

December 12, 2016

We've been back for 9 days. It's been surreal. Many of our neighbors rang bells and horns as we rode down to our house. My mom, bro, and Yaki welcomed us with hugs, kisses, and tears. This trip has been rather difficult on all of us. And now the transition of living in our home all together has been difficult, but we've tried to stay busy. We removed those two dead palms that the world map was hung on. We've cleaned our gear and have packed it away. We've donated many of our old clothing and things. Living on our bikes has taught us we don't need those material things. We've participated in the daily chores of keeping the house in order. We've both been running or walking on the beach every morning, and I've been cooking many meals in our kitchen, something I have missed. I guess we are enjoying living rather normally. The end, or not!

Epilogue

As children in school, we learned about the great world explorers. I have to admit that those explorers instilled dreams of my own exploring on that grand scale. History has provided many vehicles for this purpose of which a simple bicycle is very capable. At first you think about a small cycling trip that may take a day, but then you wonder, *Why not many days?* Suddenly that thought mushrooms in your mind. It starts to take over your thoughts and life until the day you start the wheels rolling and don't look back.

Why did we ride our bicycles around the world? We were asked this question countless times. People are surprised when we say that we did not ride for a charity, had no sponsors, and did not solicit publicity. We rode for ourselves to explore the world in this vastly unique way. We rode for discovery. We rode to meet the peoples of the world. After arriving home I read a travel article on CNN.com that listed and rated the most dangerous countries in the world as evaluated on violence and disease. Of the 37 countries we bicycled through, 21 countries were on that list.

Everywhere people asked, "Where are you from?" and, "Where are you going?" When we replied, no matter what the language, we were looked at in disbelief or they walked away shaking their head. The next question was, "How?" Our reply was always, "One day at a time." It is that easy, in the sense that you get up each morning, get on your bike, and ride. Suddenly, after weeks, months, and years, the miles add up. It is a slow process, and we told each other from the beginning that if this ever turned out to be a job that we tired of performing every day, the ride is over.

I would like to once again thank my wife Andee for her understanding with us to live this adventure. In the past six years I have only been home for eight months. As I complete this book I am stationed for my third Antarctic winter at Amundsen-Scott South Pole Station. I arrived on the last flight in February 2017, and since the station doesn't open until

November 2017 it will be another eight months until I return home. Andee is the reason we completed this journey. She kept us together and made light of stressful situations. She calmed us when 'the world overwhelmed us.' I would also like to thank my son Cary for looking after things at the house and helping his mom. There were many times we Skyped Cary with computer/website issues, and he always came through. In some respect we had the easy part of just riding our bikes every day. Both of them were on our cycling team taking care of the home front and those details that we didn't want to be bothered with.

And once again I would like to thank Jocelyn for being my traveling partner and wingman. I know I was a real pain at times and sometimes I said hurtful words. But we persevered and had fun exploring the world together. If it wasn't for your steady navigation and extra eye on me, I would be lost somewhere on Earth. We did have difficult moments where we almost separated and went our own ways. A journey like this can be stressful and stretch relationships sometimes to an almost breaking point. On the open road, it is just you and your bicycle, and each decision you make may be your last. We had good times together, but occasionally we needed our own space and would ride apart. Some of our rides were talkative and some were plain quiet as we absorbed the beauty of the moment. At times, one of us would just stop and would not start again until we were ready. The other knew to just wait. But through it all, we never complained of the daily routine of getting back on the road. It became second nature and we greeted each morning as a new day of discovery.

"Mom and Dad, we once again kept the wheels going round and round. Thank you for being our guiding light as we traveled the world."

"Mom Polly – We thank you for your continuing inspiration in our lives, especially with Cary and Jocelyn."

> *"Twenty years from now you will be more disappointed by the things you didn't do than by the ones you did do. So throw off the bowlines. Sail away from the safe harbor. Catch the trade winds in your sails. Explore. Dream. Discover."*
>
> – Mark Twain

Afterword from Andrea Rice, August 2017

My mother, Polly, advised Mike before our wedding to keep a watchful eye on me because I was known to wander and loved to plan adventures. Her advice proved to be true, but the wonderful adventures were not always together as a couple. Mike has spent many months in different locations while I have managed a career in education, two athletic and artistic children, and a home in Florida. We spent many summer vacations traveling back to the West Coast, always with family and friends, to visit and share memories. Our parents provided the support and encouragement to explore the world where there are many ways to learn from each other. Cary and Jocelyn have both been supportive of me, especially when Mike has been working far from home. Perhaps my real part in this fantastic world tour was the "encourager" as I would not have ventured on all the paths they rode.

I am truly grateful that Mike and Jocelyn allowed me to be a "sag" driver for several weeks on two of their routes, following them daily, and attempting to make the burdens less cumbersome. We all benefitted from this world exploration, and I hope the future will find us on the road together again. I am grateful that after 28,000 miles on their bicycles they returned home safely.

Final note: Polly gave us a plaque with The Marriage Creed, and one of the points is most apt for our partnership:

Cherish your union... Let no one come between your togetherness, not child, not friend, not worldly goods. Yet maintain enough separateness to allow each other his or her own unique oneness.

–Ginny and Manny Feldman

World Tour Mileage Summary

September 6, 2011 to December 3, 2016

COUNTRY	BICYCLE MILES	DAYS
United States	6,686	195
New Zealand	1,099	42
Morocco	323	13
Spain	823	26
France	483	11
Monaco	2	2
Italy	337	8
Slovenia	55	2
Croatia	369	12
Bosnia	35	1
Montenegro	149	8
Serbia	95	5
Romania	112	2
Bulgaria	194	5
Greece	230	6
Turkey	760	57
Georgia	215	14
Azerbaijan	439	14

World Tour Mileage Summary

COUNTRY	BICYCLE MILES	DAYS
Iran	1,004	33
Tajikistan	320	20
Kyrgyzstan	40	23
China	702	30
Vietnam	231	9
Laos	308	10
Thailand	1048	24
Mexico	2,434	67
Guatemala	395	14
Honduras	213	16
El Salvador	82	3
Nicaragua	363	22
Costa Rica	280	51
Panamá	251	8
Colombia	575	17
Ecuador	623	22
Perú	1,380	50
Chile	2,045	56
Canadá	3,334	90

Total bicycle miles: 28,034 (45,116 km)

Highest climb: 14,212 feet (4331 m)

Number of countries: 37

Time on bicycles: 33 months

Final Thoughts

This adventure has changed our view of the world. Life carries on no matter where you are. We are no longer in a hurry. Our lives were totally contained on our bicycles. We were content with what we had. We did not need any more than what our bicycle panniers contained. How simple is that? We rode when we wanted to and took breaks wherever we decided to explore a part of the world and history. We also embraced an amazing amount of nature that only a touring bicyclist encounters, and these sights, smells, and sounds will always be with us. Along the way, happiness was found in little things — sunrises and sunsets, camping in deserts, mountains, and beaches, meeting new people, a constant stream of fresh air and exercise, different foods, and making progress to our goal of circling the planet, however slowly. I came up with a rough estimate that we performed over eighteen million pedal rotations during our 28,000 miles. I wonder if after that first rotation we had known that we had about eighteen million more to go would we have continued. That first rotation sure added up over the long haul!

Many people are afraid of the unknown and they hesitate after considering all the potential problems and pitfalls that may lie ahead. We embraced the unknown every day and awoke wondering what we would see and who we would meet that day. Most days we never knew where we would sleep that night. It all eventually worked out with our minimal planning. As the old saying goes, "Plan roughly, and execute superbly." Thank you Jocelyn. We felt very fortunate for our health and returning home to our family safely. Only one tragic incident marred our journey and that one incident will live with us forever. But we learned from that and carried on. Would we do it again? Obviously there are many areas of the world we did not cycle. Maybe we will travel more of this wonderful world in the future by bicycle or other means. We both miss the road and the simple life.

Jocelyn still has her whole life ahead of her and is more resilient and less afraid of the future because of this journey. She knows she can pretty much do anything after her life around the world on a bicycle. Cary is now more interested in adventure travel after seeing our pictures, videos, and hearing our "Tales from the road." I believe that both of my children will experience life "on the road less traveled."

"Be infinitely flexible and constantly amazed."
—Jason Kravitz

South Pole Mike Winter 2017

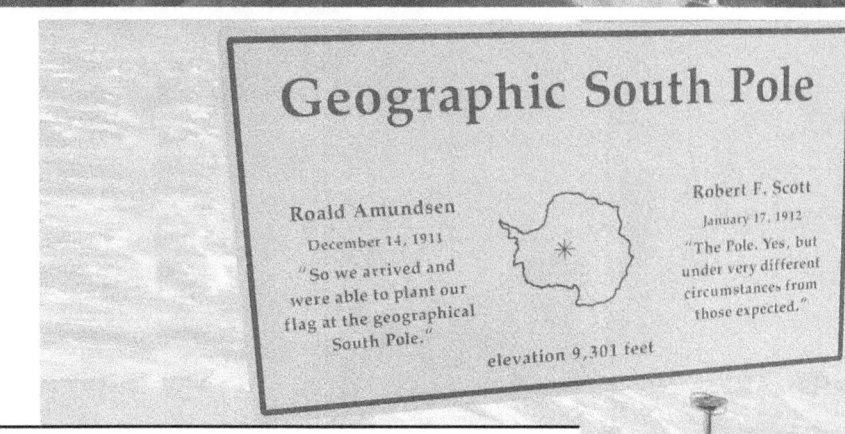

Visit SouthPoleMike.blogspot.com